NEW REALITIES IN THE MANAGEMENT
OF STUDENT AFFAIRS

NEW REALITIES IN THE MANAGEMENT OF STUDENT AFFAIRS

Emerging Specialist Roles and Structures for Changing Times

Edited by

Ashley Tull and Linda Kuk

STERLING, VIRGINIA

Sty/us

COPYRIGHT © 2012 BY
STYLUS PUBLISHING, LLC.

Published by Stylus Publishing, LLC
22883 Quicksilver Drive
Sterling, Virginia 20166-2102

Library of Congress Cataloging-in-Publication Data
New realities in the management of student affairs :
emerging specialist roles and structures for changing times /
edited by Ashley Tull and Linda Kuk.—1st ed.
　　p.　cm.
Includes bibliographical references and index.
ISBN 978-1-57922-575-9 (cloth : alk. paper)
ISBN 978-1-57922-576-6 (pbk. : alk. paper)
ISBN 978-1-57922-577-3 (library networkable e-edition)
ISBN 978-1-57922-578-0 (consumer e-edition)
1. Student affairs services—United States—Administra-
tion.　2. Organizational effectiveness—United States.
I. Tull, Ashley, 1972–　II. Kuk, Linda, 1950–
LB2342.92.N38　2012
371.4—dc23　　　　　　　　　　　　　　　　2011028480

13-digit ISBN: 978-1-57922-575-9 (cloth)
13-digit ISBN: 978-1-57922-576-6 (paper)
13-digit ISBN: 978-1-57922-577-3 (library networkable
e-edition)
13-digit ISBN: 978-1-57922-578-0 (consumer e-edition)

Printed in the United States of America

All first editions printed on acid free paper
that meets the American National Standards Institute
Z39-48 Standard.

Bulk Purchases

Quantity discounts are available for use in workshops
and for staff development.
Call 1-800-232-0223

First Edition, 2012

10　9　8　7　6　5　4　3

We would like to thank Nick Rammell, law student at Brigham Young University, and Rosa Edwards, administrative assistant in the Campus Life Center at the University of Arkansas, for their editorial assistance throughout the preparation of the book.

CONTENTS

PART ONE: INTRODUCTION, CONTEXTS, AND CURRENT PRACTICES WITH SPECIALIST ROLES AND STRUCTURES

I. THE CHANGING NATURE OF STUDENT AFFAIRS   3
   Linda Kuk

2. THE CONTEXT FOR USING SPECIALIST ROLES AND MATRIX STRUCTURES IN STUDENT AFFAIRS ORGANIZATIONS   13
   Linda Kuk

3. SURVEY OF CURRENT PRACTICES WITH SPECIALIST ROLES AND STRUCTURES   34
   Ashley Tull and Nick M. Rammell

PART TWO: EMERGING SPECIALIST ROLES WITHIN STUDENT AFFAIRS ORGANIZATIONS

4. EMERGING ROLES AND RESPONSIBILITIES OF THE STUDENT AFFAIRS TECHNOLOGY OFFICER POSITION   49
   Leslie Dare and Kyle Johnson

5. EMERGING ROLES AND RESPONSIBILITIES OF THE STUDENT AFFAIRS DEVELOPMENT OFFICER/DIRECTOR OF DEVELOPMENT   58
   James Rychner and Linda Clement

6. EMERGING ROLES AND RESPONSIBILITIES OF THE STUDENT AFFAIRS COMMUNICATIONS OFFICER   68
   Chris Heltne

7. CHANGING ROLES AND RESPONSIBILITIES OF THE "ASSISTANT TO"   76
   Sherry Mallory, Evette Castillo Clark, and Bernie Shulz

8. CHANGING ROLES AND RESPONSIBILITIES IN
    STUDENT AFFAIRS HUMAN RESOURCES AND
    PROFESSIONAL DEVELOPMENT   *84*
    Allison Hawkins Crume

9. EMERGING ROLES AND RESPONSIBILITIES OF THE
    STUDENT AFFAIRS CHIEF OF STAFF/DIRECTOR OF
    ADMINISTRATION   *94*
    Cynthia Bonner and Allyn Fleming

10. CHANGING ROLES AND RESPONSIBILITIES OF
    STUDENT AFFAIRS AUXILIARY SERVICES   *103*
    Jerrid P. Freeman and Dean Bresciani

11. CHANGING ROLES AND RESPONSIBILITIES IN
    STUDENT AFFAIRS RESEARCH AND ASSESSMENT   *114*
    Marilee J. Bresciani

**PART THREE: INSTITUTIONAL AND ORGANIZATIONAL
IMPLICATIONS OF EMERGING SPECIALIST ROLES AND
STRUCTURES IN STUDENT AFFAIRS ORGANIZATIONS**

12. FACILITATING ORGANIZATIONAL CHANGE TO
    INCORPORATE SPECIALIST ROLES AND MATRIX
    STRUCTURES IN STUDENT AFFAIRS ORGANIZATIONS   *129*
    Kathy Cavins-Tull

13. EMERGING ROLES AND STRUCTURES IN STUDENT
    AFFAIRS ORGANIZATIONS AT SMALLER COLLEGES
    AND UNIVERSITIES   *149*
    Frank P. Ardaiolo and Kathleen M. Callahan

14. EMERGING SPECIALIST ROLES AND STRUCTURES IN
    STUDENT AFFAIRS ORGANIZATIONS AT COMMUNITY
    COLLEGES   *169*
    Bette M. Simmons

15. PREPARATION FOR NEW AND EMERGING ROLES AND
    RESPONSIBILITIES   *188*
    Linda Kuk

16. CONCLUSIONS AND RECOMMENDATIONS   *206*
       Ashley Tull and Linda Kuk

     ABOUT THE EDITORS   *215*

     ABOUT THE CONTRIBUTORS   *217*

     INDEX   *227*

PART ONE

INTRODUCTION, CONTEXTS, AND CURRENT PRACTICES WITH SPECIALIST ROLES AND STRUCTURES

This is a book about change, not solely about transformational change, but also about what the authors refer to as adaptive change. Transformational change can be viewed as a revolutionary process, dramatic and extensive. Transformational change seems to be a popular and an often presented and written about approach to implementing and managing change. Yet it rarely occurs naturally in organizations, and researchers have found that it is not used successfully very frequently within higher education organizations (Kezar, 2001). Most change that does occur in higher education organizations, especially within student affairs organizations, has not been transformational, but rather more incremental and modest in scope.

Adaptive change is ongoing and occurs as part of the day-to-day life of an organization, as individuals and units respond to new demands, challenges, and problems within and outside the organization. Adaptive change is subtle, incremental, and evolutionary and is often visible through the emergence of new roles, responsibilities, and structural shifts within organizations. In most cases, this type of change is incremental, sporadic, and often goes unnoticed. It is rarely systemic or strategic in scope or planning, so it is not always managed effectively. Yet over time, this type of change can have tremendous consequences for the performance and success of an organization.

As a result, this book also focuses on *planned change*, which can be either transformational or adaptive. The book examines some of the ways processes of planned change occur, how this type of change can be understood and managed, and what needs to be done to achieve desired outcomes through intentionally focusing on and directing change in student affairs organizations. It also identifies how planned change can be become transformational and yield successful change within student affairs organizations.

Reference

Kezar, A. J. (2001). Understanding and facilitating organizational change in the 21st century. *ASHE-ERIC Higher Education Report.* San Francisco: Jossey-Bass.

I

THE CHANGING NATURE
OF STUDENT AFFAIRS

Linda Kuk

As we enter the second decade of the 21st century, student affairs organizations are at a crossroads. They are facing increasing challenges in terms of expanding enrollment; changing demographics; the shifting and demanding nature of responsibilities; and increased expectations related to programs and services from the greater campus community, parents, and external constituents.

In the past decade considerable emphasis has been placed on increasing enrollment, which has helped fend off the catastrophic effects of dwindling tax-based funding. However, these increases have also placed greater demands on student services. More students equate to greater needs for services. In most cases, student affairs organizations have been expected to absorb these increased demands within existing resources and, in some cases, with even fewer resources. During the most recent economic recession, the squeeze caused by increasing enrollment has intensified due largely to the numbers of students returning to higher education as a result of job losses as well as those entering higher education for the first time.

The squeeze on services caused by enrollment expansion is also inte
fied by increases from groups of students that have not traditionally ?
higher education. The diversity of students on campuses is incr
their varied needs are increasing as well. The demographic p
education continues to expand to include more students
underrepresented groups, more students with disab
from across the spectrum of social economic stra
students based on age and academic needs. A

the nature, amount, and type of services expand, requiring new approaches and services.

At the same time, students are accessing existing services in greater numbers and with more serious and time-sensitive issues. The complexity of issues that students bring with them to campuses, and the expectations that students and their families exhibit in receiving services, has created new challenges to the knowledge and level of competencies of practitioners. Students are bringing the pains, problems, and realities of the increasingly violent and depersonalized world to the college campus. Mental illness; physical abuse; drug and alcohol use, abuse, and dependency; crime, sexual assaults; domestic violence; suicide; stalking and harassment; invasions of privacy and other issues related to the misuse of social media; and, in some cases, mass murderous attacks against fellow students and faculty, are becoming commonplace on many campuses. Student affairs staffs are often the first responders and/ or points of contact in addressing these incidents and their aftermath. They are expected to address these issues, often with little advance training or personal support for the tolls these encounters take on their personal lives. The need to provide opportunities to develop the knowledge, skills, and competencies required to address both the increasing complexity and the continual evolution of issues and problems is ongoing. Institutional structures for continuing professional development and support personnel need to be incorporated more intentionally into the fabric of higher education and student affairs organizations as the demands to address these emerging issues accelerate.

In the face of increased challenges, new roles and responsibilities are also emerging to address changing needs. In most cases existing student affairs professionals are not adequately trained or experienced to assume these roles and responsibilities, and individuals from outside the profession are being hired. In some cases, existing student affairs staffs are selected to take on these new roles and responsibilities with insufficient opportunities to acquire needed professional training. In other cases, these responsibilities are added on to practitioners' existing roles, adding stress and new challenges to human resource issues in student affairs organizations.

The challenges facing student affairs organizations are intensified by the ccelerating speed of advancements in technology, globalization, innova ns, and student consumerism. The use of technology has essentially nk the world, compressed our expectations of time, and intensified stu ability to be knowledgeable and at times aggressive consumers. These phenomena are only expected to increase as technology becomes even more sophisticated and user-friendly.

Access to information from all corners of the globe is now achieved through technology at our fingertips. We can hold courses and access services from nearly anywhere with the click of a mouse or the use of our 10 digits. Students do not need to engage in face-to-face interaction and are increasingly preferring to engage with each other through social media and virtual worlds and realities. Most students can interact with their parents and families daily no matter where they live, and this enables parents to continue to play an active role in their children's lives, often making those children overly dependent and less self-reliant into adulthood. The speed of technological advancements and innovation, and the generational expectations related to its use, has placed considerable pressure on both faculty and student affairs professionals to adapt quickly and implement new and wider technological use.

Most higher education institutions are beginning to use these advances to improve administrative processes and educational delivery, but these innovations are expensive to purchase and upgrade, and faculty and administrative units are not always quick to accept them. Many, non-early-technology adaptors learn how to use new software and/or equipment, and then it changes and these users have to upgrade to and learn new versions. At the same time, early adaptors, generally the younger generation, are quick to adapt use of these technological changes and to expect them to be implemented in instruction and service delivery, or they are easily dissatisfied.

Societal expectations related to communication have become nearly immediate and always available, and this now affects the availability of the services and educational offerings. When someone sends a communication via any form of current technology, email, texts, photo, social networks, and so on, that individual expects an almost immediate answer. When such individuals ask a question, request a change, or demand a solution to a problem, they also expect to receive a near-immediate response. These service-oriented enhancements, initiated to compete in the private marketplace of the service industry, are becoming the expected standard for service delivery everywhere. Some marketing campaigns now claim their service "never sleeps" or is available "24/7." This sense of immediate and constant availability and access regarding service-related expectations is making its way into expectations about student services and instructional response on college campuses as well.

At the same time, student affairs organizations face the reality of dramatically shrinking resources and strain on the ability to increase tuition and fees. Given current economic realities, it is a near certainty that resources will not be returning any time soon, and in some cases, may never return as they were before. Such realities, while troubling and in some cases devastating, also present new opportunities to view and design organizational realities differently. They provide a wake-up call to begin to understand and take charge of the adaptive changes that have been occurring and to develop new strategies for managing these changes to enhance the effectiveness and efficiency of student affairs organizations.

These challenges and expectations will require new ways to organize services, to respond to student needs and prioritize the use of limited resources, and to assess changing needs and develop new services. They will require increased lateral collaboration between units within student affairs and across the entire institution (Kezar & Lester, 2009). This demand for increased collaboration and for sharing information and resources will place new demands on student affairs organizations that have been traditionally siloed and vertically oriented in the way they interact within the institution. It probably will require new approaches to organizing and result in new roles and responsibilities for student affairs practitioners.

Many higher education organizations have already begun institutional restructuring processes, and more will take place in the years to come. Student affairs organizations will be asked, if they have not already been part of these processes, to reduce fiscal and human resources significantly and, in some cases, to substantially restructure their organizational units. This work is intended to share new ideas regarding organizational design and restructuring of roles and responsibilities that might enable student affairs organizations to respond to these demands more effectively.

In the face of new and emerging challenges, student affairs organizations will continue to face redesigning their organizations and repositioning existing resources, and each organization's issues and needs will be different. The way a student affairs organization is structured and the positions that are created are often influenced by internal and external environmental factors as well as the institution's mission and history. At the same time, each organization can learn from the experiences of others and adapt ideas and solutions to meet their specific needs. This work is intended to provide and discuss a number of dimensions of change and present them as examples and models that might assist student affairs leaders and practitioners to understand and more effectively manage the change that is occurring in their organizations and to borrow effective ideas and solutions from others within the profession.

Change Within Student Affairs Organizations

Since its inception, the student affairs organization has been evolving and adapting. As higher education has grown, student affairs organizations have also grown and adapted to meet changing needs and challenges. Today's student affairs organizations are complex and include larger staffs, greater resources, very sophisticated and complicated work, and numerous facilities to manage (Hirt, 2006; Kuk, Banning, & Amey, 2010; Manning, Kinzie, & Schuh, 2006). While traditional student affairs functions have remained somewhat unchanged, how they are conducted, managed, and organized is beginning to shift. At the same time, new challenges are emerging and the demands being placed on these organizations are increasing.

Student affairs leaders are beginning to develop and implement new organizational designs and structures and are shifting resources to meet emerging challenges while dealing with the decrease in overall resources. Such adaptive shifts have often occurred out of necessity, urgently and/or in isolation, have not always been fully recognized as organizational structural changes, and have not been widely shared throughout the profession (Kuk & Banning, 2009). By sharing the emerging and adaptive changes that are occurring and presenting discussions of theory and research that support these changes, they can be viewed and understood more clearly and be used more effectively throughout the profession.

Student affairs organizations have been and continue to be organized as hierarchical, functional structures, with units that provide highly differentiated programs and services to students. As these organizations become more complex, they have added programs and services while retaining their traditional hierarchical and functional focus. As a result, they have also developed multiple layers of management staff to supervise and coordinate roles and responsibilities among staff. Organizational specialists argue that these types of organizational structures no longer address the needs of modern organizations effectively and have become inefficient in addressing changing and time-sensitive demands (Galbraith, 2002; Keeling, Underhile, & Wall, 2007; Kezar & Lester, 2009; Kuk, Banning, & Amey, 2010).

There is some evidence that new elements of organizational design are emerging in student affairs organizations. These shifts and applications probably are early forms of new structural redesign and adaptation. This book explores the elements of organizational design, especially those that are beginning to appear within the profession, to identify their advantages and disadvantages and discuss how they might assist student affairs organizations in their restructuring efforts.

Another element of organizational restructuring is the appearance of cross-organizational positions. The increase in these types of positions is also an early sign of the evolution of organizational expectations and needs that represents an initial adaptation to needed skills and competencies within student affairs units. These processes are generally a first step in a shifting organizational redesign effort and can enlighten other student affairs organizations as they struggle with adjusting their own organizations in the midst of uncertain and emerging demands.

There are a number of different types of positions within student affairs organizations. The "traditional type of position," which appeared in the literature over time, can be categorized by both *function* (i.e., admissions, housing, etc.) and *populations* served (i.e., women; racial, ethnic and cultural groups; college- or discipline-specific students; etc.). Those professionals who work with students in a functional capacity must have a firm grasp of the particular service they are providing to serve students effectively (Hirt, 2006). Likewise, those professionals who work with students in a population capacity must have a firm grasp of the particular population they serve. In many cases, professionals in the population group also need a working knowledge of the functional aspects of student affairs units to make appropriate referrals and help their students acquire appropriate services to meet their needs.

In recent years a third type of student affairs position has emerged and has been labeled the *cross-organizational specialist*. This position/role is neither essentially function- or population-oriented. These positions/roles are being added to student affairs organizations primarily to address emerging challenges and enhance the use of resources by sharing roles and resources laterally across student affairs units and organizations. The professionals hired for these roles and responsibilities often come into student affairs work from other professions and training and generally are not trained in student development or student affairs administration. These staff possess the competencies and expertise needed in student affairs, but they also must be brought up to speed on the purpose and theories underlying student affairs work. These new roles and responsibilities also provide new opportunities for expanding the expertise and contributions of existing student affairs staff who demonstrate the knowledge, competencies, and potential to perform these emerging roles. These emerging challenges, and the roles and responsibilities needed to address them, require new ways of conceptualizing and addressing professional staff development and effective use of human resources.

In recent years, senior student affairs officers (SSAOs) have been hiring specialists to conduct such activities as fund-raising and development; research and assessment; technology integration; communication and media relations; professional development and training initiatives; budget and financial management; auxiliary and facilities management; and human resources. They have also been redesigning their administrative structures to include chiefs of staff, and assistants to the SSAO positions. Given available fiscal resources and the size of staffing resources, these roles and responsibilities have been fashioned at times into stand-alone positions, with unique sets of responsibilities, or in other cases, they have been combined or added to existing traditional positions. This book describes and discusses a number of new roles and provides insights into how they are being designed and staffed to enhance efficient use of human resources in both large and small student affairs organizations.

Exploration of the changing dynamic within student affairs organizations begins by examining current student affairs organizations in the context of new and emerging organizational design theory and approaches to organizational design. In this chapter we discuss the changing needs and challenges facing student affairs organizations and how current functional, hierarchical structures no longer adequately address the demands placed on these higher educational units. Chapter 2 discusses the need for organizational structures that are flexible and adaptive within the environmental context, less hierarchical or vertically focused, and structured to be increasingly collaborative and laterally focused. It explores new emerging structural elements, including hybrid and matrix structures, as potentially effective changes to existing organizational designs.

Chapter 3 presents an overview of how student affairs organizations currently use cross-specialist positions. It discusses the results of a national study of more than 250 senior student affairs officers (SSAOs) are discussed and presents examples of how they view the use of specialist positions within the context of their organizations' challenges.

Part two of the book (chapters 4 through 11) presents detailed examples of a variety of roles and responsibilities that have emerged or have changed significantly within student affairs organizations. Practitioners who occupy the roles and, in some cases, their supervisors present and discuss these descriptions. While a number of new roles and responsibilities probably are emerging in different sectors of student affairs practice, the authors have chosen to focus on eight different sets of roles and responsibilities, which include: technology, development and fund-raising, communications and public relations, assistant to the SSAO, human resources and professional development, the chief of staff or director of administration, director of auxiliary services, and director of research and assessment. These positions represent both emerging and changing roles and responsibilities within student affairs units. Each chapter presents a history of how the role emerged, how and why it was designed, what competencies and skills are needed to perform the roles and responsibilities, and how the role has been integrated into the existing organizational structure and context. Each chapter concludes by discussing emerging needs for the role and responsibilities in the context of anticipated changes.

Part three of the book discusses the implications of change both in organizational structure and in the emergence of new and changed roles and responsibilities within student affairs organizations. Chapter 12 discusses various theories and types of change and how they can be identified and applied to student affairs organizations. It addresses the intra-and interorganizational environmental factors that should be considered when addressing different forms of change issues related to structure and emerging roles and responsibilities, especially those related to planning, budgeting, and resource allocation.

Chapters 13 and 14 discuss the implications of change for specific types of college organizations, such as small colleges and community colleges, where limitations on resources or organizational missions and structures may not permit or support specific positions to accommodate these roles and responsibilities. These chapters discuss and present examples of how to address emerging needs in light of limited resources as well the use of cross-training and ongoing staff development as tools to assist in addressing and managing these changes.

Chapter 15 discusses preparation, ongoing professional development, and maintaining practitioner competencies in managing change as the profession looks to the future. It also explores the current roles of professional preparation programs, professional associations, and individual student affairs organizations in providing professional preparation and development across the student affairs practitioner's life span. It discusses the shortcomings within each of the various professional components and discusses how a more collaborative and systematic approach to ongoing professional development is needed to address the needs of student affairs organizations' professional development into the future. Finally, it suggests how the profession might make better use of the expertise present in professional preparation programs to better serve practitioners ongoing staff development needs. Chapter 16 discusses the projected impact change is likely to have on the future of student affairs and how student affairs organizations might use elements of organizational design and cross-functional staffing arrangements to address the challenges facing student affairs organizations.

Conclusion

This is a book about change—adaptive, planned, and transformation forms of change—applied to the student affairs organization context. It examines how change occurs; how the types of change can be identified, understood, and managed; and what needs to be done to achieve desired outcomes through intentionally focusing on and directing change in student affairs organizations.

Student affairs organizations are at a crossroads. They are facing increasing challenges in terms of expanding enrollment and changing demographics, nature and demands of responsibilities, and expectations related to programs and services from the greater campus community, parents, and external constituents. The complexity of issues that students bring with them to campuses, and the expectations that students and their families exhibit in receiving services, has created new challenges to the knowledge and level of competencies of practitioners. These challenges are intensified by the accelerating speed of advancements in technology, globalization, innovations, and student consumerism. Societal expectations of immediate and constant availability and access regarding communication and service are making their way into expectations about student services as well. This is changing the dynamics of student affairs roles and responsibilities and how resources need to be allocated.

At the same time, student affairs organizations face the reality of dramatically shrinking resources and strain on the ability to increase tuition and fees. Such realities, while troubling and in some cases devastating, also present new opportunities to view and design organizations differently.

This work explores the elements of organizational design, especially those that are beginning to appear within the profession, identifies their advantages and disadvantages, and discusses how they might assist student affairs organizations in their restructuring efforts.

This work also describes and discusses a number of new roles and provides insights into how they are being designed and staffed to enhance efficient use of human resources in both large and smaller student affairs organizations. Overall the work is intended to explore and discuss a number of dimensions of change and present them as examples and models that might assist student affairs leaders and practitioners to understand and more effectively manage the change that is occurring in their organizations and to borrow effective ideas and solutions from others within the profession.

References

Galbraith, J. R. (2002). *Designing organizations.* San Francisco: Jossey-Bass.

Hirt, J. B. (2006). *Where you work matters: Student affairs administration at different types of institutions.* Lanham, MD: University Press.

Keeling, R. P., Underhile, R., & Wall, A. F. (2007, Fall). Horizontal and vertical structures: The dynamics of organization in higher education. *Liberal Education, 93*(4), 22–31.

Kezar, A. J. (2001). Understanding and facilitating organizational change in the 21st century. *The ASHE-ERIC Higher Education Report.* San Francisco: Jossey-Bass.

Kezar, A. J., & Lester, J. (2009). *Organizing higher education for collaboration: A guide for campus leaders.* San Francisco: Jossey-Bass.

Kuk, L., & Banning, J. H. (2009). Designing student affairs organizational structures: Perceptions of senior student affairs officers, *NASPA Journal, 46*(1), 94–117.

Kuk, L., Banning, J. H., & Amey, M. (2010). *Designing organizations for sustainable change.* Sterling, VA: Stylus.

Manning, K., Kinzie, J., & Schuh, J. (2006). *One size does not fit all: Traditional innovative models of student affairs practice.* New York: Routledge.

THE CONTEXT FOR USING SPECIALIST ROLES AND MATRIX STRUCTURES IN STUDENT AFFAIRS ORGANIZATIONS

Linda Kuk

An organization's structure is much more than the framework or shell on which the organization rests; it is actually more like a human organism. This organism has a skeleton, but the real structure of the body consists of a number of systems—of which the skeleton is only one—that are interconnected and function as a whole. The skeleton gives the body shape and support, but the other units of the body and the interconnected systems together give it functionality, identity, and life. So, too, organizations comprise positions (roles and responsibilities), work units, and systems that together give it structure, functionality, and purpose. It is the organization's structure as a whole that enables, and in some cases limits, the organization's ability to adapt and respond to the demands and expectations placed upon it.

Members of the organization, usually the leadership, craft organizational structures, and they adapt over time to the changing environment in which they exist or they cease to function effectively (Bowditch, Buono, & Stewart, 2008). Sometimes, this adaptation is slow and hardly noticeable; other times, it appears to be quick and chaotic. Change within organizations is inevitable, yet adaptation is often a resistive rather than an enabling response. At the same time, the results of change and adaptation can be more effective and productive if they are understood and managed than if they are left to chance and reaction. This is true for student affairs organizations as well as for the larger collegiate organizations of which they are a part.

Roles and responsibilities take shape within the organizational construct of positions that consist of a grouping of work tasks. These positions are a fundamental component of an organization's structure; however, positions have relevance only in relation to other positions in an organization. Together they are formed and shaped into the skeleton or framework of an organization. As in the human organism, collectively they represent a part of the organization's structure. The presence and emergence of new roles and responsibilities and the reconfiguration of traditional roles and responsibilities with emerging roles and responsibilities into new positions is a sign of organizational adaptation. However, these adaptations may be occurring in an isolated and unintentional way and may not result in greater organizational efficiency and effectiveness.

This chapter provides the organizational context for understanding these structural changes by exploring student affairs organizational structures and the organizational paradigms that have been used to create and sustain these structures. This chapter explores the more macro context of why current structures may no longer be sufficient to enable the organization to respond and adapt to changing demands from both the internal and external environment. Emerging ideas and theories related to organizational design are presented and applied to understanding how to use the resources and elements of organizational design more effectively to craft more adaptive and effective organizational structures for student affairs organizations. The chapter also explores the concepts of hybrid and matrix structures as structural approaches to enabling student affairs organizations to retain some past strengths, and at the same time become more adaptive to the changing demands and challenges they face. Finally, the chapter discusses how the use of more flexible structural design and work flow analysis (changing roles and responsibilities) can enable student affairs organizations to achieve greater effectiveness.

The chapter begins by exploring the history and development of student affairs organizations and some of the challenges they have faced. Through growth and adaptation, these organizations have developed strengths and complexity that are reflected in their current organizational forms.

The Historical Development of Student Affairs Organizations

Student affairs organizations have been developing over the last 50 years as predominantly hierarchical, functional structures. These organizational structures originally evolved out of the need for student and administrative services, such as housing, advising, health services, and admissions in the collegiate setting and the specialization of faculty toward a greater academic focus (Hirt, 2006; Komives, Woodward, & Associates, 2003). These organizations' expansion and complexity were propelled by tremendous growth in numbers, diversity, and needs of students accessing higher education after World War II (Kuk, 2009; Kuk, Banning, & Amey, 2010; Manning, Kinzie, & Schuh, 2006). Student affairs organizations, like other administrative units at that time, were organized according to existing organizational theory and knowledge that supported a mechanistic and functional alignment of units to provide the increasing array of specialized programs and services that students required and expected (Ambler, 1993, 2000).

As needs grew, new units or services were added to the mix and aligned as separate operations providing a special program or service (Clark, 1983; Gumport, 1993; Kezar, 2001). As the number of programs and services expanded, mid-level functional managers were added to organizations to supervise an increasing array of programs and services. Communication was essentially vertical in nature and often top-down in process. This resulted in hierarchical student affairs organizations that were functional in purpose and able to deal with very specialized issues and concerns brought on by increasing numbers of students.

The focus of these organizations was on serving students through administrative and student development activities, and they were structurally unique and separate from other administrative and academic units within the collegiate organization. Student behavior and student life became the organizational domain of student affairs, while academics, curriculum, instruction, and research became the domain of the faculty and academic administrative units (Komives et al., 2003; Manning et al., 2006).

Functional units within student affairs organizations continued to expand as separate, independent, and specialized units with a focus on vertical communication and interaction between units initiated through senior-level administrative action or requests. Organizational leaders prided themselves on the number of layers, and the complexity of their organizations was seen as a mark of quality. More became better, and the extent of the portfolio and the number of functional areas supervised were more highly rewarded and praised.

Roles and responsibilities moved from being generalist to more specialized with very little crossover in either hiring or training. Each unit, and the staff within it, was expected to have and was rewarded for its specific knowledge and ability to execute its specialization efficiently. Smaller institutions that were unable to attain a high level of specialization because of fewer resources often felt less sophisticated or even less able because they had to wear "many hats." Collegiate organizational units became increasingly insular and prided themselves on being independent both academically and administratively. For example, housing staff were housing professionals, and counseling staff were counseling professionals. Throughout student affairs organizations, professional personnel identified with their specialization first and foremost.

A Shifting Paradigm for Understanding Organizational Structure

In recent decades, the pendulum has begun to swing away from increasing specialization. This was sparked by changing demands from the environment, squeezed and limited resources, and shifts in the organizational paradigms that were fostered through our understanding of organizational design and structures.

For example, the demands of consumer-oriented students and their families for greater access and additional educational services and amenities, and shifting needs from increasingly diverse populations of students created enormous competition among institutions to offer higher-quality, costlier, and more individualized programs, services and facilities to lure and retain students (Kuk, 2009; Kuk et al., 2010; Manning et al., 2006). Expectations from state legislatures and the public for greater accountability and greater attention to institutional costs placed considerable pressure on institutions to become more concerned about use of contracting resources and assessment of outcomes (Balzer, 2010; Burke & Associates, 2005; Malloy & Clement, 2009).

These expectations and demands have gradually shifted the focus of once isolated, specialized units to an awareness that more cross-unit collaboration is now required to meet these expectations and to achieve an institution's mission and goals. Student affairs units are reaching out to academic units to foster a greater focus on student learning and success, and academic disciplines are fostering cross-discipline and interdisciplinary studies, and research granting agencies are demanding interdisciplinary teams on major funded research projects. In recent years efforts to collaborate with other units within student affairs and across division boundaries have increased, but they have not been sustained by current organizational structures (Kezar & Lester, 2010). So what is going on, and why do current functional, hierarchical structures no longer work as effectively as they did in the past? Are student affairs organizations at a point where changes to organizational structure are needed to adapt to the needs of the organization and to the new focus on collaboration?

Organizational theorists and researchers believe we are in the midst of a major paradigm shift in how we understand and view organizations and their designs (Allen & Cherrey, 2000; Galbraith, 2002; Goold & Campbell, 2002; Kezar, 2001; Kezar & Lester, 2010; Wheatley, 2006). These new understandings of organizational structure and how they can assist in designing more effective organizations probably will have a significant impact on improving organizational functioning. So what has changed with regard to our knowledge and understanding of organizational structures?

"The basic tenet of organizational structure theory is that an organization's structure should divide the work of an organization and then differentiate, coordinate and integrate the work at all levels within the organization to best meet the mission and goals of the organization" (Kuk et al., 2010, p. 112). What has been changing in modern-day organizations, including student affairs, is the way *differentiation* and *integration* might be accomplished within organizations as a response to how interaction with the environment occurs.

Early organizational theorists viewed organizations as machines that required boundaries between units and the external environment to be productive. They relied on predictability and accuracy, achieved through control, specialization, vertical communication, and limited exchanges with the external environment (Foyol, 1949; Taylor, 1911; Weber, 1947). This worked well when the operating environment was somewhat predictable and the boundaries between the organization and the environment were fortified, clear, and easily managed from the top of the organization.

In today's organizations the boundaries between the organization and the external environment are beginning to blur and in some cases merge (Ashkenas, Ulrich, Jick, & Kerr, 2002). Dynamic and rapid changes in the external environment require organizations to respond more quickly and differently from how they have in the past. These required responses to the environment have begun to shift the paradigm of how organizations are being viewed, what roles they play, and how they need to be structured to be successful. This relatively new *success paradigm* has shifted away from controlling, hierarchical structures that rely on high levels of specialization and differentiation. Organizations are beginning to see the value of and need for shared decision making, more transparent and lateral communication, and more flexible and collaborative operational processes. As a result, the organizational structural paradigm is shifting. Organizations are starting to be viewed as open, organic systems that are in a constant state of change and require the ability to transform continuously (Wheatley, 2006).

Organizational theorists, through their research and theory building, have envisioned new ways of viewing organizational structures (Ashkenas et al.,2002; Bess & Dee, 2008; Galbraith, 2002; Goold & Campbell, 2002; Helgesen, 1995; Wheatley, 2006). First, researchers have discovered that factors important to organizational success have changed in recent decades. These factors include demands for increased response time, adaptability and flexibility in interacting with the external environment, integration of work throughout and across the organization, and the ability to innovate. They have also found four main factors that influence how organizations are structured; the dynamics and nature of the external environment in which the organization operates, the organization's size, the nature of the work it performs (its technology), and how it strategizes its work to accomplish its goals and objectives all influence how the organization should be structured (Bess & Dee, 2008; Galbraith, 2002; Goold & Campbell, 2002). Others have suggested that changes in organizational boundaries are needed to make the organizations flatter, more cross-functional and lateral in focus, more engaged with the external environment, and more global in focus (Ashkenas et al., 2002). Theorists also hold that organizations should be designed to be less hierarchical and more networked in the way they make decisions and the way work flows within the organization (Allen & Cherrey, 2000; Helgesen, 1995; Wheatley, 2006). Higher education organizations in particular need to be designed to be more collaborative (Kezar & Lester, 2010). According to Galbraith, "Organizational designs that facilitate variety, change, speed and integration are sources of competitive advantage" (2002, p. 6). Such changes would make organizations more adaptive to the demands of a rapidly changing environment, and as a result they would become more effective.

Theorists have also proposed new paradigms for the process of organizational design and what constitutes structural design in organizations (Galbraith, 2002; Love & Estanek, 2004; Wheatley, 2006). In the past organizational structures have been viewed as fortified, seldom changing, and highly specialized frameworks, with solidly defined hierarchical reporting relationships and defined spans of control. Organizational redesign generally consisted of changing reporting relationships or merging units within an organization. Within higher education, structural redesign has seldom been thought of outside the realm of changing reporting relationships. However, finding solutions to the demands placed on modern organizations, including student affairs, are going to require more than moving relational reporting lines. They are likely to be closely tied to adapting new ways of understanding organizational redesign and its processes, and effectively integrating them in redesign efforts.

New Approaches to Organizational Redesign

Organizational design has been defined as the deliberate process of configuring structure, processes, rewards, systems, people, and strategies to create an effective organization (Galbraith, 2002). Researchers (Bess & Dee, 2008; Galbraith, 2002; Goold & Campbell, 2002) have offered a number of emerging design and assessment principles that might be attended to with regard to organizational redesign. First, organizations should be designed to effectively address their institutional mission and goals. This would require attention to the unique circumstances related to the specific organization, its specific mission and goals, and its encounter with unique elements in the external environment. There are no cookie-cutter templates for how to design an organization or a structure that works effectively for all organizations (Galbraith, 2002).

However, organizational design is as much about process as it is outcome. The strategies of design should be intentional and systematic and as transparent and engaging to the organization's members as possible. There are a number of models for designing organizations, and four very different approaches are summarized in this chapter. The intent is to get readers to begin to think about what type of approach to redesign is most appropriate for their organization. The four design approaches are summarized in the following section.

Galbraith

Galbraith (2002) proposed a five-point process for organizational design that he calls the "five point star model." The five points include the following:

Strategy—Strategy, the basis for organizational success, is important because it establishes the criteria for choosing among alternative organizational forms. Strategy dictates which organizational activities are most necessary and sets the stage for making necessary tradeoffs in design.

Structure—Structure determines the placement of power and authority in an organization. Structural arrangements include specialization, shape, distribution of power, and departmentalization. Specialization refers to the number and type of specialized jobs needed to perform the work. Shape includes the span of control (the size of reporting groups within a unit) at each level of the organization. Distribution of power has two dimensions: vertically, it addresses the issue of centralization or decentralization related to decision making and control; laterally, it deals with moving power to the unit dealing with the issue or situation. Departmentalization addresses the dimensions on which a department is formed within the organization.

Process—Process addresses the functioning of the organization through vertical and lateral managerial activities. Vertical functioning deals with allocation of resources and budgets, and lateral processes address work flow issues.

Rewards—Rewards include aligning the employees' goals with the goals of the organization. They provide a systematic approach to providing motivation and incentives for completion of the strategic direction. Rewards generally include salaries, promotions, recognitions, and enhancements to work or positions. Such systems must be congruent with strategy and structure to influence goals and direction.

People—This area of design focuses on building and sustaining the organizational capacity to execute the organization's strategic direction. It produces the talent the organization needs through hiring, training and development, and rotating human resources. Again, this area needs to be consistent with the strategy and structure of the organization to be effective.

Draft and Noe

Draft and Noe (2001) define an optimum organic organizational design as

> One that is free flowing and adaptable, has few rules and regulations, encourages teamwork that crosses functional and hierarchical boundaries and decentralizes authority and responsibility to lower level employees, job responsibilities are broadly defined and spans of control are generally wide. (pp. 529–530)

A mechanistic structure is characterized by "rigidly defined tasks, many rules and regulations (high formulization), little teamwork, and centralized authority. There is a clear chain of command and a narrow span of control" (p. 530). Theorists view organizations as falling somewhere along this continuum from organic to mechanistic and clearly believe that organizations are optimized if they are designed to be closer to the organic model.

Bess and Dee

Bess and Dee (2008), building on the work of a number of organizational theorists, including Draft and Noe (2001), Mitzenberg (1983), and others, offer a design model that focuses on creating organizational effectiveness and greater employee satisfaction within higher educational organizations. They indicated the need to focus on five major contingencies for creating the optimum design for a particular organization: (1) the external environment with which it must deal, (2) the technology it uses, (3) its goals, (4) its culture, and (5) its size. They provided a series of principles they associate with crafting effective organizations, the first of which is matching the design of the organization to the environment. The second is that the organizational design must be appropriate to the organization's technology. (In this context, *technology* is defined as the function the organization performs that defines the production process in which it engages. For example, the technology within higher education is teaching to achieve student learning.) The third principle states that an organization's goals have a profound effect on the structure of the organization. The fourth, that the design of an organization is influenced by its own norms and values. The fifth and final principle is that organizational design must take into consideration the size of the organization.

Some higher education theorists argue that higher education is different with regard to its culture, its structure, and its interaction with the environment from business organizations and, as a result, requires very different approaches to change (Allen & Cherrey, 2000; Kezar, 2001). These differences may also affect the extent to which higher educational structures can change or need to change (see chapter 12).

Orton and Weick

Orton & Weick (1990) and Weick (1976, 1991) indicate that higher education organizations are loosely coupled structures. "Loosely coupled systems are uncoordinated, and have greater differentiation among components, high degrees of specialization among workers, and low predictability of future action including change" (Kezar, 2001, p. 70). Weick (1991) holds that within loosely coupled systems,

> major change is not necessary because continuous change is more likely. However, diffusion within the system is disparate; many changes will not be fully integrated across the system. Large- scale change will be difficult to achieve. Due to the independence within the system change is likely to occur in pockets continuously; independence encourages opportunistic adaptation to local circumstances. (Kezar 2001, p. 70)

Weick (1969), along with other social constructionists, argues that structure within organizations is enacted through what the organization does. From this perspective, structure exists in the minds of the organization's members and has little to do with a structure prescribed by organizational leaders. It is the cognitive map that preserves previous action, sorts, and arranges current experiences and produces expectations of future actions (Bess & Dee, 2008; Kuk et al., 2010; Weick, 1988).

Kezar (2001), Weick (1991), and others argue that structural change in higher education is more likely to be successful if strategy and process focus on changing the cognitive maps of members of the organization of how they interact with each other and how they view the organizational structure (Kuk et al., 2010, p. 121). This suggests that student affairs organizations might want to focus more on changing the way student affairs staff see their work in relation to others, how they work together, and how they can be coached to see the dynamic of change needed in their roles and responsibilities, rather than focusing on changing reporting relationships through formal organizational charts.

Why Design Student Affairs Organizations Differently?

Student affairs organizations, like other modern organizations, are facing increasingly demanding challenges in their efforts to realize the mission and goals of their institutions. Recent economic conditions have reduced necessary fiscal and human resources, thereby exacerbating the difficulties in addressing these challenges effectively. The populations and needs of students and student demographics are changing, creating new demands on and challenges to existing programs and services. Expectations of families and other outside constituent groups to provide consumer-friendly, individualized services that are timely and focus on enhancing student learning, success, retention, and safety are stretching the competencies of student affairs staff. Expectations from within the institution to provide closer collaboration, less duplication of services, more timely responses to crises, and other service demands are straining available resources with which to address these demands within the current organizational structures.

Student affairs organizations have been served well by their traditionally hierarchical, functionally specialized organizational structures. Over the years they have become complex organizations that have learned how to function with few and often decreasing resources. Their functional orientation of operation has been instrumental in developing sophisticated and reputable sets of services and programs that have adapted well to the increasing demands of large numbers of students. In most cases, these organizations have built strong student life programs that have grown to meet the needs of students by adding more specialized services and programs as needed.

Today these organizations face new challenges that require new levels of collaboration and new ways of responding across organizational boundaries that are not easily managed and addressed by existing hierarchical and functional structures. Kezar and Lester (2010) have made a strong case for the need for more collaborative structures within higher education. They cite examples of how collaboration across higher educational organizations enhances student learning, improves research and research productivity, improves governance and management, and can create greater organizational effectiveness and efficiency. They argue that higher education needs to reorganize to form more collaborative organizational forms.

While student affairs organizations are part of the collegiate organization in which they exist, they are also organizationally and culturally quite different from academic organizational units in their institutions. On the structural continuum of organic to mechanistic organizations, student affairs is likely to be more mechanistic than academic departments. As administrative units, such organizations are likely to be somewhat bureaucratic, less democratic in decision making, and more hierarchical than academic units. They are generally more dependent on student fees and fees for service to support their operations, have been the first to experience budget reductions in tough financial times, and have not always been valued for the work they do to support the institution's mission.

In recent years, they have worked hard to be more collaborative and have been the units that have reached out to academic units to enhance programs and services for students. However, these efforts have been less systemic and strategic and more personal, individual, and specific faculty/ academic unit focused, and they have rarely been maintained through the organization's structure.

It is becoming more apparent that current structures are not able to respond to the new challenges and demands student affairs organizations are facing. Functional structures do not easily promote vertical communication or advance the use of work teams that cross unit boundaries. As a result they are less able to deal with individual multidimensional issues in a timely and effective way. Students are often forced to approach multiple offices to get adequate solutions to their problems or wait unacceptable periods of time to resolve an issue due to the unit boundaries and levels of hierarchy that must be crossed to secure a solution. This is becoming increasingly less acceptable to students, faculty, and other constituents.

Functional structures often act to protect their own identity and interests and are less engaged and interested in fostering the success or other units or forming ongoing collaborations. Since they are specialized and busy with their own interests, which rarely have much to do with those of other units, they often have little time to engage in issues or problems that extend beyond their boundaries. As a result they identify with their specialization and generally have limited knowledge of units or issues that fall outside their scope of work. This generally interferes with the idea of collaboration, which requires that time, energy, and focus extend beyond one's own unit and may take time and resources away from the home functional unit. The issue of cross-unit collaboration becomes even more problematic when resources are strained or staff time and energy is demanded.

Functional specialization also makes it difficult to use limited resources and respond to new challenges effectively with existing resources. Functional specialization makes it difficult to cross-train or share existing resources, to provide vertical growth opportunities for staff, and to alter roles and responsibilities to meet changing demands. Specialization also breeds greater hierarchy and managerial levels that focus communication and decision making vertically, thereby reducing collaboration across the organization and requiring limited resources to be expended for management rather than for working directly with students.

Today student affairs organizations sit at a perplexing juncture, facing a challenging future and the realization that they need to adapt their organizations to better serve the needs of their students and their institutional mission. In some cases this change has started to happen, at times out of necessity due to shrinking resources, and at other times out of the need to manage the complexity of the organization more effectively. Some of these efforts occur without the organization's leadership actually being aware or at least naming what is happening (Kuk & Banning, 2009). So how can student affairs organizations seek to address this growing need to adapt their organizations to become more responsive to the changing environmental demands and to become more collaborative?

Effective Use of the Matrix Structure in Student Affairs Organizations

Organizational researchers and theorists have offered a number of new organizational structure models to address the evolving changes of modern organizations (Bess & Dee, 2008; Galbraith, 2002; Weick, 1991). While these new models offer solutions to existing organizational issues, no organizational structure is perfect or can effectively address all organizational issues (Galbraith, 2002). This suggests that each organizational structure has its strengths and its flaws, and that organizations need to craft structures that can enable them to address their mission and goals, address the challenges and opportunities they face strategically, and make the best use of limited resources.

While it is clear that hierarchical, functional structures are no longer adequately equipped to address the changing demands placed on student affairs organizations, it is also clear that these structures do have some strengths that have served these organizations well and might be retained. These types of structures are also the most dominant form and are not going to disappear totally from use. As a result, the functional structural form is beginning to be combined with alternative structural forms to address the challenges that functional structures alone cannot adequately address. These new structural forms, called hybrid structures, are actually structures that result from combining the principles and elements of two or more organizational models. This enables the new structure to retain the strengths of all of the structures that comprise it and minimize the inefficiencies or problems with using only one of the structures. It also enables suborganizations to have different structural forms within the larger organization so that it can match its structure to its strategy for addressing its challenges.

The *matrix structure* is a hybrid structure formed by combining the *functional structure* with the *process structure*. The process structure, a relatively newer structural model that can take many forms, focuses on the complete flow of the work process. It is often referred to as the horizontal structure where a team is given end-to-end responsibility for a work product. The matrix structure provides for the design of a functional structure along with a lateral structure, which enables the traditional functional structure to have cross-unit communication, coordination, and collaboration.

Kezar and Lester (2010) suggest that matrix organizational structures provide a number of benefits for addressing the challenges facing higher education organizations:

> Organizations that are set up in matrix fashion (have both horizontal and vertical linkage and connections among staff), with cross functional structures (different functions within organizations work together and report to each other), or are team based (units work collaboratively rather than individually and in various functional areas) and encourage more interaction, information sharing, communication, and collective problem solving result in innovation and learning. (p. 10)

The addition of lateral processes and structures to functional structures through the matrix structure also enables decentralization of decision making and increases organizations' ability to respond effectively. This can result in more effective use of resources, greater ability to respond in a timely and efficient manner, and more effective use of human resources. Denison, Hart, and Kahn (1996) hold that working in a matrix organization enlarges a staff member's experience, usually increases responsibility and involvement in decision making, and generally results in higher staff morale. Exposure to cross-divisional roles and responsibilities can ease cross-training and enable staff to enlarge and enrich their roles across organizational boundaries.

Within student affairs organizations these structures probably will take different forms or may be used only in certain areas within a division. Generally a matrix structure is constructed by placing a lateral structure in an integrated fashion over existing functional structures. This may include creating cross-divisional roles that serve all units within an organization and work across the entire division to achieve certain goals and strategies. It can also be designed to use cross-organizational work teams that work collaboratively to complete work goals and strategies from beginning to end. The work flow is lateral rather than solely vertical and enables those involved in cross-divisional roles to be involved in decision making, allocation of resources, and assessment of outcomes as they implement their work strategies.

The matrix structure has already been adopted to some extent within some student affairs organizations and shows promise as an effective model for organizing student affairs to address many of its new challenges. Examples of these structures are seen in some of the emerging roles highlighted in this book. These roles have emerged based on the changing demands student affairs organizations are facing and are addressing the need for student affairs organizations to adapt to changing roles, increasing demands, and the quest for greater cross-unit collaboration.

Work Flow in Organizational Design

One primary area of organizational restructuring has to do with analysis and redesign of roles and responsibilities within an organization. The actual organizational structure is created to hold the work tasks assigned to people together and focuses on the strategy for achieving the mission and goals of the organization. The organization's structure should be designed around the flow of work, communications, and processes associated with work tasks, and should enable those performing the various work tasks to perform their tasks effectively and work with others within and across the organization. Work flow should also focus on how staff work together effectively as they interact with the internal and external environment and how they can be adaptive to the dynamic changes that occur.

This suggests that positions need to be configured and designed in relation to each other and not as isolated job descriptions, which is what usually happens. The current paradigm for position design focuses on creating positions that are tightly designed and descriptive of specific responsibilities and expectations. When positions are designed or redesigned, they are generally created with a focus only on the current need or the vacancy that has occurred. Generally the position is recreated similar to what existed before, or it may be combined with other responsibilities, especially if gaps in service or problems have occurred or positions are being merged. Rarely are positions crafted in relation to the other positions in an organization in recognition of their collaborative or lateral connection to other roles and responsibilities.

Positions in student affairs, like those in most organizations, are also generally designed with a vertical organizational orientation. They are placed at a certain level of the organization and are given titles and compensation that match their level of responsibility within the organization. It is often said that positions, not people, are crafted, reviewed, or redesigned. Under this paradigm, little attention is supposed to be given to the persona or competencies of the individuals who occupy the roles or to the potential for advancement, retraining, or repositioning of either the position or the person as the role and/or responsibilities change. How often do we hear people say, "That's not in my job description"? Yet at the same time, how many staff actually have current and updated job descriptions, and how frequently are incumbent job descriptions actually updated? In current organizations we live very comfortably with the false notion that our job description, with fairly specific job responsibilities, defines who we are in our work lives.

We also become confused and anxious, and at times reactionary, if someone asks us to do something different or tries to change what we perceive to be our roles and responsibilities. This is especially true if the potential task disrupts our vertical orientation too much. For example, if a staff person is asked to supervise more people or manage more responsibilities, that person expects a title change and/or increased compensation. If the reverse occurs, that individual sees it as a demotion. Rarely do we restructure roles in relation to lateral work flow needs or to flatten the organization so people can work more effectively across organizational boundaries or with students.

In most organizations the organizational structure is created, and then positions are crafted to fit the structure. As needs arise or evolve, new positions are created or replaced in isolation from the analysis of work flow across the organization. It makes sense that organizations that are designed and rewarded with positions that have a predominantly vertical orientation in how they perform and communicate would have a difficult time adjusting to a more horizontal or collaborative approach to work flow or even a more complex orientation that has elements of both vertical and horizontal work flow expectations.

So how do we change this paradigm and begin to help our organizations understand and accept a more lateral, or at least both a vertical and a lateral, orientation to how they work and how they see the value of their work within their organizations? As theorists have suggested, changing the cognitive maps of the staff may be the key to crafting more collaborative and flatter structures within student affairs organizations. This is especially true in relation to their own organizational roles and responsibilities.

The Process of Position and Organizational Redesign

The first step is to recognize that roles and responsibilities only exist in relation to others in the organization and are generally connected to each other in some systematic way. In hierarchical and bureaucratic organizations, roles are tightly connected through formal authority relationships, while in more organic organizations, roles tend to be connected more loosely (Bess & Dee, 2008). Social constructionists (Rice, Sorcinelli, & Austin, 2000; Tierney & Rhodes, 1994) and others suggest that role determination is often negotiated with some obligation to perform formal role expectations but also have the ability to shape roles in ways that are consistent with the individual's interpretation and expectation of the role (Bess & Dee, 2008). Roles and responsibilities can be crafted and reinforced through rewards and other activities that promote changing the orientation of roles and responsibilities to be more lateral in their focus. Second, these changes can be reinforced by giving individuals greater decision making and resource sharing responsibilities that are collaborative in nature and more team-focused. Reporting relationships could be shared or alternated to create less of a vertical focus with regard to communication and reward structures. Work teams could be designed across organizational boundaries, with projects and work tasks being team oriented with control for decisions and resources in the hands of the team. Changes in roles and responsibilities might change frequently or as the need for new sets of skills and competencies emerge. Movement among and between units could be encouraged and cross-training routinely provided. Rewards, salaries, and titles could be more about the quality of work or collaborative results of work than on where one resides in the organizational hierarchy or how long one has been with the organization. Collaboration, flexibility, attention to work flow, and innovation could be symbolically valued by all levels of the organization. From redesign of the role and responsibility orientation, an organizational structure probably would emerge that facilitates the ability of the work to flow and collaboration to occur both across the organization and between various levels within the organization. By making these efforts intentional, adaptation and change could be managed and the results would likely produce more effective change than if left to chance. There is no one way to engage in an organizational or work flow redesign process. Roles and responsibilities can be organized and designed very differently in different types of organizations and using different approaches.

Weisbord (2006) has proposed a set of collaborative strategies for redesigning organizational roles and work flow. He suggests that some key principles should be attended to in creating a process. First, the process needs to focus on how the entire system works together, not on how a single person or team works independently. Second, individuals need to be engaged in redesigning their work. Third, design teams should cut across all levels of the organization and all functional areas. Weisbord holds that "this type of social learning, unavailable in traditional systems, changes management, and worker perception of the problem and the nature of the solution" (2006, p. 584).

Redesign involves viewing the entire organization and what demands are being made of it from within the organization and the external environment. Second, it charts how the current organization works, the current roles and responsibilities, and how these positions relate to each other both vertically and horizontally in the organization. Third, it examines each role and determines whether it is organized and structured effectively. How does it work in relation to other roles and responsibilities in the organization? The team should also evaluate how the role or position as constructed provides a set of satisfying tasks for the worker, whether it is balanced in demands and expectations, and what skills and competencies are required to perform it. Finally, the team asks the question, are the right organizational members matched appropriately with specific roles?

Once the initial analysis is complete, the team develops scenarios of new configurations of roles and work flows that may better serve the strategic needs of the organization and effectively align the work flow, organizational structure, and human resources with the strategic mission of the organization. The team may also define the gaps in the match and determine what training and competencies are needed to complete the work flow organizational structure of the organization.

The process of how the redesign team engages in analysis and development of alternative models of organizational redesign is as critical as the end product. It is the responsibility of the team to engage the rest of the organization in the process and to seek out ideas and strategies from across the organization as it works to analyze the existing organization and builds new alternative structures. It is critical that every aspect of the organization is considered in the new scenarios that are constructed, and that the team continually seeks out innovative ideas and alternate approaches that stretch traditional thinking and push the organization to optimize its resources. This process should not be a temporary or one-time event, but should be integrated into the fabric of the organization's life. Organizational redesign should come to be seen as a continuous way for the organization to adapt and engage in double-loop learning (Argyris & Schon, 1978), which has become fundamental to organizational innovation and effectiveness.

Conclusion

The chapters that follow present some of the adaptations that occur within emerging positions and/or the design and integration of new roles into traditional student affairs roles and responsibilities. Behind many of these roles are the beginnings of new structural forms and adaptations. For all practical purposes, this is often how adaptation begins and change occurs. It starts out of necessity, and in loosely structured organizations, such as student affairs, it takes place in pockets, not systematically or uniformly, and clearly not as large-scale change. But if it is to take hold and be effective, it requires a new way of viewing what we do; how we are organized to do it; and how our roles, orientations, and structures must adapt to support our changing organization's roles and responses to our dynamic environments.

References

Allen, K. E., & Cherrey, C. (2000). *Systemic leadership: Enriching the meaning of our work.* Lanham, MD: American College Personnel Association and the National Association for Campus Activities.

Ambler, D. A. (1993). Developing internal management structures. In M. J. Barr (Ed.), *The handbook of student affairs administration* (1st ed.). San Francisco: Jossey-Bass.

Ambler, D. A. (2000). Organizational and administrative models. In M. J. Barr & M. K. Desler (Eds.), *The handbook of student affairs administration* (2nd ed., pp. 121–133. San Francisco: Jossey-Bass

Argyris, C., & Schon, D. (1978). *Organizational learning: A theory of action perspective.* Reading, MA: Addison-Wesley.

Ashkenas, R., Ulrich, D., Jick, T., & Kerr, S. (2002). *The boundaryless organization: Breaking the chains of organizational structure.* San Francisco: Jossey-Bass.

Balzer, W. K. (2010). *Lean higher education: Increasing the value and performance of university processes.* Boca Raton, FL: CRC Press.

Bess, J. L., & Dee, J. R. (2008). *Understanding college and university organization: Theories for effective policy and practice. Volume 1: The state of the system.* Sterling, VA: Stylus.

Bowditch, J. L., Buono, A. F., & Stewart, M. M. (2008). *A primer on organizational behavior* (7th ed.). Hoboken, NJ: Wiley.

Burke, J. C., & Associates (2005). *Achieving accountability.* San Francisco: Jossey-Bass.

Clark, B. R., (1983). *The higher education system: Academic organization in cross national perspective.* Berkeley: University of California Press.

Denison, D. R., Hart, S. L., & Kahn, J. A. (1996). From chimneys to cross-functional teams: Developing and validating a diagnostic model. *Academy of Management Journal, 39*, 1005–1023.

Draft, R. L., & Noe, R. A. (2001). *Organizational behavior.* Fort Worth, TX: Harcourt College Publications.

Foyol, H. (1949). *General and industrial management.* London: Pitman (first published in 1919).

Galbraith, J. R. (2002). *Designing organizations: An executive guide to strategy, structure and process.* San Francisco: Jossey-Bass.

Goold, M., & Campbell, M. (2002). *Designing effective organizations.* San Francisco: Jossey-Bass.

Gumport, P. (1993). Academic restructuring: Organizational change and institutional imperatives. *Higher Education, 39*, 67–91.

Helgesen, S. (1995). *The web of inclusion: A new architecture for building great organizations.* New York: Doubleday/Currency.

Hirt, J. B. (2006). *Where you work matters: Student affairs administration at different types of institutions.* Lanham, MD: University Press of America.

Kezar, A. (2001). Understanding and facilitating organizational change in the 21st century. *ASHE-ERIC Higher Education Report.* San Francisco: Jossey-Bass.

Kezar, A., & Lester, J. (2010). *Organizing higher education for collaboration: A guide for campus leaders.* San Francisco: Jossey-Bass.

Komives, S. R., Woodard, D. B., & Associates, (2003). *Student services: A handbook for the profession* (4th ed.). San Francisco: Jossey-Bass.

Kuk, L. (2009). The dynamics of organizational models within student affairs. In G. S. Kuk, L., & Banning, J. H. (2009). Designing student affairs organizational structures: Perceptions of senior student affairs officers. *NASPA Journal, 46*(1), 94–117.

Kuk, L., Banning J. H., & Amey, M. (2010). *Positioning student affairs for sustainable change.* Sterling, VA: Stylus

Love, P. G., & Estanek, S. M. (2004). *Rethinking student affairs practice.* San Francisco: Jossey-Bass.

Malloy, S. L., & Clement, L. M. (2009). Accountability. In G. S. McClellan & J. Stringer (Eds.). *The handbook of student affairs administration* (3rd ed., pp.105–116. San Francisco: Jossey-Bass.

Manning, K., Kinzie, J., & Schuh, J. (2006). *One size does not fit all: Traditional and innovative models of student affairs practice.* New York: Routledge, Taylor, and Francis.

Mitzenberg, H. (1983). *Structure in fives: Designing effective organizations.* Englewood Cliffs, NJ: Prentice Hall.

Orton, J. D., & Weick, K. (1990). Loosely coupled systems: A reconceptualization, *Academy of Management Review, 15*, 203–223.

Rice, E., Sorcinelli, M. D., & Austin, A. E. (2000). *Heeding new voices: Academic careers for a new generation.* Washington, DC: American Association for Higher Education.

Taylor, F. (1911). *The principles of scientific management.* New York: Harper.

Tierney, W., & Rhodes, R. (1994). Faculty socialization as cultural process: A mirror of institutional commitment. *ASHE-ERIC Higher Education Report,* 93–96. Washington DC: The George Washington University.

Weber, M. (1947). *The theory of social and economic organization.* Glencoe, IL: Free Press (first published in 1924).

Weick, K. (1969). *The social psychology of organizing.* Reading, MA: Addison-Wesley.

Weick, K. (1976). Educational organizations as loosely coupled systems. *Administrative Science Quarterly, 21*(1), 1–19.

Weick, K. (1988). Enacting sensemaking in crisis situations. *Journal of Management Studies, 25*(4), 305–317.

Weick, K. E. (1991). The nontraditional quality of organizational learning. *Organizational Science, 2*(1), 116–124.

Weisbord, M. (2006). Designing work: Structure and process for learning and self-control. In J. Gallos (Ed.), *Organization development: A Jossey-Bass reader* (pp. 583–601. San Francisco: Jossey-Bass.

Wheatley, M. J. (2006). *Leadership & the new science: Discovering order in a chaotic world* (3rd ed.). San Francisco: Berrett-Koehler.

3

SURVEY OF CURRENT PRACTICES WITH SPECIALIST ROLES AND STRUCTURES

Ashley Tull and Nick M. Rammell

Introduction

As stated in chapter 1, student affairs organizations are at a crossroads, faced with numerous challenges from all sides. How they respond, particularly as organizations in a human resource-intensive profession, will ultimately affect the college students they serve. At the same time they face the realities of shrinking resources, a strain on the ability to increase tuition and fees and the existing staff's ability to continue to address increasing demands within the current functionally based, siloed structures that dominate student affairs and higher education organizations. New structural models for addressing these issues are beginning to emerge, but they are not widely known or even identified (Kuk & Banning, 2009).

Evolution of Staffing in Student Affairs Administration

The evolution of the field of student affairs administration has not occurred overnight, yet new elements of organizational structure and the use of specialized positions are emerging quickly to meet mounting needs. While the traditional functions of student affairs have remained somewhat unchanged, how they are managed and organized is beginning to shift. Senior student affairs officers (SSAOs) are beginning to develop new elements of organizational design structures and to shift resources to meet new and emerging challenges. In most cases these changes have not been fully recognized as such and are not widely shared throughout the profession (Kuk & Banning, 2009). Each student affairs organization is challenged with responding to its environment, which includes groups of diverse stakeholders and a rapidly changing student body (Manning, Kinzie, & Schuh, 2006). Many new and/ or emerging cross-functional specialist roles may be fashioned into stand-alone positions, with unique sets of responsibilities, or they may be combined with or added to existing positions. Student affairs structures will also be challenged to redesign their organizations to address these challenges by addressing organizational structural and resource issues more effectively and creatively.

Factors Contributing to Evolution

Several new and not-so-new factors have contributed to the emergence of cross-organizational specialized positions within student affairs administration, and they exist both within and outside higher education institutions. Internal factors have included matching models to institutional goals and cultures, transforming from traditional models to innovative models; leadership; institutional crisis; technology; and professional development (Manning et al., 2006). External factors to institutions have included "technology, globalization, online learning, and students as consumers" (Dungy, 2003, p. 354). External factors beyond the control of student affairs and higher education have included "economic conditions, eroding public confidence, accountability demands, and demographic shifts resulting in increased numbers of people from historically underrepresented groups going to college" (Manning et al., 2006, p. 145).

With many states reducing their contributions to public institutions, colleges and universities have faced uncertainties that limit their ability to do their work. This can be seen in the creation of development roles and structures within student affairs organizations whereby units are expected to bring in private support for their operations. The result of not doing this is strained resources and an inability to address new priorities while meeting existing demands. Many institutions have also faced additional scrutiny from external constituencies evidenced by new laws and policies developed at the state and national levels that have implications for colleges and universities. In addition, calls for greater accountability have come from national and regional accrediting bodies. In some cases both internal and external influences may be intertwined and overlapping. Both of these factors have much to do with the conceptualization of the student affairs organization, institutional mission, support for student learning, and formation of partnerships and collaboration with those in academic affairs (Manning et al., 2006).

Organization/Reporting of Cross-Organizational Specialist Positions

The design of each student affairs organization is different and specific to a campus's mission. The ways a student affairs organization is shaped and the administrative staff who are hired are often influenced by the internal and external factors outlined previously. Increased competition for resources, greater student expectations, increased external scrutiny, and technology are all factors that have influenced the organization and hiring of staff (Sandeen & Barr, 2006). Hiring good student affairs professionals involves identifying those who have the necessary experience and skills to accomplish the task. The decision to establish specialty positions for particular administrative functions should occur based on organizational and institutional mission, needs, and responsibilities. The *Student Personnel Point of View* (1937) stated,

> [T]he principle of definiteness of assigned responsibility for each personnel function should be clearly established, even though only one member of a staff may be available to perform the function. In larger institutions, the volume of work permits, and sometimes compels, more formal organization and greater degrees of specialization. (p. 30)

The student affairs profession has long operated under the philosophy of hiring trained professionals and providing them with resources, development, and support (Carpenter, 2003). By practicing this philosophy with those who are not traditionally from a student affairs or higher education background, we can ensure the best service to our students, institutions, and the larger public—for example, enabling those who are not skilled in research and assessment techniques to take courses or attend special institutes on the topic for training.

Several positions have been a regular part of the fabric of student affairs organizations for some time. Outlined in chapter 1, these include both functional and population-specific types of positions. The argument can be made that a third type of position has begun to emerge within student affairs, the cross-organizational specialist. These roles are being added to integrate the specific expertise needed to address emerging challenges and to enhance the use of resources by sharing roles across functional units. These professionals in many cases may come into student affairs work from a different field and may not be trained in student development or higher education administration. For example, the media relations coordinator may have worked in journalism or public relations outside the university, or the development coordinator may have worked for a local or national nonprofit organization. These new types of professional positions justify our need as a profession to facilitate multiple entry points into the student affairs profession for those who are qualified and interested in these positions (Carpenter, 2003). These new professionals must also be brought up to speed on the purposes and theories underlying student affairs work.

At the same time, existing staff and those being educated in student affairs may be coached and trained to assume many of these cross-organizational roles. These changes in operational responsibilities will provide challenges and opportunities for professional development of student affairs staff. While each student affairs organization should mold itself based on distinctive institutional aspects, each should be attuned to consistent characteristics of effectiveness and should be measured against those of the profession (Dungy, 2003). Through anticipating future roles and responsibilities within student affairs organizations, SSAOs might best structure their organizations to meet emerging needs. In some cases, such has those at small colleges and universities, this may mean developing new knowledge and skill sets among existing staff members.

Current Practices in the Use of Specialist Positions

A national study of senior student affairs officers (SSAOs) was conducted to gain a better understanding of current practices in the use of specialist positions within student affairs organizations. Two hundred fifty voting delegate members of the National Association of Student Personnel Administrators (NASPA), those who serve as SSAOs at their institutions, indicated those specialist position types they hired, at least three-quarters time, within their organizations from a list provided. SSAOs represented a variety of institutional types, including four-year, public; four-year, private; four-year, private, religiously affiliated; and community colleges. Specialist position types included in the study were development, research and assessment, technology, communications and outreach, human resources and professional development, auxiliary services, and assistant to/chief of staff.

Because specialist positions vary by type, SSAOs received a list of tasks commonly associated with each position type to help them respond to the study questions. Additionally, SSAOs were asked to indicate any additional specialist position types they hired within their organizations. We discuss the results of the national study of SSAOs throughout the remainder of the chapter as they relate to each specialist position type. SSAOs provided information for several specialist position types that were not included on the national study, and those are highlighted later in the chapter.

Cross-Organizational Specialist Positions in Student Affairs Administration

Development

SSAOs were asked to indicate whether their respective institutions employed a student affairs development officer. Common tasks for such a position were enumerated and include alumni relations and development, program sponsorship, annual campaigns, donor relations, corporate and foundation relations, grant proposals, and coordinating phone-a-thons.

Among SSAOs who participated, 46 (13.14%) said they had a position employed at least three-quarters time (30 hours per week) responsible for development. The majority of student affairs development officers ($N = 35$, 76.09%) were employed at public, four-year colleges or universities, followed by private, four-year colleges or universities ($N = 10$, 21.74%). Among community college administrators, only one (2.17%) reported employing a development officer, and no administrators from private, four-year, religiously affiliated colleges or universities employed this position.

SSAOs should be strong advocates for the programs and services in their portfolios. This includes allocation of existing resources and accumulation of new ones. SSAOs in essence have to be entrepreneurial in their efforts to secure additional resources from external sources (Sandeen & Barr, 2006). To do so, many SSAOs hire development offers with training in development tactics and who have contacts in business and industry. Several skills and characteristics for successful development officers have been identified that include: "desire to succeed; communication skills; partnering skills; willingness to ask; and perseverance and persistence," (Penney & Rose, 2001, p. 3).

Technology

SSAOs were asked whether their respective institutions employed a student affairs technology officer. Common tasks for such a position were enumerated and include those mentioned previously. Among administrators who participated, 67 (19.14%) indicated they had a position employed at least three quarters of their time (30 hours per week) responsible for technology. The majority of student affairs technology officers ($N = 46$, 68.66%) were employed at public, four-year colleges or universities, followed by private, four-year colleges or universities ($N = 13$, 19.40%). Community college administrators employed a small percentage ($N = 5$, 7.46%), and among private, four-year, religiously affiliated administrators, only 3 (4.48%) reported employing a technology officer.

Barratt (2003) identifies several competencies necessary for technology officers in student affairs, including

> selecting software; operating systems; general applications; spreadsheet and data analysis; database management; presentation software; communication; audio-video and graphics software; information retrieval; campus software systems; groupware; web site design and maintenance; instructional software; confidentiality and data security; virus protection; PDAs and hand-helds; assistive technology; and use of information technology to enhance work processes. (pp. 385–393)

Student affairs professionals should acquire the skills and knowledge required for program delivery and enhanced communication, which can best be achieved by technology officers in student affairs organizations (Upcraft & Goldsmith, 2000). By doing so, student affairs organizations are able to develop efficient methods of interaction with their students to achieve learning and student development (Barratt, 2003).

Communications and Outreach

SSAOs were asked whether their respective institutions employed a student affairs communications and outreach officer. Common tasks for such a position were enumerated and include serving as media relations coordinator, maintaining relationships with external media, working collaboratively with university communications or media relations groups, producing press releases, editing annual reports and/or divisional newsletters, and developing and delivering presentations.

Among SSAOs who participated, 39 (11.14%) said they had a position employed at least three-quarters time (30 hours per week) responsible for communications and outreach. The majority of student affairs communication and outreach officers ($N = 24$, 61.53%) were employed at public, four-year colleges or universities, followed by private, four-year colleges or universities ($N = 8$, 20.51%). Private, four-year, religiously affiliated administrators employed a small percentage ($N = 4$, 10.26%), and a smaller percentage of community college administrators ($N = 3$, 7.69%) reported employing a research and assessment officer.

Colleges, universities, and their constituencies are under constant media scrutiny for many reasons. An institution's prominence in its community is a main reason for much of this attention (Montgomery & Snyder, 2002). Student affairs professionals are increasingly expected to respond directly to print and broadcast media in a variety of circumstances. Montgomery and Snyder state that the rules of media engagement should "stick to the message; move the students into the community; know the difference between rural and urban media outlets; team up with your media relations officer; let your media relations officer run interference; get the message out; and conduct media training" (pp. 27–38). Student affairs organizations hiring communication and outreach officers are best positioned to interact with media representatives in ways that are informative, accurate, and meaningful.

Human Resources and Professional Development

SSAOs were asked whether their respective institutions employed a student affairs human resources officer. Common tasks for such a position were enumerated and include coordinating division-wide and/or departmental recruiting, hiring and training staff, coordinating payroll and benefits for divisional and/or departmental staff, and coordinating annual evaluation processes.

Among SSAOs who participated, 32 (9.14%) said they had a position employed at least three-quarters of their time (30 hours per week) responsible for human resources. The majority of student affairs human resource officers ($N = 23$, 71.88%) were employed at public, four-year colleges or universities, followed by private, four-year colleges or universities ($N = 7$, 21.88%). Among administrators from religiously affiliated colleges or universities, only 2 (6.25%) reported employing a human resources officer, and no administrators from two-year community colleges indicated employing this position.

Effective management of personnel requires staff trained in human resource management. Today's student affairs organizations are hiring human resource officers to manage staff recruitment, hiring, performance appraisals, benefits, and other common human resource functions. These individuals are best able to stay abreast of legal and other policy implications that affect employees (Rosse & Levin, 2003). Some who hold this role are also charged with talent development as it relates to work in student affairs administration (Dalton, 2003).

As a human resource-intensive field, student affairs administration has historically emphasized formal and informal professional training and development. SSAOs should be concerned with providing direct and indirect support for staff development on several levels, including departmental, organizational, institutional, and profession-wide. This should also include philosophical and budgetary support for staff development (Grace-Odeleye, 1998). Through their investment in staff training and development, SSAOs encourage growth and development that pays dividends to both staff and students the student affairs organization serves. These tasks are often assigned to a professional development officer in some capacity in today's student affairs organization.

Among SSAOs who participated, 30 (8.57%) said they had a position employed at least three-quarters of their time (30 hours per week) responsible for professional development training. The majority of student affairs professional development training officers ($N = 17$, 56.67%) were employed at public, four-year colleges or universities, followed by private, four-year colleges or universities ($N = 10$, 33.33%). Among community college administrators, only 2 (6.67%) reported employing a professional development training officer, and 1 administrator (3.33%) from a private, four-year religiously affiliated college or university indicated employing this position.

SSAOs were asked whether their respective institutions employed a student affairs professional development training officer. Common tasks for such a position were enumerated and include coordinating and implementing new staff orientation, student staff training and development, professional development planning, coordinating the training calendar, technology training; retreat planning and implementation; individual and group consultations; and developing and managing resource libraries.

Auxiliary Services

SSAOs were asked whether their respective institutions employed a student affairs auxiliary services officer. Common tasks for such a position were enumerated and include managing financial and/or operations of campus recreation center; housing, union, intramural, and dining services facilities; campus card offices and/or other auxiliary services.

Among SSAOs who participated, 81 (23.14%) said they had a position employed at least three-quarters time (30 hours per week) responsible for auxiliary services. The majority of student affairs auxiliary services officers ($N = 47$, 58.02%) were employed at public, four-year colleges or universities, followed by private, four-year colleges or universities ($N = 26$, 32.10%). Administrators from community colleges ($N = 4$, 4.94%) and religiously affiliated colleges or universities ($N = 4$, 4.94%) indicated employing a small number of auxiliary services officers.

Auxiliary services officers in student affairs organizations manage a diverse array of facilities and fiscal resources, which include renovation and/ or construction and oversight of new facilities in the student affairs inventory. Having an officer to handle these tasks is essential because staff should have knowledge and understanding of the strategic and operational considerations that come with these responsibilities (McClellan & Barr, 2000). Some of the tasks for which auxiliary services officers are charged with include: developing a budget; budgeting for utilities, overhead, and equipment replacement; budget implications for deferred maintenance; establishing a maintenance cycle; staffing; training programs; professional staff issues; contract services; and legal issues (pp. 201–205).

Assistant to/Chief of Staff

SSAOs were asked whether their respective institutions employed any individual(s) at least three-quarters' time (30 hours per week) to serve as an "assistant to the vice president/chancellor" or "student affairs chief of staff." Because duties assumed in these positions vary greatly by institution, the survey did not enumerate primary tasks. Administrators were asked what duties individuals serving in such a capacity fulfilled.

Among SSAOs who participated, 121 (34.57%) said they had a position employed that served as an assistant to the vice president/chancellor or chief of staff. Most administrators ($N = 101$, 83.47%) identified this position as assistant to the vice president/chancellor, with no exceptions among institutional type. The majority of assistants to the vice president/chancellor or chief of staff officers ($N = 62$, 51.24%) were employed at public, four-year colleges or universities, followed by private, four-year colleges or universities ($N = 36$, 29.75%). Among administrators from private, four-year, religiously affiliated colleges or universities, 13 (10.74%) reported employing such an officer, and a smaller number of community college administrators ($N = 10$, 8.26%) also answered affirmatively.

SSAOs identified an array of duties specific to such a position, although some common ones did emerge, including budget and financial oversight, representing vice president/chancellor in absence, institutional committee work, overseeing capital projects and development; managing judicial affairs functions, and all others as assigned by vice president/chancellor.

Research and Assessment

SSAOs were asked whether their respective institutions employed a student affairs research and assessment officer. Common tasks for such a position were enumerated and include accreditation; measurement of learning outcomes; assessing enrollment and/or retention, programs, and satisfaction; and strategic and long-range planning initiatives.

Among SSAOs who participated, 57 (16.29%) said they had a position employed at least three-quarters time (30 hours per week) responsible for research and assessment. The majority of student affairs research and assessment officers ($N = 36$, 63.16%) were employed at public, four-year colleges or universities, followed by private, four-year colleges or universities ($N = 15$, 26.32%). Private, four-year, religiously affiliated administrators employed a small percentage ($N = 5$, 8.78%), and among community college administrators, only one (1.76%) reported employing a research and assessment officer.

Student affairs administrators have become involved in research and assessment at a rapid pace largely because of a greater push for accountability, cost effectiveness, and equity, along with accreditation concerns (Upcraft & Schuh, 1996). These practices, long considered as the work of academic affairs and institutional research, are now common in student affairs organizations. "Colleges and universities are expected to provide evidence to their internal and external constituencies that the quality of education and the student experience is commensurate with rising costs, with their statement of excellence, and with their desire to retain the competitive edge," (Bresciani, Zelna, & Anderson, 2004, p. 1).

Additional Specialist Positions in Student Affairs Organizations

SSAOs were asked to identify other specialized positions employed by their respective institutions and to briefly describe the assigned duties for those positions. Although the titles used to identify such positions varied greatly, there was a measure of consistency in assigned duties for similar positions and in the institutional role these specialists assumed. As student affairs organizations become increasingly complex, such specialist positions may merit further research.

Multiple SSAOs identified similar duties for specialist positions: campus-community liaison, civic-student outreach coordinator, conference and event coordinator, director of academic skills and student support, and student information coordinator. The national study of SSAOs discovered the existence of each of these. Campus-community liaison positions are thought to be increasing as town-gown relationships become even more important. Students have lived off-campus in college and university settings for as long as postsecondary institutions have existed; however, with new demands for on-campus living going unmet, many students will find themselves living off-campus and commuting. This is also thought to be an important consideration as colleges and universities tackle other societal issues affecting college students, such as alcohol and drug use, sexual assaults, noise ordinances, traffic connections, and others that surround some colleges and universities. A greater connection to community resources will prove beneficial when working on these challenges.

Roles and structures emerging around academic skills and student support are not surprising, given greater efforts by many colleges and universities toward retention and graduation rates. This has come through greater calls for accountability from state and federal governmental agencies as well as creditors. Many states have explored or implemented funding formulas based on these rates, thus some institutions' renewed focus on retraining and graduating students. In many cases this will lead to assigning specialist roles and structures.

Conclusion

As explained in chapter 1 and this chapter, student affairs organizations are at a crossroads, brought on by both internal and external demands and new realities. Staffing student affairs organizations, over time, has been a direct result of these demands and new realities. While many student affairs organizations have operated with functional and/or population-specific staffing practices, a third type, the cross-organizational specialist position has continued to emerge as a result of heightened demands for new specialized work and economic concerns, among others. The design and staffing practices of student affairs organizations vary by individual institution and should be predicated on each organization's mission and populations served. This notion dates back many years to the *Student Personnel Point of View* (1937).

As we said previously in this chapter, cross-organizational specialist positions have emerged recently in student affairs organizations. Each organization has developed its specialist positions to meet the needs of its campus constituencies. While we have reported on several in this chapter, including development, research and assessment, technology, communications and outreach, human resources and professional development, auxiliary services, and assistant to/chief of staff, others continue to emerge. We covered some of these previously under additional specialist positions in student affairs organizations. Some of these will be addressed in later chapters in the book. It is not certain how many different cross-organizational specialist positions will to emerge, but we can be certain that others will arise to meet the needs of internal and external constituents of student affairs organizations and higher education institutions.

References

Barratt, W. (2003). Information technology in student affairs. In *Student services: A handbook for the profession* (4th ed., pp. 379–396). San Francisco: Jossey-Bass.

Bresciani, M. J., Zelna, C. L., & Anderson, J. A. (2004). *Assessing student learning and development: A handbook for practitioners*. Washington, DC: National Association of Student Personnel Administrators.

Carpenter, S. (2003). Professionalism. In *Student services: A handbook for the profession* (4th ed., pp. 573–591). San Francisco: Jossey-Bass.

Dalton, J. C. (2003). Managing human resources. In *Student services: A handbook for the profession* (4th ed., pp. 397–419). San Francisco: Jossey-Bass.

Dungy, G. (2003). Organizations and functions of student affairs. In *Student services: A handbook for the profession* (4th ed., pp. 339–357). San Francisco: Jossey-Bass.

Grace-Odeleye, B. (1998). A model for staff development in student affairs. In *Strategies for staff development: Personal and professional education in the 21st century* (pp. 83–93). New Directions for Student Services, 84. San Francisco: Jossey-Bass.

Kuk, L., & Banning, J. H. (2009). Designing student affairs organizational structures: Perceptions of senior student affairs officers, *NASPA Journal, 46*(1), 94–117.

Manning, K., Kinzie, J., & Schuh, J. (2006). *One size does not fit all: Traditional and innovative models of student affairs practice*. New York: Routledge.

McClellan, G. S., & Barr M. J. (2000). Planning, managing, and financing facilities and services. In M. J. Barr & M. K. Desler (eds.). *The handbook of student affairs administration* (pp. 197–215). San Francisco: Jossey-Bass.

Montgomery, T., & Snyder, M. B. (2002). Student affairs professionals and the media. In *Student affairs and external relations* (pp. 27–38). New Directions for Student Services, 100. San Francisco: Jossey-Bass.

Penney, S. W., & Rose, B. B. (2001). *Dollars for dreams: Student affairs staff as fundraisers.* Washington, DC: National Association of Student Personnel Administrators.

Rosse, J. G., & Levin, R. A. (2003). *Academic administrators guide to hiring.* San Francisco: Jossey-Bass.

Sandeen, A., & Barr, M. J. (2006). *Critical issues for student affairs: Challenges and opportunities.* San Francisco: Jossey-Bass.

Student Personnel Point of View. (1937). Retrieved February 24, 2011, from http://www.myacpa.org/pub/documents/1937.pdf

Upcraft, M. L., & Goldsmith, H. (2000). Technological changes in student affairs administration. In M. J. Barr, & M. K. Desler (Eds.), *The handbook of student affairs administration* p. 216–228). San Francisco: Jossey-Bass.

Upcraft, M. L., & Schuh, J. H. (1996). *Assessment in student affairs: A guide for practitioners.* San Francisco: Jossey-Bass.

PART TWO

EMERGING SPECIALIST ROLES
WITHIN STUDENT AFFAIRS
ORGANIZATIONS

Authors of the chapters that follow will describe several emerging and changing specialist roles and structures. Authors were selected based on their personal experiences in holding these specialist roles and/or structures or because they are knowledgeable about them. In each case chapter authors were identified after the national study of senior student affairs officers (SSAOs), through recommendations from their SSAOs, or identifying their prior scholarship and presentations on their specialist roles and/or structures. Authors were asked to provide a historical background on the development or influences that led to the creation of their particular roles and responsibilities; discuss organizational reporting structures; provide sample job or position descriptions for persons serving in the particular specialist role; and identify challenges, successes, and future trends or anticipated needs with regard to the role and/or structure. They were also asked to provide specific examples of their specialist roles and structures based on their work in student affairs organizations. This process resulted in both personal and organizational insights and context for the specific roles and structures being described. In most cases authors discuss specific roles and structures at particular colleges and universities (see chapters 4–11).

Chapters on emerging and changing specialist roles and responsibilities in student affairs organizations include technology, development, communications, "assistant to" positions, human resources and professional development, chief of staff and director of administration, auxiliary services, and research and assessment. The editors of this book have labeled chapters as either emerging or changing (see individual chapter titles) based on their history and presence within student affairs organizations. Some have existed for some time, but their role or structures may still be evolving (i.e., changing roles and responsibilities in student affairs research and assessment), while others are newly emerging in their role or structures (i.e., emerging roles and responsibilities in student affairs communications). Each of these, as you will read, have significantly changed the way student affairs administrators work within their organizations. The editors predict that these will continue to change and emerge and that roles and structures not covered in this book or yet conceptualized will transpire.

4

EMERGING ROLES AND RESPONSIBILITIES OF THE STUDENT AFFAIRS TECHNOLOGY OFFICER POSITION

Leslie Dare and Kyle Johnson

T he technology officer position has become more prevalent in student affairs organizations during the past decade. This chapter traces the historical development of the position, provides two institutional examples and three sample position descriptions, and discusses future trends and challenges.

The role of technology in higher education is widely studied and embraced. When looking at the evidence—campus units dedicated to information technology and teaching, learning with technology, and terminal degrees in learning technologies—it is clear that technology is indeed fully embedded in higher education and integrated into most aspects on the academic side of the house.

Depending on several factors, the technology officer position in student affairs is viewed as a necessity by some and as a luxury by others. The size of an organization can be a factor as well. Larger institutions tend to have technology leadership roles embedded in the student affairs organizations at a higher rate than smaller institutions (Dare, Thomas, & Zelna, 2005). In either case, it is a fairly new administrative role in the student affairs profession. This chapter explores the evolution of a leadership position that is closely tied to one of the most popular and challenging areas for student affairs—technology. We provide examples of typical position duties, along with our individual experiences in this role.

Historical Development Within the Profession

Technology in higher education is generally well funded and integrated in administration, planning, and decision making at the campus level, particularly as it relates to teaching and learning. There are well-established national professional organizations (e.g., EDUCAUSE, Association for the Advancement of Computing in Education, Association for Information Communications Technology Professionals in Higher Education) and their regional and local counterparts. Research centers (EDUCAUSE Center for Applied Research, The Campus Computing Project); scholarly journals (*Journal of Computing in Higher Education, The Internet and Higher Education*); practitioner publications (campustechnology.com, campus-technology.com, *EDUCAUSE Quarterly*); and news and opinion periodicals (*The Chronicle of Education*'s *Wired Campus, Inside Higher Ed's In-Focus*) abound.

There has been a parallel focus on technology in student affairs, starting with sporadic articles in the 1970s and 1980s on the emergence of computing, including Peterson's (1975) discussion of management information systems, Penn's (1976) overview of computing hardware and software, and the technology theme at the 1983 American College Personnel Association (ACPA) annual conference that featured sessions on microcomputers and videotapes. New themes surfaced in both the literature and professional organizations (e.g., ACPA and National Association of Student Personnel Administrators [NASPA]) in the 1990s regarding the impact of technology on student behavior (e.g., isolation and electronic stalking) and using technology to provide student services, including housing, counseling, and disability services. Both themes became even more popular in the 2000s with the growth of distance education (Dare, Zapata, & Thomas, 2005) and the critical analyses of legal, ethical, and policy issues, such as plagiarism, illegal file sharing, and accessibility. The concept of "high tech, high touch" surfaced during this time with the philosophy of using technology to supplement in-person services, not replace them (Benedict, 2001). During the latter part of this decade, Internet access has become ubiquitous and social media have burst forth, evoking the following:

- research on new issues, such as the Pew Internet Project's research on social networking (2007);

- resources, such as the creation of the NASPA Technology Knowledge Community and its Tech Tools (http://naspatechtools.org); and
- discourse, such as *Inside Higher Ed*'s "Student Affairs and Technology" blog (http://www.insidehighered.com/blogs/student_affairs_and_technology); the "Student Affairs Women Talk Tech" blog (http://sawomentalktech.com/blog/); and the aptly named "Mistaken Goal: Where Student Affairs & Technology Meet" blog (http://mistaken goal.com).

Likewise, there has been a call for student affairs professionals to increase their technology skills and use resources strategically. For example, Komives and Peterson (1997) called for ongoing professional development and consultation with campus information technology practitioners, and Barratt (2001) explored staffing as a key component in technology administration in student affairs.

While the profession overall has embraced the notion that resources should be dedicated to technology administration, full-time positions for technology leadership are still the exception rather than the rule. Dare, Thomas and Zelna (2005) found that of 402 ACPA and NASPA member institutions, only 18% had a technology officer position, with 48% using either a committee or assigning additional duties to an identified staff member for technology leadership; 33% percent indicated no technology leadership existed for their student affairs organization. From a 2010 informal poll conducted through Twitter (http://www4.ncsu.edu/~ladare/techleadership.html) with 152 respondents, 18% indicated their student affairs organization had a permanent position dedicated to technology leadership, with 31% using the committee or "additional duties" approach; 51% percent indicated no technology leadership existed for their student affairs organization.

Institutional Examples of the Technology Officer Position

We discuss two examples of the technology officer position in this section, the first at Duke University in Durham, North Carolina, and the second at North Carolina State University (NCSU) in Raleigh, North Carolina. Based on research and discussions with peers, these examples are fairly representative of similar positions in higher education.

At Duke University, the position of manager of student affairs information technology was created in the mid-1990s when the first desktop computers were deployed in the division. The primary role of this individual was to install and maintain those new computers, and the position was created because the central information technology (IT) organization did not provide desktop support for individual departments. The position has always reported to the director of resource administration, a position very similar to the chief of staff role described in chapter 9.

By 1997, the position expanded to include Web and file server support as well as database and Web development. As the division's technology needs evolved, the IT unit hired additional staff. In 1999, the position was retitled director of student affairs information technology. By 2008, the department included six full-time staff, and the director focused on institutional partnerships and strategic direction. Certain services such as email hosting and physical server maintenance were passed to the central IT organization, while shared service opportunities allowed the division to deploy services such as email and Web content management more efficiently than they could have alone.

At NCSU, the director of student affairs technology services position developed in a similar fashion. The first networked desktop computers were deployed in the early 1990s, resulting in the establishment of an advisory team (Student Affairs Information Technology Advisory Committee) to determine which departments and staff would receive the first ones. That committee continued to provide guidance on technology issues for several years.

Separately, the distance education (DE) coordinator position was established in 2000; while that position required an understanding of technology, technology leadership was not its primary responsibility. However, the need for technology leadership was readily apparent, and the position was retitled director of distance education and technology services in 2002, with a focus on representation in institutional governance and strategic planning. A critical responsibility added to the director's position during this time was membership on permanent and ad hoc committees across campus. As a result, decisions about technology resources made by the central IT operation now take into account the needs of student affairs.

In 2008, three positions previously administered through central IT were moved under distance education and technology services. Operating budgets for each position and funding for part-time student positions were also established. In 2009, the name of the department was changed to student affairs technology services to accurately reflect the scope of activities.

The position now has responsibility for both tactical and strategic operations. The director serves as an IT manager for staff who are embedded in departments and provide daily desktop and systems support. The director also serves as a leader of the division in securing technology resources, such as centralized support services, hosted systems and servers for special applications, file storage, Web and application development, and software licensing. The director also participates in development of new resources on campus, such as managed desktop support, classroom technology, and learning management systems. Since its inception as the DE coordinator, the position has reported to the associate vice chancellor for student affairs.

In both cases, the organizational structure of the central campus IT operation had a direct impact on the evolution of the position. Likewise, the individuals serving in those positions had the trust of and support from direct supervisors and senior student affairs leadership to grow their respective units. These positions as they now exist were uncommon when originally established, but there numbers have grown, especially in larger institutions.

Sample Position Descriptions

In the course of networking with peers, the authors have encountered three variations of the technology officer position, each of which correlates with the degree to which the student affairs organization relies on the institution's central IT resources. A common theme is that positions become established through the efforts of a student affairs professional who champions technology use. These positions attract candidates with technical expertise as well as "tech-savvy" student affairs professionals.

Sample Job Description #1: Technology Leadership as Primary Responsibility (Administrative Focus)

In this example, the technology officer tends to have a student affairs background, with an interest in technology. This position carries with it the following responsibilities:

- Provide strategic and long-range planning for technology use in student affairs.
- Develop and articulate strategy to support organization's technology infrastructure.
- Act as project manager for significant technology projects within the area.

- Act as liaison to central IT organization and other campus IT organizations.
- Provide representation on institutional governance and advisory committees.
- Coordinate data exchange between institutional and local systems.
- Manage other IT staff in area.
- Evaluate new technologies for their utility in providing student services and developmental programs.
- Educate student affairs staff regarding students' use of technology.

Sample Job Description #2: Technology Leadership as Primary Responsibility (Technical Focus)

In this example, the technology officer tends to have a technical background; experience and understanding of the student affairs profession are secondary. Duties of this position include:

- Provide strategic and long-range planning for technology use in student affairs.
- Develop and articulate strategy to support organization's technology infrastructure:
  - desktop support;
  - systems/networking;
  - software; and
  - asset management.
- Act as project manager for significant technology projects within the area.
- Act as liaison to central IT organization and other campus IT organizations.
- Provide representation on institutional governance and advisory committees.
- Coordinate data exchange between institutional and local systems.
- Manage other IT staff in area, including:
  - desktop support manager and/or desktop support staff;
  - systems/networking staff;
  - software/applications development staff; and
  - Web development staff.
- Plan and manage desktop support for area.
- Provide server support as needed for the area.

Sample Job Description #3: Technology Leadership as Secondary Responsibility ("Hat" Role)

In this example, the technology officer tends to be a student affairs professional who has some technology leadership duties in addition to the other regular duties (another "hat" worn by the employee). Sometimes this is a technical person embedded within a department (such as a departmental Web developer) or someone in senior leadership who can represent the student affairs organization more broadly. Experience and understanding of the student affairs profession can be primary or secondary. Responsibilities of this profession include:

- Act as liaison to central IT organization and other campus IT organizations.
- Provide representation on institutional governance and advisory committees.
- Chair student affairs advisory group regarding technology.
- Stay abreast of technology trends and communicate them to student affairs staff.

Challenges and Future Trends

Several environmental conditions and trends will change the nature of the technology officer position in the future. First, the growing national focus on measurable outcomes means that more of what student affairs organizations do will be data-driven, in terms of both inputs and outputs. The use of specialized systems to collect and maintain counseling data, internship information, judicial records, housing activities, and a myriad of other information about a student's interaction with the institution is already aiding in the day-to-day activities of student affairs staff. At the same time, all of these new data can and should be integrated into early warning systems that will assist institutions in identifying at-risk students and, by doing so, increase retention rates. Predictive modeling of prospect data can assist admissions areas in targeting and recruiting students better.

Second, the economic landscape forces institutions to consider a number of cost-saving options. At many larger institutions, consolidation of IT services is seen as one such option. Student affairs areas that currently have staff to maintain their desktop computer and server resources may find they are being asked to fold those resources and responsibilities into the central IT operation to provide more cost-effective service in that area. While this trend could be seen as a threat, this strategy, when implemented properly, can leave the remaining student affairs IT staff with more time to focus on issues that have more direct impact on services to students.

Third is the recent rise of cloud computing. EDUCAUSE ("7 Things You Should Know . . . ," 2009) defines *cloud computing* as "the delivery of scalable IT resources over the Internet, as opposed to hosting and operating those resources locally, such as on a college or university network." This new model enables functional areas to deploy technology solutions without requiring the traditional internal server support. While cloud computing does alleviate resource concerns for student affairs IT staff, it also introduces new complexities, including legal, contractual, and data exchange issues. As more functional areas take advantage of this model, the technology officer will need to ensure that student affairs IT staff have the requisite skills for supporting cloud computing, and that student affairs staff understand the benefits and risks of this model.

Fourth, mobile computing will grow tremendously, which will have an effect on all aspects of technology: hardware, software, infrastructure, support, development, and security. Tim O'Reilly, the founder and CEO of O'Reilly Media, recently stated, "The biggest thing that's next, that's on everybody's mind is the transition to mobile" (Siegel, 2010). The implications are significant for higher education because students use mobile devices for the many facets of their daily lives, both in and outside the classroom. The technology officer will need to ensure that resources are dedicated to accommodate this emerging trend.

Fifth, the impact of technology on college students continues to be of interest to many, and concern for some, especially given the recent advent and growth in social media. For example, Seider (2009) posits the "Fragmented Generation" moniker to describe the current generation of young adults and the effect of enormous amounts of information available through technology. The technology officer will need to monitor research in this area constantly to advise student affairs departments and staff.

Conclusion

The technology officer position is not yet widely established in student affairs organizations, but it is reasonable to expect its numbers to increase greatly in the near future. The position is well suited to bring cohesiveness and efficiency to a student affairs organization through strategic planning and building a partnership with the campus IT organization. However, keeping pace with continually evolving technologies, and their impact on students, will be a primary challenge for those serving in this position. Technology is a crucial and omnipresent resource for student affairs staff and organizations and ultimately plays an essential role in the development, retention, and success of students. Senior student affairs officers must find a way to allocate permanent resources to support this critical function within student affairs organizations.

References

7 things you should know about cloud computing. (2009, August). EDUCAUSE. Retrieved from http://net.educause.edu/ir/library/pdf/EST0902.pdf

Barratt, W. (2001). *Managing information technology in student affairs: A report on policies, practices, staffing and technology.* Retrieved from http://www.studentaffairs.com/ejournal/Spring_2001/will2.html

Benedict, L. G. (2001). Technology and information systems. In S. Komives & D. Woodard (Eds.), *Student services: A handbook for the profession* (3rd ed., pp. 476–493). San Francisco: Jossey-Bass.

Dare, L. A., Thomas, A. G., & Zelna, C. L. (2005, March). *Technology administration in student affairs.* Paper presented at the annual meeting of the National Association of Student Personnel Administrators, Tampa, FL.

Dare, L. A., Zapata, L. P., & Thomas, A. G. (2005). Assessing the needs of distance learners: A student affairs perspective. In K. W. Kruger (Ed.), *Technology in student affairs: Supporting student learning and services* (pp. 39–54). New Directions for Student Services, 112. San Francisco: Jossey-Bass.

Komives, S. R., & Peterson, R. J. (1997). Values and principles guiding technology decision making for the future. In C. M. Engstrom & K. W. Kruger (Eds.), *New directions for student affairs: Using technology to promote student learning: Opportunities for today and tomorrow* (pp. 17–30). San Francisco: Jossey-Bass.

Penn, J. R. (1976). Dealing with the computer. *NASPA Journal, 14*(2), 56–58.

Peterson, M. (1975). Implications of the new management technology. *NASPA Journal, 12*(3), 158–170.

Seider, S., & Gardner, H. (2009). The fragmented generation. *Journal of College and Character, 10*(4), 1–4.

Siegel, R. (Reporter). (2010, November 15). Debating the next phase of the web [Radio series episode]. In A. Silverman (Producer), *All things considered.* Washington, DC: National Public Radio.

5

EMERGING ROLES AND RESPONSIBILITIES OF THE STUDENT AFFAIRS DEVELOPMENT OFFICER/ DIRECTOR OF DEVELOPMENT

James Rychner and Linda Clement

No matter what the term used—*fund-raising, development,* or *philanthropy*—incorporating a structured program of strategically asking individuals, foundations, and corporations for support is a clear and growing trend within student affairs operations nationwide. Many alumni cite their out-of-classroom experiences as their fondest memory and often point to them as critical to their current life success (Cockriel & Kellogg, 1994). Whether serving as a resident assistant; holding office in the student government; or being involved in student groups, clubs, or organizations on a college campus, "student affairs–related experiences" have long been critical to alumni engagement and financial support. Yet, student affairs administrators rarely have had significant roles and professional development staff to assist in garnering financial support for student affairs programs, services, or related priorities. Over the past two decades development professionals, officers, or directors of development have begun to play an emerging role in assisting student affairs leadership and programs as they begin to view fund-raising as part of the student affairs enterprise.

The development officer (DO) position is increasingly emerging as a significant member of the student affairs leadership team. This chapter provides a brief historical overview of development and the development officer role; discusses reporting lines and typical responsibilities; and briefly explores some challenges, successes, and trends related to this new student affairs role.

Historical Background

Colleges and universities have had a tradition of raising funds for academic programs and colleges, alumni associations, and athletic programs (Kroll, 1991). Fund-raising at private institutions has a long history with Harvard, purported to be in 1641 the first institution to raise funds for educational purposes (Worth, 1993). In the public sector, with few exceptions, fund-raising began during the mid-1970s (Cook & Lasher, 1996).

Fund-raising or development has a shorter history in student affairs. But there seem to be expectations that student affairs raise funds to support student services programs (Barr, 2009). As recently as 1991, Terrell and Gold (1993) observed that the number of development officers hired to raise funds for student affairs was small. Their number had increased significantly by 1997 when NASPA surveyed a limited number of its members on the issue of fund-raising and found the following results:

- 85% were involved in fund-raising on their campuses;
- 74% were seriously considering or were in the process of establishing a fund-raising function for their student affairs division; and
- 30% had a full-time fund-raiser assigned to their division (Penney & Rose, 2001, xxiii).

Although this 1997 survey has not been replicated, there are clear indications that staff in student affairs are increasingly interested and actively involved in fund-raising:

- The 2010 National Association of Student Personnel Administrators (NASPA) Conference offered a record nine programs and meetings with presentations or meeting agendas including fund-raising/development.
- In 2007, NASPA developed a knowledge community, "Student Affairs Development and External Relations," and now hosts an annual development conference.

Reporting Structures

In creating a development function, relationships must be forged between student affairs staff and staff in the Institutional Advancement Division (Terrell & Gold, 1993). Student affairs can be an asset in the institution's efforts to raise funds, and institutional advancement can be an asset in student affairs efforts to advance its fund-raising agenda.

There are numerous successful models for reporting structures for staff who are raising funds for student affairs. Staff can report to the campus institutional advancement operation or the Division of Student Affairs. There can also be dual reporting structures. The reason for these reporting structures relates to the culture of an institution and the financial support for the position(s) (Morgan & Policello, 2010). In a recent informal survey conducted by the NASPA Student Affairs Development and External Relations Knowledge Community (2010), a variety of hybrid relationships/reporting structures between the institutional advancement and student affairs division were reported. Variations of reporting and communications systems include:

- Development officer reports to student affairs vice president with monthly or quarterly updates provided to institutional advancement.
- Development officer is based in institutional advancement and serves as a liaison to student affairs and raises funds for student affairs priorities as part of the position's overall portfolio.
- Development officer works within student affairs and has little or no contact with institutional advancement.

Whatever reporting structure exists, there needs to be steady and consistent communication among development officers and senior student affairs administrators.

Development Position at the University of Maryland

At the University of Maryland, in the Division of Student Affairs, the development function has evolved and increased in size and scope over time. It began as a part of a development officer's portfolio reporting directly to the vice president for institutional advancement. When the evolution of the function did not move rapidly, a position description was formulated for the director of development for the Division of Student Affairs, reporting directly to the vice president for student affairs with a dotted line reporting relationship to institutional advancement and jointly funded by both divisions. Over the past five years, the function has developed into a three-person operation supplemented by student staffing.

This unit consists of a director of development, an assistant director, and a second assistant director for grants and scholarships. The director provides leadership and works with directors in other units in student affairs. The assistant director works with special projects, for example, young alumni board and parents association. The assistant director for grants and scholarships identifies funding opportunities for the departments in student affairs and works with department staff to secure appropriate campus support and approvals. While similar structures are in place at other institutions, including the University of Illinois, Duke University, and Virginia Tech, there are other successful models reporting to institutional advancement or other parts of the intuition.

Sample Job Descriptions for Development Officer/Director of Development

Sample Job Description #1: Assistant Vice Chancellor for Student Affairs Advancement, University of Illinois at Urbana-Champaign

The assistant vice chancellor for student affairs advancement is a full-time academic professional position. This position reports to the vice chancellor for student affairs and the vice chancellor for institutional advancement. Substantial travel is required to carry out the responsibilities of the position, which include:

- Providing leadership to the student affairs advancement program while supporting the broader institutional advancement goals.
- In consultation with the vice chancellor for student affairs and the vice chancellor for institutional advancement, developing the annual advancement plan for student affairs, participating in formulating campaign goals, and directing student affairs efforts in the university's comprehensive campaign.
- Initiating proposals to corporations and foundations for support of innovative programmatic initiatives in student affairs that emphasize student learning, personal development, and collaborative work.

- Identifying, cultivating, and closing major gifts with special attention to leadership development programs, designated facilities, endowed internships, programming funds, and recognition awards.
- Directing the annual fund, which includes direct mail and telemarketing using targeted solicitation approaches; analyzing the outcome of each annual fund; and initiating appropriate changes to increase results.
- In consultation with the vice chancellor for student affairs and the Parent Programs Office, developing and supporting a campaign for parents of university students.
- Continuing to expand the constituency base with particular emphasis on identifying alumni who have benefitted from leadership, mentoring, scholarship, employment, or internship opportunities provided by student affairs.
- Working closely with the vice chancellor and members of the Student Affairs Advisory Council on strategic goals, communication, alumni relations, fund-raising, and expanding the constituency base.
- Planning and implementing an exemplary stewardship program; using stewardship as a basis for generating expanded private support in the future.
- Advising the vice chancellor on new approaches for fund-raising, trends, and progress in meeting annual and/or campaign goals.
- Hiring, training, supervising, and providing performance reviews for the staff in the Student Affairs Advancement Office. (Staff includes three full-time academic professionals and one full-time civil service secretary.)
- Serving as liaison for student affairs with the University of Illinois Foundation and the Office for Institutional Advancement and building positive, collaborative work relationships with campus and foundation regional gift officers.
- Planning and overseeing production of quality advancement publications and electronic communications.

Sample Job Description #2: Director of Development and External Relations, Division of Student Affairs, University of Maryland

Reporting to the vice president for student affairs, the director of development and external relations provides division-wide leadership and support in fund-raising and external relations. Through strategic planning, research, and assessment, the director oversees an aggressive development program. By establishing and cultivating relationships with friends, parents, alumni, foundations, and corporations, the director leads efforts to create shared interests with prospects with the goal of philanthropic support for division-wide and departmental priorities.

The duties and responsibilities of this position include:

- Identifying, cultivating, and soliciting philanthropic support by developing and maintaining relationships with corporations, foundations, and individuals.
- Generating revenue for Division of Student Affairs (DSA) priorities through outright gifts, foundations grants, gifts-in-kind, and corporate support.
- Serving as a Division of Student Affairs resource regarding funding sources, fund-raising fundamentals, ethical and legal issues regarding donations, and donor relationships.
- Assisting department staff in establishing relationships and partnerships that enhance the student experience through cash gifts, corporate sponsorships, internships, speakers, gifts-in-kind, and grants.
- Providing assistance in soliciting foundation grants, including research, strategy development, and proposal writing and review.
- Recording all prospect activity and track donation information for gifts to the Division of Student Affairs.
- Monitoring DSA staff fund raising activity to ensure compliance with DSA, Division of University Relations, and University of Maryland policies and procedures.
- Serving as Division of Student Affairs liaisons to Division of University Relations Development Office, Alumni Association, Office of Research Administration and Advancement, and Office of Contract and Grants.
- Supervising assistant director for grants and scholarships and assistant director for development.

Challenges and Future Trends

With any significant change or growth in the structure of an organization come accompanying challenges. Student affairs professionals need to be aware of some of the major obstacles when entering the fund-raising field.

Finding the funding necessary to start a development operation can be the first challenge. As you have read throughout this book, finding funding for any new position is sometimes difficult, and in the case of a development officer can be an even more difficult proposition. As the old adage goes, "You have to spend some to make some"; this is true of a development operation and office. When the University of Maryland established a development program in 2003, with the help of a consultant a benchmark was set and the newly hired development officer was given clear and reasonable dollar goals and other assigned outcomes. Knowing that success does not come in the form of major gifts the first few years is important. When a new development program begins, it often takes three to five years to develop a structured and successful program (Morgan & Policello, 2010).

Another challenge for the student affairs development officer and fund-raising effort is that development is often a new concept to many leaders and other staff in student affairs enterprises. Staff seldom receive training in their graduate course work or other professional studies in fund-raising/development. In fact, the term development in the student affairs profession connotes student growth. If staff view fund-raising as an add-on responsibility and do not understand how or why they need to be involved, their chances of succeeding are very slim. Organizations that add fund-raising and development responsibilities to division-wide job descriptions and strategically bring staff on board have a much better chance of succeeding and raising significant dollars over time. Awareness and buy-in also help remove the stigma some feel the fund-raising field. Some in the field still believe that development work is "selling out and inappropriate for student affairs"; but as administrators see dollars making a difference in the lives of students and helping create and support priorities, the stigma can be lessened.

The development officer must also be aware that competing priorities on campus and competition for donor dollars can present major roadblocks. On most campuses, guidelines are in place that clearly govern the fund-raising process (Schuh, 2009). Guidelines prevent different development staff from approaching the same donor for support without a comprehensive plan in place. On many campuses the competition to "claim" a donor is fierce, and without support from campus leadership, student affairs might have trouble gaining access to higher-level prospects and donors. Making the case for student affairs priorities and helping potential donors understand that student affairs has critical, and fundable, needs is essential.

As we see more student affairs organizations entering the fund-raising and development arena, and as such programs begin to mature, success becomes more evident. Both the University of Illinois and University of Maryland have programs that began with one development officer and have grown to multiple staff members with specialized positions seeking to increase donor numbers and dollars raised for student affairs priorities.

As development officer roles expand within student affairs, the need for administration to be trained and aware of development becomes increasing critical. According to Cathy Engstrom, associate professor and chair of the Department of Education at Syracuse University, students increasingly are entering higher education programs with knowledge of and interest in development, and in particular the role of the development officer in student affairs. "Young professionals seem to understand that as practitioners, fund-raising will likely be part of their job responsibilities and seem to have a comfort level with that fact," states Engstrom. As student affairs administrators enter the field understanding the role development, and the development officer, plays within the organization, we will begin to see greater sophistication of and increasing dollars going to student affairs development programs.

Additional trends and issues related to the student affairs development function include:

- As development functions emerge, the time commitment of all student affairs staff involved in fund-raising will increase. The development officer does not raise money in a vacuum, and others in student affairs will be called on to assist in the cultivation, solicitation, and stewardship of donors. When organizations accept gifts, follow-up is required, and the time of nondevelopment student affairs staff often will be needed to ensure commitments are honored. For example, if a grant is received, unit staff may need to draft the required reports, or when the development officer finds a sponsor for a particular program unit staff might be responsible for ensuring that all terms of the sponsorship agreement are met.
- Grants and corporate sponsorship will be increasingly important parts of the student affairs development officer portfolio. Most current programs concentrate on the individual donor, but sponsorships by and partnerships with corporations and foundations are largely untapped resources.
- The competition for donors on campuses will require that we have clearly articulated needs, cases for support, and, often, defined outcomes. Today's donor wants to have a direct impact and will often

give to the program or service with the most passionate case for support.

- Specialized development officers probably will emerge as we see continued success. Development staff or administrators with development responsibilities within a student affairs program or department are beginning to emerge. Career centers, Student Unions, and parents' programs are areas where these development specialists have been created.

Conclusion

Current trends point to student affairs organizations' weaving development initiatives and the development officers into the fabric of the organization. Administrators may need to grow accustomed to these activities occurring within their specific enterprise (Miller, 2010). As student affairs leaders look for ways to supplement budgets and expand programs and services, adding a development officer function is worthy of discussion.

References

Barr, M. (2009). Budgeting and fiscal management for student affairs. In G. S. McClellan, J. Stringer, & Associates (Eds.), *The handbook of student affairs administration* (pp. 481–504). Hoboken, NJ: John Wiley.

Cockriel, I., & Kellogg, K. O. (1994). *Fund raising: Building constituency groups in student affairs.* Paper presented at the West Regional Conference of the National Association of Student Personnel Administrators, Aspen, CO.

Cook, W., & Lasher, W. (1996). Toward a theory of fundraising in higher education. *The Review of Higher Education, 20*(1), 33–51.

Kroll, D. M. (1991). Role expansion in student affairs: Student affairs officers and fund raising in selected Midwestern liberal arts colleges (Doctoral dissertation, The Ohio State University, 1991). *Dissertation Abstracts International, 52,* 1656.

Miller, T. E. (2010). Summary and suggestions for the path ahead (pp. 71–74). New Directions for Student Services, 130.

Morgan, M. F., & Policello, S. M. (2010). Getting started in student affairs development (pp. 9–18). New Directions for Student Services, 130.

Penney, S. W., & Rose, B. B. (2001). *Dollars for dreams: Student affairs staff as fundraisers.* Washington, DC: National Association of Student Personnel Administrators.

Schuh, J. H. (2009). Fiscal pressures on higher education and student affairs. In G. S. McClellan, J. Stringer, & Associates (Ed.). *The handbook of student affairs administration* (pp. 81–104). Hoboken, NJ: John Wiley.

Terrell, M. C., & Gold, J. A. (1993). *New roles for educational fundraising and institutional advancement.* San Francisco, CA: Jossey-Bass

Worth, M. J. (1993). *Educational fund raising: Principles and practice.* Washington, DC: American Council on Education Series on Higher Education.

6

EMERGING ROLES AND RESPONSIBILITIES OF THE STUDENT AFFAIRS COMMUNICATIONS OFFICER

Chris Heltne

Communications positions in student affairs organizations encompass a variety of responsibilities and functions, including branding and marketing; public and media relations; print and online graphic identity and design; writing and editing; and other roles, depending on the structure of the organization. The centralized communications model provides an organizational and institutional vision and strategy for student affairs outreach that increases quality of content, creates consistency among messages, addresses audience needs, and breaks down silos to better coordinate information. The position considers continuity of messages, methods of distribution, audience demographics, statement of intended outcomes, assessment, emerging technologies and market spaces, and more characteristics that fill out the bones of the information exchange. These considerations change the discussion from merely delivering information to *exchanging* information *effectively*.

This is the crux of the expertise communications professionals bring to the team, transforming the mass of information generated in the student affairs organization into an effective outreach model that achieves established strategic goals.

The consistent messaging at the core of communications work plays a role at all touch points with all student affairs audiences and beyond, and can be highly effective in helping define and guide outreach to these audiences to elicit intended outcomes.

While all departments within a given student affairs structure can benefit from communications expertise, the need per unit may not merit a full-time position dedicated to this function. If such a position does not exist, communications responsibilities are often carried out by unit-level staff with varying levels of communications knowledge and training, and with an eye only toward outreach for the department for which they work. This structure can lead to inconsistencies and redundancies among departments with repercussions for the organization as a whole.

The value of the expertise provided by the functional areas within student affairs is critical to the success of the centralized communications position. The individual in this position depends on these areas to provide subject area knowledge and deliver that knowledge as promised, while the communications effort works to coalesce that knowledge from across the organization and magnifies it in ways that are easily accessed by all constituencies and through all venues.

Historical Developments

Modern communications training incorporates many fields of study. A review of communications programs at schools across the country reveals course requirements and electives in journalism, media studies, popular culture, statistics, economics, research methodology, sociology, demographic studies, business, ethnography, public policy, child and adolescent development, law, and much more. Further, studies in psychology, psychoanalysis, sociology, anthropology, linguistics, and other fields inform the history of and establish the foundation for the concept of branding, a holistic approach to communications that pervades the industry. Thus the concept of branding that influences so much of the communications, marketing, and public relations landscape today is rooted in part in the seminal ideas of other fields (Moor, 2007).

Most Fortune 500 companies today have high-level, even executive-level positions such as a chief communications officer or chief branding officer whose role it is to develop and nurture the company's brand strategy. This trend is manifesting itself even more so today in colleges and universities. Brand strategist Martin Jelsema (2010) lists a variety of elements that all brand strategies should consider. These include existing audience perceptions and expectations, analysis of competition, service attributes, relationship with the audiences, organizational image, and much more. Student affairs administrators would be well served to consider these elements as well when building their own brands.

In a brand's best proactive iteration, individuals with media relations responsibilities pitch the best stories to appropriate media to direct a picture that is consistent with brand goals. More often, however, media relations is reactionary, responding to an inquiry from one or more media outlets about an emerging story. In these instances, a solid messaging foundation is critical.

This has been in evidence on campuses across the country throughout the current economic downturn. Public and private universities have multiple constituencies to inform constantly, as the outlook and facts shift almost daily. Consistent and clear messages are paramount, ensuring that whoever is speaking, wherever the messages are appearing, whatever the statement being made, everyone is saying the same thing (Masterson, 2009).

The centralized communications role consolidates these messages into a consistent brand strategy that aligns with university and division-level strategic goals, while keeping in mind the relationships that departments, programs, and individuals build with various campus constituencies. Without a centralized approach to help coalesce the many messages from the individual departments within the division, community understanding of the division and the departments becomes confused and fractured, and success of outreach efforts is diminished.

Reporting Structures for Communications Officers in Student Affairs

The following position for Duke University reports to the vice president for student affairs. While no other formal reporting relationship exists, the position is required to build strong relationships with colleagues within the division and throughout the university to ensure effective communications. This includes regular interactions with the Office of Public Affairs and Government Relations, which oversees university communications; the Office of News and Communications, which is the primary communications conduit for external communications; and the Office of Alumni Affairs as well as the communications liaisons at the various schools and other administrative units throughout the university. Further, the individual in this position is a member of both the university crisis communications team and the student affairs crisis response team during emergency response procedures, a time when consistent and clear communications can be both critical and exceedingly difficult.

Sample Job Descriptions for Communications Officers in Student Affairs

The following represent two job descriptions for current communications officers working within student affairs organizations.

Sample Job Description #1: Director of Communications for Student Affairs, Duke University

The director of communications for student affairs at Duke is a full-time position that reports to the vice president for student affairs. Duties and responsibilities of this position include:

- Develop communications goals and measurable outcomes for the division. Consult with internal and external stakeholders to identify needs; discern objectives; and, in consultation with appropriate university partners, develop effective approaches to communications with students and other stakeholders. Assess effectiveness of communications strategies and modify approaches as necessary.
- Develop and maintain collaborative relationships with the Office of News and Communications (ONC), Office of the Dean for Undergraduate Education, DukeEngage, and other key communications contacts within the university. Work with these colleagues in the development, delivery, and assessment of key institutional messages to students, parents, and other internal and external constituencies.
- Serve on the university's Crisis Communications Team. Carry out assigned tasks when the team is convened in response to a crisis situation. Develop a crisis communications plan for student affairs and coordinate development and delivery of critical messages to internal constituents during crisis periods.
- Define and implement division branding concepts and design standards and update as needed. Provide consultation to departments with regard to application of branding and design standards to department websites, publications, and other outreach.
- Oversee the division's major publications and communications efforts to ensure alignment with institutional messages. Provide consultation

on the creation and/or revision of departmental publications or communications, including determining content and design as well as editing and production. Provide consultation to departments regarding the use of technical consultants, graphic designers, photographers, and freelancers as needed. Edit bulletins and other university publications containing information about student affairs.

- Plan, implement, and assess communications campaigns for special projects or initiatives in student affairs.
- Initiate articles and news items of interest for university print and electronic publications, in coordination with the ONC and others, as appropriate.
- Coordinate format and presentation of background materials for key audiences, such as senior administrators, board of trustees, and others, including but not limited to reports and white papers. Oversee preparation and production of division annual report. Assist with internal communications efforts related to policies, processes, and operations.

Sample Job Description #2: Associate Director of Administration for Communications and Marketing, Division of Student Affairs, Virginia Tech

The associate director reports to the director and chief of staff in the office of the vice president for student affairs. As the chief marketing, media relations, information technology, and communications officer for the Division of Student Affairs, the associate director of administration for communications and marketing:

- Develops, implements, and maintains a comprehensive public relations plan and advises and assists the vice president for student affairs and the president with public relations and information technology matters. This includes performing or supervising the following activities: (a) market research and customer profiling; (b) strategic market planning for organizations in the division; (c) promotional and publicity and communication strategies; (d) content and design of websites; (e) overview presentations; (f) graphic design of all printed materials; and (g) special projects, as assigned.
- Develops and recommends information technology policies and procedures, analyzes the IT needs of departments and establishes priorities for company's IT expenditures, and, with technology, develops and implements communications strategies.

- Creates new opportunities to showcase facilities and publicize features of programs to increase sales and awareness.
- Designs and oversees implementation of Division of Student Affairs events such as Family Day/Weekend, reunions, and opening week events.
- Identifies and implements community relations opportunities, both locally and globally.
- Enhances the strategic direction of all areas within the Division of Student Affairs through appropriate and effective communication strategies.
- Oversees and administers budget requests and expenditures, while enhancing new revenue opportunities.
- Directs and supervises a full-time staff of eight; part-time staff of four; and intern staff of four to 20 in graphic arts, marketing, conference management, information systems management, and marketing assistance event management. A student staff of 10 supports these same areas.
- Provides research information services and consulting for a variety of programs and services.
- Serves as a member of the Division of Student Affairs Leadership Group and works, as a part of this team, to provide a positive experience to students and other clients.

Anticipated Needs for the Future

Without a doubt communications has become increasingly immediate and varied in form over the past few decades. From a focus on printed materials as a means of communication on campus, to the explosion of the Internet, blogs, Facebook, Twitter, and flickr, communication is coming faster, and there's more of it. Messages are everywhere, all the time, and the competition for attention is formidable.

Communications officers in student affairs need to keep up with this new and emerging technology. As outlets multiply, student affairs offices must adjust their outreach efforts, particularly given the backgrounds and needs of their primary audiences for programs and services. Each new entering class will potentially have a new favorite medium. Meeting its members on their turf is critical to delivering information successfully. In this new world of social media, the role of websites is changing. While still important for delivering information and providing a format for transactions, they are no longer being surfed and browsed the way they once were.

In light of this situation, any communications strategy must be flexible and have the ability to incorporate emerging technologies and changing use of existing technologies, as discussed in chapter 4. Communications officers in student affairs must also be willing to play with new tools that might make it big, or might go bust: Second Life, Foursquare, SCVNGR, and Tumblr, among others. Those responsible for communications must stay abreast of the use of, audiences for, and popularity of these technologies to ensure maximum effectiveness (Comm, 2010).

Conclusion

The student affairs organization performs many different functions across the university landscape. These functions are divided among departments that are responsible for delivering programs and services to their identified populations. As departments promote their offerings to the university community, they compete for attention among the many other messages audiences receive each day, including those that other student affairs offices deliver. Multiply that same approach by the number of departments in the organization, and within student affairs alone, the competition for audience attention begins to build, and then increases exponentially.

More communication is not the answer, per se; the answer lies in *effective* communication. Sending information and blanketing the communications avenues does not ensure success. "While it's great to have a large following on Twitter and Facebook, the value of your followers list is all about quality, not quantity" (Gerber & Toren, 2010). In fact, much research says more actually damages the sender's ability to get a message across. Audiences tune out overused listservs or twitter feeds, ignoring messages they have grown to devalue. They simply stop listening.

Communications professionals at the organizational level play an integral role for student affairs offices. They provide an organization-wide view of communications outreach; develop consistent messages from the student affairs strategic plan; translate those messages into language that is accessible for target audiences; reduce the noise caused by too many messages created in silos; and increase message effectiveness through consolidated outreach. They also help departments and the organization create relationships with those communities that will allow student affairs to develop an effective, responsive, and trusted brand for the division and for the departments that team members can share.

If the communications effort is successful, the brand the audience thinks of when its members encounter student affairs will be exactly the association the division intended. A student affairs office that communicates effectively with the university community will be better positioned to provide the full value of its programs and services to campus, and thus reach its strategic goals.

References

Comm, J. (2010). *Twitter power 2.0: How to dominate your market one tweet at a time.* Hoboken, NJ: John Wiley.

Gerber, S., & Toren, A. (2010). How to: Get the most from a small business social media presence. *Mashable.* Retrieved from http://mashable.com/2010/11/10/small-biz-social-media/

Jelsema, M. (2010). The elements of a branding strategy. *The Sideroad.* Retrieved from http://www.sideroad.com/Branding/branding-strategy-elements.html

Masterson, K. (2009, November 29). Harsh economy drives new brand of communication from the top. *The Chronicle of Higher Education.* Retrieved from http://chronicle.com/article/Economic-Crisis-Creates-a-N/49286/

Moor, L. (2007). *The rise of brands.* New York: Berg.

7

CHANGING ROLES AND RESPONSIBILITIES OF THE "ASSISTANT TO"

Sherry Mallory, Evette Castillo Clark, and Bernie Shulz

Introduction

As higher education has become increasingly complex, and the responsibilities of the senior student affairs officer (SSAO) have continued to evolve, the role of the "assistant to" has taken on greater importance in student affairs. The "assistant to" position, which reports directly to the SSAO and often has flexible assignments, with little or no line responsibility, is not new to higher education; Giddens (1971) and Stringer (1977) first wrote of it nearly four decades ago. It is, however, still relatively new as a specialist position within student affairs organizations.

A unique aspect of the position is that, like snowflakes, no two "assistant to" job descriptions are exactly alike. While we can identify a few common roles and responsibilities, the position often varies greatly depending on the needs and priorities of the SSAO, the division, and the institution. In this chapter, we explore the historical development and influences of the "assistant to" position; describe its most common roles and responsibilities; provide sample titles and job descriptions; and discuss the position's successes, challenges, and anticipated future needs.

Historical Development/Influences

The "assistant to" position has its origins in business. In the 1950s and 1960s, it was not uncommon for high-level executives to have a personal assistant, or "assistant to." The role tended to vary greatly, in both scope and influence; as Whisler (1960) noted, "The role [varies] enormously . . . from organization to organization. Probably no other management title can match it in this respect" (p. 182). A fair amount of controversy initially surrounded the role. Some felt the presence of an "assistant to" was evidence of managerial malpractice; others noted the critical impact of the position on communications and information flow within an organization.

In his study of the "assistant to" in four settings—business, the military, the federal government, and city government—Whisler (1960) identified several features common to the position. These included: (1) having influence "stemming from . . . being interposed in the line of information transmission between a person of high authority and those of lesser authority"; (2) being flexible, with "activities continually varying"; and (3) serving in the role of an "intermediary between the executive and those with whom the executive must interact" (p. 207).

He also identified a key function of the "assistant to" position as ensuring open communication lines and managing the flow of information within the organization. High-level executives, according to Whisler (1960), often receive a large volume of communications and are asked to evaluate a wide range of events. The "assistant to" can assist with these responsibilities, by "being observant, talking with other individuals, learning additional details, and getting the whole picture, . . . interpreting messages, and keeping subordinates informed and reassured about the [executive's] intentions" (pp. 185, 186).

By the mid-1970s, according to Stringer (1977), the "assistant to" position had become fairly common in higher education. Yet, the prevalence of the position in student affairs at that time is not known. An informal survey of two dozen SSAOs revealed that most created their "assistant to" positions in the past two decades; however, some—such as the University of Miami and the University of North Carolina at Chapel Hill—have had an "assistant to" in place since the late 1970s or early 1980s.

In 2009, Tull et al. surveyed 250 SSAOs at two- and four-year colleges and universities across the country on the use of specialist positions in student affairs. They found that roughly one-third (31%) reported having an "assistant to." Reasons cited for creating the position included the need to have a strong staff person who can handle the day-to-day operations of the vice president's office; to have someone with the flexibility to move in different directions and take on a variety of projects; and to have someone who could assist with communication details—drafting letters, speeches, and presentations—and respond to inquiries from the campus and surrounding community.

As noted in chapter 9, the increased prevalence of the "assistant to" position—like the chief of staff position—probably is related to changes in the higher education landscape over the last decade or so that have increased the complexity and scope of student affairs work" (Bonner & Fleming, 2011, p. 96). Over time, student affairs divisions have developed a range of new programs and services in response to emerging student needs, and have formed partnerships with academic affairs focusing on an increased emphasis on student learning (Kuk & Banning, 2009; Manning, Kinzie, & Schuh, 2006).

In addition, the role of the SSAO has fundamentally changed, with greater emphasis on accountability, transparency, managing multiple budgets, seeking external funds, and navigating a complex political climate (Grund, 2009). As demands on the SSAO have grown and shifted, so too has the need for a staff member who can serve as a "utility infielder" or "go to" person for the SSAO and the division, stepping in where needed and assisting with critical issues such as accreditation, assessment, budget management, crisis management, grant writing, information technology, internal and external communications, strategic planning, and professional development.

Titles, Reporting Structures, and Areas of Responsibility

A review of 25 "assistant to" position descriptions at 22 four-year colleges and universities revealed a range of titles and job responsibilities. However, a common thread connected all positions reviewed: in every case, the "assistant to" reported directly to the SSAO. Titles tended to vary greatly, ranging from "assistant to the vice president" and "special assistant to the vice president," to "executive associate to the vice president" and "director of strategic initiatives and planning."

Fifteen shared areas of responsibility emerged among the positions reviewed. Given the importance of assessment and communication with a range of stakeholders, it was not surprising to see assessment (84%) and communications (56%) emerge as the top two areas of responsibility. Also common are serving as an ombudsperson/addressing student concerns (52%) and providing professional development oversight (52%). A summary of areas of responsibility is presented in table 7.1.

TABLE 7.1
"Assistant To" Areas of Responsibility

Areas of Responsibility	Number (N = 25)	%
Assessment	21	84
Communications	14	56
Ombudsperson/Student Concerns	13	52
Professional Development	13	52
Budget Management	12	48
Strategic Planning	12	48
Technology/Web Development	12	48
Development/Fund-raising/Scholarships	7	28
Human Resources	6	24
Diversity Initiatives	6	24
Parent/Family Programs	5	20
Board of Trustee/Related Tasks	5	20
Judicial Hearing Officer	4	18
Facilities/Space Management	3	14
Enrollment/Admissions	2	9

Although not formally captured in most job descriptions, special projects or new initiatives are often a critical area of responsibility for those in the "assistant to" position. There also seems to be a fair amount of evolution of "assistant to" roles and responsibilities that may not be captured accurately in the job description. Just under half (44%) of those in the "assistant to" positions reviewed reported that they were frequently asked to perform responsibilities that fell outside their job description.

Job Descriptions for the "Assistant To"

Sample Job Description #1: Assistant to the Vice President

- Acts in place of the vice president in his or her absence and at his or her request.
- Coordinates the division budget request process.
- Assists the vice president in policy development and revision.
- Researches best practices on behalf of the vice president.
- Coordinates division assessment activities.
- Researches grant opportunities relevant to student affairs.

- Assists the vice president in evaluating and revising the strategic plan.
- Meets with individual students, when necessary, to assist in solving problems.
- Works with faculty and parents to support student success and safety.
- Advocates for students' interests.
- Follows up with student affairs directors to ensure completion of assigned tasks.

Sample Job Description #2: Special Assistant to the Vice President

- Serves as a member of the division's senior leadership team, setting budget priorities, meeting agendas, and division priorities.
- Serves as divisional representative for the university's strategic planning process.
- Manages technology for the division, including centralized Web oversight.
- Leads divisional and departmental assessment-related projects with the Office of Institutional Assessment and Research.
- Chairs the Staff Development Advisory Committee, charged with coordinating professional development programming for the division.
- Coordinates fund-raising efforts with the Office of Development.
- Serves as the division's representative in the university communications group, charged with central coordination of internal and external media coverage.
- Represents the division on the university committees and project teams that develop policies and programs and include issues of technology, faculty/staff benefits, and strategies to enhance the student experience.

Successes and Challenges of the "Assistant To" Position

The "assistant to" position covers a wide range of responsibilities, initiatives, and oversight areas to meet emerging demands and changes within student affairs organizational structures. While more traditional student affairs programs and services seem preserved in the fabric of the profession with defined roles (e.g., housing and residence life, student activities, and counseling), the "assistant to" position has progressed into a rapidly growing and evolving role that addresses and responds to changing demographics, environments, resources, and needs. Several successes and challenges of the "assistant to" position are worth noting.

Successes

Divisional scope

A great reward of the "assistant to" role is the opportunity it offers to work on a broader scale on behalf of the division of student affairs. Providing support to the SSAO in planning, problem solving, and decision making on critical agendas and initiatives is an important task. Often, the "assistant to" advises the SSAO on the "pulse" of the division, helping to set direction and identifying key colleagues to connect with on certain projects.

Point person for everything and everyone

The "assistant to" is often seen as the SSAO's "go to" person, trusted to make things happen in a timely manner. He or she is often also the person whom colleagues approach to get an assessment of the SSAO or a particular direction. The "assistant to" can be extremely supportive to others and answer questions quickly on behalf of the SSAO, thus serving as a point person for everything and everyone.

The ability to address emerging demands

The "assistant to" can help address a multitude of concerns as well as solve problems, develop new initiatives, and translate the SSAO's vision into action. It is not uncommon for SSAOs to delegate major roles and responsibilities, such as strategic planning, emergency preparedness, retention, technology, and assessment activities, to senior leaders. When an "assistant to" position exists, SSAOs have a designated professional who can help them carry out major tasks that might be viewed as "other duties as assigned" and given lower priority.

Challenges

Constant change

The roles and responsibilities of the "assistant to" can and do change quickly. Professionals filling the role must learn to adapt and adjust to shifting demands, organizational restructuring, and new ideas and initiatives. The "assistant to" may be asked to oversee a one-time or pilot project with no sustainable commitment, or to oversee an area or supervise colleagues during a vacancy or while filling a temporary role. Without substantial budgets or resources such as staff support to assist them, the "assistant to" should be able to use resources creatively and manage time well.

Staying proactive, not reactive

The "assistant to" can easily be expected to absorb new initiatives and projects, while juggling a vast array of ongoing areas of responsibility. As this happens, and the workload increases, it can be difficult to remain proactive and forward-thinking. It is important that the SSAO and "assistant to" work together to provide direction for the division, doing what is necessary to remain proactive and shifting responsibilities as needed.

Best practices are hard to generate

Given the wide range of duties the "assistant to" performs, it can be difficult to generate best practices for or research on the position's roles and responsibilities. Professionals serving in the position tend to be resourceful and generally find the information they need to complete a specific task or assignment through casual contact or communication, researching campus websites, attending annual student affairs professional conferences, or referrals. However, they may be "reinventing the wheel" when they could benefit instead from the work done on other campuses.

What makes generating best practices for or research on the "assistant to" more complex, is that—as noted previously—titles tend to vary greatly and are not as standardized as other positions that oversee specific student affairs areas. Often, "assistant to" roles and responsibilities fall under a director or executive director, assistant or associate dean, assistant or associate vice president, or even a chief of staff, which makes it difficult to find colleagues who perform specific responsibilities of interest.

Anticipated Needs for the Future

Given the increasing complexity and scope of student affairs work, and the fundamental shifts that have occurred in recent years in the SSAO role, "assistant to" positions have become a viable and important staff role. To perform these jobs well, and to address emerging trends and respond effectively to changing needs and demands, a more formal approach to professional development is called for.

In recent years, the authors have convened meetings of those serving in an "assistant to" capacity or performing related roles/responsibilities at annual student affairs conferences. However, no additional training or development occurs beyond these gatherings. What is needed is a professional development institute, webinar, seminar, or online discussion that addresses the most critical concerns and needs of the "assistant to," thus enabling professionals serving in this capacity to connect with others who have similar roles/responsibilities so they can begin to identify best practices.

References

Bonner, C., & Fleming, A. (2011). Emerging roles and responsibilities of the chief of staff-director of administration. In A. Tull & L. Kuk (Eds.), *New realities in the management of student affairs: Emerging specialist roles and structures for changing times* (pp. 94–102). Sterling, VA: Stylus Publishing.

Giddens, T. R. (1971). The assistant to the president: Who is he? *Educational Record*, *52*(4), 357–360.

Grund, N. (2009). The continuing evolution of student affairs: A roundtable discussion with SSAOs. *Leadership Exchange*, *6*(4), 24–28.

Kuk, L., & Banning, J. H. (2009). Designing student affairs organizational structures: Perceptions of senior student affairs officers. *NASPA Journal*, *46*(1), 94–117.

Manning, K., Kinzie, J., & Schuh, J. (2006). *One size does not fit all: Traditional and innovative models of student affairs practice*. New York: Routledge.

Stringer, J. (1977). The role of the "assistant to" in higher education. *The Journal of Higher Education*, *48*(2), 193–201.

Tull, A., Brazzell, J. C., Harbin, J. J., Broyles, P., & Flanagan, S. (2009, March). *Trends in the use of specialist positions in staffing student affairs organizations*. Presented at the NASPA National Conference, Seattle, WA.

Whisler, T. L. (1960). The "assistant-to" in four administrative settings. *Administrative Science Quarterly*, *5*(2), 181–216.

8

CHANGING ROLES AND RESPONSIBILITIES IN STUDENT AFFAIRS HUMAN RESOURCES AND PROFESSIONAL DEVELOPMENT

Allison Hawkins Crume

The roles and responsibilities of student affairs human resources have grown beyond traditional employee and labor relations aspects. Human resources has expanded to include ongoing staff training and professional development as integral functions. Most higher education institutions have human resources departments that fall under a division of finance, administration, or support services. This chapter explores the historical development of the human resources position within student affairs, describes current human resources positions with professional development responsibilities, and presents ideas and challenges for future growth in this area.

Historical Development of Human Resources

Alagaraja and Dooley (2003) asserted that a global perspective is needed to truly understand the history and formation of human resources development (HRD). The roots of HRD can be traced back to the earliest technological revolutions and civilizations from 5,000,000 BCE to 1250 BCE. There is evidence of training in survival skills and organizational behaviors in the earliest cultures. For example, Syrian, Egyptian, and Chinese societies had peer education, apprenticeship, and business models. Western literature identifies the Industrial Revolution, 1763–1871, as a pivotal shift for U.S. industrialization. In particular the American Civil War, 1861–1865, led to a high demand for warfare materials quickly and at low cost. In addition, job opportunities expanded from skilled trades to assembly line workers, and human resource positions increased as well to handle pay and benefits (Alagaraja & Dooley, 2003; Storberg-Walker & Bierema, 2008).

The introduction of the managerial role created a class system within the workforce, further dividing supervisors from employees. The need for a separate entity to advocate for workers became more apparent as management felt time spent on personnel issues was money lost. Employees started unions to voice their concerns to disconnected supervisors, and the breakdown of the employer-employee relationship was the impetus for creating human resources as a work organization position (Losey, 1998).

The formation of unions and worker strikes caught the attention of the U.S. government. Several initiatives and legislation were passed to protect and advocate for employees, including formation of the U.S. Department of Labor; passage of the National Labor Relations Act, or Wagner Act; and creation of the National Labor Relations Board (NLRB) (Losey, 1998). The human resources role expanded to provide overall administrative support for personnel matters, including equity. In 1946, the College and University Professional Association for Human Resources (CUPA-HR) was formed; its mission is:

> to provide dynamic leadership to the higher education human resources profession and the higher education community by delivering essential knowledge, resources and connections that enhance individual and institutional capacity and effectiveness. (College and University Professional Association for Human Resources [CUPA-HR], 2010)

Human resources in higher education mirror the human resources role in business. Human resources departments at colleges and universities vary in size and responsibility, but they continue to serve the traditional functions of employee and labor relations and payroll and benefits. However, some institutional human resources departments have expanded to include equity and access, organizational and staff development, employee assistance, and staff recruitment and retention programs. As the role of student affairs expanded on campuses, human resource needs increased to support the growing administration. Many student affairs job descriptions included human resource responsibilities, such as strategic planning, personnel support, and professional development.

History of Professional Development

Professional development emerged to provide professionals with mandated and educational training. Licensures, certifications, and standardized exams are required for some professions and must be renewed throughout one's career. These additional trainings, recertification, and continuing education opportunities are considered to be the original professional development programs (Carpenter, Miller, & Winston, 1980; Carpenter & Stimpson, 2007). The Council for the Advancement of Standards in Higher Education (CAS) established competencies and standards in 1979 supporting the professionalization of student affairs. The *CAS Professional Standards for Higher Education* provide national standards for student affairs professionals to learn and master collectively and individually throughout their careers (CAS, 2009).

Graduate programs in student affairs provide preparation for practitioners and researchers, and assistantships and internships allow students to gain professional experience in educational settings prior to graduation. In addition, graduates from outside disciplines find that the field of student affairs complements their career aspirations, which include psychology, health sciences, sociology, and business. As a result, student affairs practitioners adhere to multiple professional standards depending on their functional areas (Carpenter, 2003; Schwartz & Bryan, 1998).

International, national, regional, and state student affairs-focused associations provide structure for professionalism through established competencies and standards. In addition to the *CAS Professional Standards for Higher Education*, the National Association of Student Personnel Administrators (NASPA) and the American College Personnel Association (ACPA) provide statements of practice and ethical conduct for student affairs professionals. These documents form the backbone of the student affairs field, guiding decision making and practices (CAS, 2009; ACPA & NASPA, 2010; Segawa & Carroll, 2007).

Human resources organizational development and training workshops offer opportunities for student affairs staff to expand their knowledge of the basic concepts, such as supervision, budget management, and hiring practices. Professional development has become an integral part of manager and leader training, and human resources departments are valuable partners for institutional departments in creating, supporting, and implementing educational programs.

Experiences in Human Resources and Professional Development

Human resources departments at institutions provide a large array of services for colleges and universities. In some cases, campus departments view human resources departments negatively because of miscommunication or misunderstanding of roles. Additionally, human resources departments have the challenge of serving the entire campus constituency. Collaboration and cross-department partnerships are integral in increasing communication and educating the campus community on the resources available. For example, at the University of Nevada, Las Vegas, human resources and academic resources departments forged a partnership under new leadership to enhance their institutional effectiveness. The two departments came together to share goals and refute stereotypes. Their conversations led to further discussions of how the teams could support each other to improve the university community (Connally & Neuman, 2006; Smallwood & Ulrich, 2006).

Human resources employees need to be proactive in communicating about the resources available to the university community. The majority of faculty and staff only work with human resources during negative incidents, which may include reporting a grievance, documenting a staff improvement plan, or handling staff conflict. Even positive incidents such as hiring new staff and salary increases can be burdened with bureaucracy and directives. Instead, human resource departments need to be more collegial and advisory, helping to remove barriers for campus partners (Connally & Neuman, 2006). Associating with positive programs and activities is one way to change how human resources are perceived on campus.

Examples of Human Resource Services

Texas A&M University's Administrative and Human Resources department encompasses employee and organizational development, policy and practice review, workforce management, human resources operations, and benefit services. In addition to supporting these areas, the department provides opportunities for employee recognition and awards. Administrative and

Human Resources provides tools to assist and encourage supervisors and staff with recognition and appreciation ideas. The department also provides links to Texas A&M employee award programs, including monetary compensation awards available to recognize outstanding accomplishments.

Professional development is a necessity throughout the university community. Seeing a need for more specialized staff training, student affairs divisions created educational models based on the profession's national standards and competencies (CAS, 2009). In particular, new student affairs professionals are considered an at-risk population for attrition and burnout. Intentional programs, such as orientation, networking receptions, and staff training, are integral to new professionals' successful transition into and retention in the field of higher education. Many institutions require all new hires to participate in a staff orientation, but more recently this session is offered online. New student affairs professionals entering their first jobs through graduate preparation programs are searching for the cohort environment they experienced as graduate students. Some institutions even create specific programs to provide a cohort experience for these staff members.

The Division of Student Affairs at Florida State University (FSU) created a New Professionals Institute (NPI) in 2009 inspired by similar professional development programs offered by NASPA and ACPA. The program consists of seven two-hour sessions held monthly throughout the fall and spring semesters, to which professionals with no more than five years of full-time experience may apply. The NPI enhances new professionals' knowledge of student affairs while educating them about institutional culture and assisting them with their personal and professional development goals.

Participants are separated into small groups led by two facilitators, and the curriculum includes sessions on professionalism, communication, collaboration, supervision, student advising, program development and implementation, diversity in the workplace, and assessment. Middle managers or senior student affairs officers conduct the sessions, the main benefit of which continues to be the networking and collaborative relationships that form as a result of the program.

Although many of the staff working in student affairs divisions hold degrees in higher education, some do not. The varying levels of education, skill sets, job duties, and interest make general professional development across the campus difficult. The Oglesby Union, a department within the Division of Student Affairs at FSU, has also developed an inclusive professional development model for diverse staff, and its "Café Conversations" provides professional development programming for 60 full-time staff members.

The program features a monthly lunch for staff highlighting programs and services provided by the university or within the community. Staff members are able to socialize with colleagues out of the office setting in a non-threatening environment. The program began in 2001 after staff criticized the lack of professional development opportunities for administrative employees. The department believed educating staff about existing university community programs and services had multiple benefits, including better-informed staff, improved customer service, and more campus and community partnerships. Staff share feedback after each session and make suggestions for future presentations. The Oglesby Union administration's investment of resources and commitment to staff development creates a team atmosphere for staff across job levels.

Job Descriptions for the Professional Development Coordinator

Job descriptions for professional development coordinators can vary based on a variety of organizational and institutional factors. The following two are provided as examples: one represents a position at a student affairs organizational level and the other on a departmental level within a larger student affairs organization.

Sample Job Description #1: Department Level

- Serve on the executive leadership team handling strategic and long-range planning, budget and fiscal management, facilities planning, contract management, and personnel issues.
- Supervise and provide leadership for research and assessment, marketing and communications, and professional development.
- Manage departmental budgets and expenditure control for activities and programs budgets unit.
- Assist in preparing and administering operating budget.
- Responsible for development and implementation of program evaluation and student learning outcome initiatives for the overall assessment of departments, programs, and services.
- Plan and facilitate professional development for student employees, graduate assistants, and full-time staff through orientations, workshops, and retreats.

- Lead monthly department directors meeting to promote proactive problem solving and increase communication.
- Collaborate with campus partners to develop assessment plans for university-wide events such as Welcome Week, Parents' Weekend, and Homecoming.
- Provide data and outcomes for internal and external constituents such as accreditation, budget, and annual reports.

Sample Job Description #2: Division Level

- Lead all Division of Student Affairs (DSA) assessment and research efforts, including planning and implementing major projects.
- Support and coordinate assessment and evaluation of DSA programs, services, and departments based on intended student learning and program outcomes.
- Plan, administer, review, and evaluate DSA strategic planning initiatives to ensure alignment with overall university mission.
- Compile and share data required for accreditation, government mandates, and trend analysis.
- Communicate impact of student engagement and learning in student affairs programs to university community through reports, presentations, and other media.
- Plan and facilitate staff training for undergraduate student employees and peer educators, graduate assistants, and full-time staff in the DSA.
- Identify and secure grant funding for DSA programs and initiatives.
- Provide support to major university-wide DSA sponsored programs and events.
- Create opportunities to share new knowledge and best practices through the DSA.

NASPA and ACPA jointly published *Professional Competency Areas for Student Affairs Practitioners* (ACPA & NASPA, 2010), which defines competency in human and organizational resources as:

> Knowledge, skills, and attitudes used in the selection, supervision, motivation, and formal evaluation of staff; conflict resolution; management of the policies of organizational discourse; and the effective application of strategies and techniques associated with financial resources, facilities management, fundraising, technology use, crisis management, risk management and sustainable resources. (p. 18)

Recommendations

The human resources role is a fundamental part of the administration, ensuring that staff are hired, paid, and adhering to numerous legalities and policies. Recently the human resources role has broadened to include staff recruitment, recognition, conflict mediation, and strategic planning, skills that are integral in many new professional and middle-manager student affairs practitioners roles. As a result, human resources responsibilities in student affairs job descriptions will continue to increase.

Human resources and student affairs need to build partnerships to empower staff to make more informed decisions. These collaborations will be mutually beneficial by enhancing all aspects of the employee-employer relationship. By increasing communication about the resources available through institutional human resource departments, student affairs divisions can expand the programs and services they offer. Human resources positions within student affairs should use institutional human resources departments and share best practices.

Professional development continues to have a major impact on institutions' annual budgets. Student affairs practitioners usually attend at least one conference a year either in their functional area or one of the annual conferences hosted by ACPA or NASPA. However, institutions and professional organizations have reduced the travel stipends available, so alternative professional development opportunities are needed. Drive-in or regional conferences provide quality networking and staff training at lower cost.

Student affairs organizations should be innovative in their staff programming to engage professionals and encourage socialization. As budgets continue to tighten, student affairs practitioners will need to be creative in continuing their professional development outside the traditional annual conference setting. More institutions are developing their own professional development initiatives, providing their staff with opportunities to present, learn, and publish on their home campuses. For example, the University of Maryland Division of Student Affairs hosts the Maryland Student Affairs Conference with NASPA Region II, ACPA, and the Maryland College Personnel Administration. Other ideas for professional development include conference calls, webinars, and interactive media forums to promote dialogue among student affairs professionals.

Conclusion

The human resources role was created to serve as a communicator between employees and employers. This role continues to be the main purpose for human resources outside of the essential administrative functions. Student affairs practitioners need to remember the importance of their relationship with their teams to the overall success of the program, service, department, and division. Professional development is a successful tool in recruiting and retaining staff and shows an investment in employees. Student affairs practitioners should take responsibility for lifelong learning and seek opportunities on their campus. Although the role and responsibilities of human resources is expanding, the foundation of staff development and human relations will continue to be at the forefront of organizational culture within higher education.

References

Alagaraja, M., & Dooley, L. M. (2003). Origins and historical influences on human resources development: A global perspective. *Human Resources Development Review, 2*(1), 82–96.

American College Personnel Association (ACPA) & National Association of Student Personnel Administrators (NASPA). (2010, July). *ACPA/NASPA professional competency areas for student affairs practitioners.* Washington DC: Authors.

Carpenter, D. S. (2003). Professionalism in student affairs work. In S. R. Komives, D. B. Woodard Jr., & Associates (Eds.), *Student services: A handbook for the profession* (4th ed., pp. 573–591). San Francisco: Jossey-Bass.

Carpenter, D. S., Miller, T. K., & Winston, R. B., Jr. (1980). Toward the professionalization of student affairs. *NASPA Journal, 18*(2), 16–22.

Carpenter, S., & Stimpson, M. T. (2007). Professionalism, scholarly practice, and professional development in student affairs. *NASPA Journal, 44*(2), 265–284.

College and University Professional Association for Human Resources (CUPA). (2010). *CUPA-HR Mission.* Retrieved from http://cupahr.org

Connally, S., & Neuman, D. (2006). HR as partner: Building strategic partnerships on campus. *CUPA-HR Journal,* Spring/Summer, 4–10.

Council for the Advancement of Standards in Higher Education (CAS). (2009). *CAS professional standards for higher education* (7th ed.). Washington, DC: Author.

Losey, M. R. (1998). HR comes of age. *HRMagazine, 43*(3), 40. Retrieved from http://search.ebscohost.com.proxy.lib.fsu.edu/login.aspx?direct = true&db = bth &AN = 370648&site = ehost-live

Schwartz, R. A., & Bryan, W. A. (1998). What is professional development? In W. A. Bryan & R. A. Schwartz (Eds.), *Strategies for staff development: Personal and professional education in the 21st century* (pp. 3–13). New Directions for Student Services, 84. San Francisco: Jossey-Bass.

Segawa, M., & Carroll, T. J. (2007). Development through professional engagement. In R. L. Ackerman (Ed.), *The mid-level manager in student affairs* (pp. 177–207). Washington DC: National Association of Student Personnel Administrators.

Smallwood, N., & Ulrich, D. (2006). How HR leaders can add value to an organization. *CUPA-HR Journal*, Fall/Winter, 12–14.

Storberg-Walker, J., & Bierema, L. L. (2008). An historical analysis of HRD knowledge: A critical review of "The foreman: master and victim of doubletalk." *Journal of European Industrial Training, 32*(6), 433–451.

9

EMERGING ROLES AND RESPONSIBILITIES OF THE STUDENT AFFAIRS CHIEF OF STAFF/DIRECTOR OF ADMINISTRATION

Cynthia Bonner and Allyn Fleming

The chief of staff (or director of administration) position has begun to emerge among student affairs management teams as an important role, usually reporting directly to the vice president or senior student affairs officer (SSAO). In this chapter we explore the historical roots of the position, describe its most common roles and responsibilities, provide background information and job descriptions for several representative positions, and discuss some issues and challenges for the future.

The chief of staff position has its origins in western military tradition. Zabecki (2008) explains that the chief of staff role was not necessary when armies were small in size and could be managed by a single commander, but as European armies began to grow in size and complexity during the 17th century, specialized staff functions began to emerge to manage administrative and supply operations. In the American military, General George Washington established the first staff position during the American Revolution, but it was not until 1903 that the title *Chief of Staff of the Army* was used. This role has flourished over the intervening years, and, in the modern context, the chief of staff "function[s] as the head of the national military staff, coordinating strategy, policy, training, organization, and equipment development and procurement" (Zabecki, 2008, p. 2).

It is no wonder that civilian organizations have followed suit and incorporated the chief of staff role into their management structures. Most notable of these is the Executive Office of the President. Until Herbert Hoover became president in 1929, the White House staff consisted of one assistant, often a volunteer or a person whose salary was paid by the president himself (Walcott & Hult, 1995). By hiring multiple staff members, Hoover began institutionalizing the White House staff. However, the chief of staff position did not officially emerge until 1953 during the Eisenhower administration, which is not surprising, given Eisenhower's military background. In his administration, the chief of staff assumed responsibility for "appointments and scheduling, patronage and personnel, press, speechwriting, cabinet liaison, congressional relations, and special projects" (Hess, 2002, p. 58).

Chief of staff positions have similarly proliferated in business and industry as well as in higher education. College and university presidents have followed the trend and added chiefs of staff to their offices during the 1990s. Often the roles emerged from an administrative assistant or executive assistant position when it became clear that a senior-level staff person was needed to manage the overall operations of the president's office. Over time, the concept took hold, and it is not unusual to find higher education institutions where several senior executive officers have a chief of staff reporting to them.

In divisions of student affairs, the chief of staff role has become more prevalent over the last 10 years. For example, an informal survey of 56 student affairs vice presidents from public and private universities across the country and in Canada indicated that 16, or 29%, have a chief of staff or a position that performs substantial elements of the job. Reasons cited for creating such a position include needing help with the administration of a large organization (500 or more employees); needing a trusted advisor who knows the "pulse" of the institution, serves as a sounding board, and works with key institutional players; and needing a communication expert, someone to create talking points, speeches, presentations, and reports for the vice president, to act as a liaison to students, faculty, community members, the press, and other administrators on the vice president or senior student affairs officer's behalf, and to serve as the hub of communication between the SSAO's office and divisional managers. Other stated needs include an effective administrator to manage the SSAO's office and help supervise unit heads; coordinate the work of the division's executive team (e.g., determining meeting agendas and creating annual and long-term goals); and oversee division-wide functions such as strategic planning, human resource management, emergency planning/crisis response, and policymaking for the organization.

Historical Influences

The increased prevalence of the chief of staff position within student affairs probably is related to changes in the higher education landscape over the last decade or so that have increased the complexity and scope of student affairs work. Many of these changes have also created a need for focused attention on staff development, division-wide communication and planning, and cross-divisional collaborations. In a modern student affairs organization that includes hundreds of employees working in distinct departments with different missions, a position that focuses on the whole organization can help create a unified vision to promote cohesiveness and encourage a culture of collaboration.

Evolving Chief of Staff Functions

A difficult resource environment in recent years has pushed student affairs vice presidents to look for new revenue sources, including donor giving, grants, and user fees. Departments are also being asked to increase efficiency and cut costs by sharing staffing and other resources. In a student affairs division, which can include departments as diverse as recreation, financial aid, and counseling services, division-wide planning and departmental collaborations are facilitated when everyone understands and is working toward the same overarching goals. A chief of staff can help lead these efforts.

Similarly, the need to keep pace with technological (and other) changes requires student affairs organizations to remain nimble and flexible. Strategic planning helps in restructuring business and administrative processes to emphasize agility, efficiency, standardization, and transparency. Coordinating investments in systems across campus departments (or even across campuses) can help lower costs and raise efficiency; a chief of staff can facilitate the cross-organizational communication that promotes these benefits.

Advances in technology and reductions in resources have encouraged some institutions to decentralize functions such as human resources and accounting to the campus divisions, furthering the need for an effective administrator to create division-wide policies, procedures, and programs to ensure policy compliance, promote diversity, and track equitable treatment of personnel across departments. The impending retirement of a generation of Baby Boomers has also encouraged succession planning and strengthening of professional development programs. The chief of staff is often uniquely positioned to lead these efforts.

The campus shootings at Columbine and Virginia Tech, along with Hurricane Katrina and the terrorist attacks of 9/11, among other recent tragedies, have increased colleges' focus on emergency planning, crisis management, and preventing and responding to potential campus violence. Division- and campus-wide planning, training, and communication, which a chief of staff can facilitate, are crucial elements in a comprehensive and effective emergency plan. A rise in serious student behavioral issues, including student mental health problems (University of California Student Mental Health Committee, 2006), has implications for crisis management, training, student conduct procedures, and communication across campus departments—all of which, again, can be facilitated by a student affairs chief of staff in regular communication with key campus personnel.

Growing complexity in the legal landscape and increased state and federal mandates and accountability expectations (e.g., the Clery Act, Patriot Act, Reauthorization of Higher Education Act, etc.) require greater staff attention to data collection and tracking across multiple departments as well as report writing and interpretation, which are often best facilitated from within the office of the vice president for student affairs.

Because student affairs organizations sometimes hold a less powerful position in the campus hierarchy than campus academic divisions, they need leverage to accomplish goals, promote values, and influence students and the larger campus community. The ability to generate and articulate a multiyear plan and goals, craft a consistent message, and communicate that message strategically—all chief of staff responsibilities—can be extremely powerful, whether the goals are promoting student wellness, increasing student retention rates, encouraging sustainability efforts, or raising donor funds.

Institutional History of Chief of Staff Roles

Virginia Tech

The chief of staff role at Virginia Tech was conceived shortly after a reorganization of the division of student affairs, which put in place a structure that encouraged a division-wide approach to issues such as budgets, salary adjustments, and space planning. When the division's director of planning and assessment position became vacant, the opportunity presented itself to establish a chief of staff position to assert a divisional direction in administrative matters and provide administrative support to all areas of the division (Virginia Tech, 2004).

The Division of Student Affairs at Virginia Tech appointed its first chief of staff in 2004. Since that time the position has evolved from one that initially coordinated just the finances and human resources managed by the office of the vice president for student affairs to a supervisory role that includes responsibility for a team of professional staff who serve a wider range of division functions, including communications and marketing, strategic planning, professional development, emergency preparedness, and assessment. For the most part this team was formed over time by incorporating existing personnel and funding from departments in the division. Factors that facilitated the centralization of functions into the office of the vice president include several changes in division leadership as well as significant budget reductions that have created a climate in which departments are willing to collaborate more closely and share resources.

The chief of staff at Virginia Tech has been instrumental in reestablishing a systematic departmental program review process; implementing a process to identify and assess student learning outcomes; developing divisional strategic goals, drafting the division's diversity commitment and goals; and initiating a systematic, division-wide process for evaluating administrative professional faculty.

University of California, Santa Barbara

The chief of staff role for the Division of Student Affairs at the University of California, Santa Barbara (UCSB), was established in 1993 when a vacant assistant vice chancellor position was replaced with one that focused on communication, policy development, grievance resolution, and oversight for the vice chancellor's office. This change was made because the vice chancellor believed his organization had become so complex that he needed a senior-level position providing leadership for his office more than he needed another line administrator. This position quickly evolved to include division-wide strategic planning and professional development functions. For example, the current chief of staff, who has held the position since its inception, has helped lead three division-wide planning efforts that resulted in centralized information technology services, shared administrative staffing among departments, a fund-raising and grant-writing operation, and a net-zero energy plan. Other chief of staff-led projects at UCSB include co-authoring a guide to departmental planning, founding a professional development program for student affairs professionals interested in higher education leadership, creating a professional development mini-grant program, and helping found an annual daylong conference for all student affairs staff, now in its 18th year.

Job Descriptions for the Chief of Staff-Director of Administration

Sample Job Description #1

- Provide leadership for the human resources, finance, strategic planning, marketing, information technology, facility planning, assessment, and emergency preparedness functions in the Division of Student Affairs.
- Supervise associate directors of administration for finance, human resources, communications and marketing, assessment, and emergency preparedness.
- Develop policies and strategic plans related to student affairs initiatives and resource allocations.
- Coordinate with university development on identifying and implementing student affairs development initiatives.
- Provide oversight for division's professional development activities and coordinate division-wide employee recognition and reward programs.
- Coordinate the division's international collaborative efforts, serve on the university council on international education, and represent the division in campus initiatives to advance and promote women and members of other underrepresented groups.
- Serve as an adjunct to the higher education graduate program.
- Serve as a member of the division's leadership teams and represent the vice president for student affairs with internal and external constituencies.

Sample Job Description #2

- Provide research, analysis, and recommendations to the vice president for student affairs on programmatic, budgetary, and administrative issues, etc.
- Direct and implement long-range planning, policymaking, and general administration for the Division of Student Affairs.
- Serve on policymaking committees addressing issues such as staff compensation, professional development, human resource policies, campus regulations applying to students, etc.

- Handle highly sensitive matters, including student grievances related to discrimination, whistle-blower complaints, student conduct and discipline issues, and student crises.
- Participate in division-wide emergency planning and campus-wide crisis response.
- Manage correspondence and communication, including creating complex public presentations.
- Serve as a member of the senior management group for the division, setting meeting agendas and promoting outcomes.
- Manage human resource functions for the division, including professional development programs and succession planning.
- Oversee all operations, budgets, and staff in the vice president's office.

Challenges and Future Trends

As divisions of student affairs move toward establishing chief of staff positions and centralizing administrative functions, challenges frequently emerge with the pooling of resources and personnel. Student affairs divisions at public institutions are often funded through a variety of revenue sources, including state-appropriated funds, tuition revenue, student fees, and auxiliary income. In many institutions these various revenue streams are not typically commingled, but are maintained and accounted for separately. This construct poses a significant challenge to divisions moving toward centralized administrative models in which resources and personnel are shared. For instance, over the past six years at Virginia Tech, division-wide coordination of support functions has taken place, but centralization of the staff under one administrative unit, supported by pooled resources, has not been entirely realized. The next step will be to develop a workable financial model by which resources from a variety of auxiliary sources can be combined with state-appropriated funds to support a centralized administrative unit. One issue that Virginia Tech and other institutions attempting such centralization must address is identifying a funding mechanism that will comply with their institutions' financial regulations, while at the same time offering the flexibility needed to create new organizational paradigms that cut across funding lines and allow the divisions to maximize their limited resources.

The basis on which revenues are shared among departments is another aspect that can pose a challenge. For example, should departmental financial contributions to a central administrative unit be proportional to the size of a department's budget, the number of staff it employs, or some other factor such as the unit's use of a particular service? And finally, should this basis of funding be consistent, or should it vary by service? For example, one might argue that centralized human resource services should be funded according to the number of employees in each department, financial services according to the size of departmental budgets, IT services by the number of workstations and/or applications supported, and communications by the time devoted to each department's projects. While each of these various funding approaches makes sense, taken together they can create a complex accounting model that is confusing and difficult to administer.

Throughout this chapter, we have referred to chief of staff and director of administration positions interchangeably. However, as divisions of student affairs begin to establish centralized administrative units, these units might become sizable organizations comprising multiple but disparate support functions. While such growth can provide increased efficiencies and greater coordination across a division, the nature of the chief of staff position will necessarily change. With a burgeoning span of control, a chief of staff will find it increasingly difficult to provide also a high level of direct support and confidential advice to the vice president. As administrative units grow in size and complexity, we are likely to see a greater distinction develop between chief of staff and director of administration roles.

The Division of Student Affairs at the University of South Florida is an example of an organization that has taken centralization of its division's support services to another level by establishing a shared services center (Meningall, 2010). This center has allowed the division to consolidate its financial, human resources, computing, audit, and assessment functions into an organizational unit led by a senior director and chief financial officer, whose role is similar to that of a director of administration. Staffing for the center comprises more than 40 employees who either were reassigned from various departments in the division or have been specifically recruited to fill vacancies as they have occurred. The center handles routine functions for the division that involve large volumes of transactions, activities that require a standard skill set, and ancillary functions and services. In the current climate of declining resources, it would not be surprising to see more shared services centers in some form emerging among divisions of student affairs, especially at large public universities.

Conclusion

The chief of staff role, which has existed in some form for many years, but has only emerged with any frequency in divisions of student affairs over the last decade, evolved from a need for greater accountability and coordination in a climate of declining resources and increasing demands and expectations. These pressures probably will persist, or even grow, and chief of staff and/or director of administration positions will continue to proliferate in divisions of student affairs, though a distinction could emerge between the role of chief of staff and that of director of administration as more administrative support services become centralized. Regardless, the student affairs chief of staff, like its military and White House counterparts, promises to play an increasingly central and strategic role in managing 21st-century organizational complexities.

References

Hess, S. (with Pfiffner, J. P.) (2002). *Organizing the presidency*. Washington, DC: Brookings Institution Press.

Meningall, J. (2010, February). *University of South Florida Student Affairs Shared Services Center*. Presented at the meeting of the Southeast Chief Student Affairs Officers, Tampa, FL.

University of California Student Mental Health Committee (2006). Final report. Retrieved from http://www.universityofcalifornia.edu/regents/regmeet/sept06/303a ttach.pdf

Virginia Tech. (2004, February). Proposal to consolidate administrative functions in the Division of Student Affairs under a chief of staff.

Walcott, C. E., & Hult, K.M. (1995). *Governing the White House: From Hoover to LBJ*. Lawrence: University of Kansas Press.

Zabecki, D. T. (2008). *Chief of staff: The principal officers behind history's great commanders. Vol. 1. Napoleonic Wars to World War I*. Annapolis, MD: Naval Institute Press.

10

CHANGING ROLES AND RESPONSIBILITIES OF STUDENT AFFAIRS AUXILIARY SERVICES

Jerrid P. Freeman and Dean Bresciani

S tudent development programs within student affairs organizations and related auxiliary services portfolios, whether in or outside student affairs areas, have been a traditional and generally well-understood domain of student affairs (Chandler, 1973; Knock, 1988; Nuss, 2003; Shaffer, 1973; Young, 2003). That said, the overall administrative organization and financial oversight of auxiliary programs and services in such settings has moved into and out of larger student affairs organizational portfolios. As institution size and subsequent organizational specialization decreases, and particularly in private college settings, oversight of such programs is more often coordinated outside student affairs portfolios, with matters of administrative and particularly fiscal responsibility generally if not almost invariably falling outside student affairs. Units most often organized outside student affairs are those with substantial facilities, revenue management, and personal aspects (e.g., housing, food services, bookstore and other retail sales, etc.).

Competing notions of auxiliary services alignment in or out of student affairs portfolios has reflected a tension between a focus of those services being on educational implications for students, against the business and technical expertise appropriately thought of as necessary for their responsible and savvy administration. Also affecting those organizational decisions are the competitive market nature of such programs, required and often specialized business knowledge, facilities construction and maintenance demands, large human resource components, and substantial revenue and expenditure features.

Those skill sets have often been deemed beyond the preparation and scope of traditional student affairs practitioners and the focus of their portfolios. While less often the case in larger settings with more potential for specialization, this perspective becomes increasingly evident as institutional size diminishes. As institutional size and complexity diminish, business specialization is less often evident within student affairs units and their staff.

The matter has become even more complicated with the steady broadening and extension of student programs and services in recent decades. These expanding programs and services reflect an increasingly competitive marketplace in which services are offered, and expectations of campus constituencies no longer made up only of students, but now also faculty, staff, and those in communities near our campuses. Examples range from recreational facilities and programs to fine and performing arts.

Historical Development and Influences

In a relatively short period, the student affairs profession has matured from a modest and narrowly focused orientation to a major foundational aspect of most higher education settings. Most academic preparation programs for student affairs professionals have adapted their curriculum to changing practitioners' responsibilities, yet it is impossible for any program to prepare students for all of the positions and skills needed in the field. However, it can be argued that the focus and nature of student affairs professionals and, in particular, their academic preparation has been and perhaps continues to be inadequate for managing large auxiliary operations, which have a strong business orientation.

With expanding accessibility and demand for higher education since the 1940s, student affairs and its practitioners' academic preparation have generally remained based in counseling, psychology, educational administration, and, most recently, student development-related disciplines. Those fields provide little if any attention to administrative much less business aspects of higher education, in spite of the fact that even relatively modest colleges and universities represent large and complex economic enterprises. At the other end of the spectrum, many colleges and universities are the largest "business" in the towns where they are located, if not one of the leading economic engines of their state's economy. More than ever, student affairs is becoming a significant contributor to the economic feasibility of individual institutions and a participant in the local market.

Arguably, that is still the case today with the emerging focus in student affairs preparation programs reflecting new priorities in learning outcomes, educational assessment, accountability, and diversity rather than business-related topic areas. While those new orientations are rational responses to the demands on student affairs practitioners, they provide limited preparation for leading the business and more specifically the auxiliary services aspects often intertwined into student affairs functional areas. Staff who aspire to be senior student affairs officers (SSAOs) also may find themselves at a disadvantage if they do not have a strong business orientation or experience in complex auxiliary environments if they lead an entire division that must balance academic and business perspectives and at the same time be competent and savvy members of the executive committee that leads an institution.

Nonetheless, a subtle but distinct change came with the increasingly diverse students and student demographics initially introduced starting with the GI Bill in the latter half of the 1940s. As discussed in literature on the topic, the resulting and still increasing shift from mass to universal accessibility of higher education has had profound implications (Trow, 2000). Along with that change in access and expectations come increasingly diverse student profiles demanding increasingly varied programs and services as well as social expectations for the quality and breadth of those programs and services.

Those changes have ultimately led to a demand for higher education administrators and, subsequently, student affairs practitioners, who offer academic and experiential paths of preparation blending educational perspectives with the business and technical expertise to deliver auxiliary goods, services, and programs. In an era of unprecedented public scrutiny of higher education costs, benefits, and business practices, criticism is clearly increasing and evident even in general media outlets. The emerging expectation, in short, is to provide programs and services in an educationally productive and business responsible manner. The resulting opportunity is for student affairs professional preparation to provide a more dynamic expertise to meet the educational and managerial expectations of higher education settings, and to do so in a way that institutional leaders coming from strict business services backgrounds cannot offer and to which they are ill-equipped to respond.

The latter lack training and a professional orientation as educators, whereas the former can bring both priorities to the table.

Traditional Versus Emerging Background Experiences in Position

A distinct functional area orientation and progression of skill development and career advancement in student affairs-related auxiliary services remains the most common practice in the field. That said, and particularly in larger settings with more opportunity and need for specialized expertise, there is an increasing trend toward academic preparation and hiring that reflects business management, accounting, law, facilities design and construction, and related fields previously thought to be outside requisite preparation for higher education, much less student affairs. As highlighted previously, a pendulum swing to a pure business administration preparation and orientation comes with its own substantial limitations and is certainly no more advantageous. As increasingly demanded in higher education and, specifically, student affairs, those responsible for educating students and administering our institutions will be expected to blend skill sets that historically have been separated.

In parallel, the desire and need to explore new and potentially more efficient organizational mechanisms, particularly given increasing expectations but diminishing resources, has contributed to consideration of new organizational models in higher education settings. We explore one such example next.

An overarching student affairs auxiliary services position was conceived at the University of Arkansas in 2009, when the campus was in the midst of declining budget flexibility and a push to cut administrative overhead. The time was right to try a different approach, as a new SSAO was appointed and one of two major student affairs auxiliary services senior staff members was resigning to take another position. The new SSAO was an internal appointment and quickly articulated numerous upper- and mid-level staff changes to make the student affairs division more effective and cost-efficient. The major focus of those changes was to get more synergy among the staff currently at the institution by bringing similar staff functions within different departments under the same leadership, and thus serve the divisional needs in student affairs auxiliary facilities more efficiently.

The divisions' auxiliary facilities were the student union, residence halls and apartments, related warehouses, dining halls, and certain Greek chapter houses. The new "blended" position was filled by the director of the Arkansas Union who had managed day-to-day operations; facility cleaning and maintenance; and the operating, capital projects, reserve, and foundation budgets. Also, already in place was a director of housing facilities who managed facilities for all residence halls and apartments, warehouses, dining, and Greek chapter houses that were contracted with the institution for funding and facility support. When those two positions were combined, oversight for all of the maintenance, custodial, and safety/security personnel in all student affairs auxiliary areas was brought under the direction of one individual.

With that change, numerous other activities were brought together and altered. The student union was restructured so that reservations and staff associated with handling reservations and customer service would come under centralized leadership. The financial, human resources, and payroll operations of the union were combined with similar functions in the housing program to create staff and financial efficiencies. During the following year, technology support for those departments was brought together as well.

With the joining of personnel and talents also came a joining of ideas. Both areas were able to take advantage of the technology advances used to improve customer service and efficiency in their individual areas. That was accomplished through shared reservation software (EMS), time-keeping software (Genesis: Time America), work order systems (TMA), and strategic planning efforts for capital projects.

Job Descriptions for Auxiliary Services

The following are two job descriptions for positions in auxiliary services in student affairs and institution-wide organizations.

Job Description #1: Director of Student Affairs Auxiliary Facilities, University of Arkansas

- Provide direction for more than 105 full-time and 43 seasonal staff and numerous student staff who support and achieve the mission and goals of the Arkansas Union, dining services, Greek life, and university housing.
- Provide direct supervision of the associate director of residential facilities, assistant director for maintenance and construction, assistant director for facilities administration, and facilities director of Arkansas Union.

- Direct central operations functions for 19 residence hall buildings, one apartment complex, seven Greek houses, one managed property, two central warehouses, and the Arkansas Union comprising more than 1.83 million square feet.
- Manage a $17-million general operating budget.
- Oversee capital planning and projects in all student affairs auxiliary facilities.
- Establish budget requirements; administer bid specifications, contract negotiation, selection, and follow-up for all university housing and Arkansas Union facilities.

Job Description #2: Assistant Vice President for Auxiliary Services, Auburn University

Auburn University Auxiliary Enterprises are university-operated or contractor-managed entities and receive no subsidy from the university's general fund. No portion of student tuition dollars **or** state appropriations goes to support auxiliary operations. All expenditures, including total personnel costs, utility charges, renovation and replacement cost, and debt servicing, are paid from revenues earned by providing affordable lodging, dining, document reproduction, academic materials, general merchandise, and related goods and services to our students, faculty, campus staff, and guests.

- Provide senior leadership in the advancement of all university goals for productivity, quality, cost, customer service, and program success for all assigned departments: housing and residence life, Tiger Dining, Copy Cat duplicating centers, TigerCard ID Office, and AU Bookstore in Haley Center.
- Responsible for fiscal oversight for assigned departments, including administrative systems and compliance regulatory and internal controls and audits.
- Correspond and meet with other senior executives, legislators, trustees, and local and state government officials to advance university initiatives, goals, plans, and agendas.
- Recommend and implement new business concepts, systems, technologies, and programs to benefit the university.
- Represent the office of the president or the executive vice president on a number of university committees

Anticipated Needs for the Future

For the foreseeable future a major shift toward staff and financial efficiencies will become imbedded in most organizational decisions made in higher education. This notion has become evident not only in student affairs, but also across all areas of higher education. Higher education budgets across the country continue to tighten in virtually all institutional areas, while public scrutiny of perceived if not real burgeoning numbers of higher education staff and associated costs continues to grow.

In public university settings, due to their largely independent funding, auxiliary units often have been spared such economic shifts. Over the past decade, however, those auxiliaries have become viable revenue streams to support broader institutional funding. Most are now charged for the competitive and operational advantages of co-location on and in collegiate settings through "administrative overhead fees" and similar mechanisms. The practice of treating auxiliaries as revenue-generating units supporting general campus operations has, of course, always and more comprehensively been the case in private university settings.

A troubling aspect to treating auxiliaries solely as revenue-producing units is the potential disassociation of the auxiliary services revenue stream from an understanding of what creates it and the educational complement that most student affairs auxiliary services use as core to their mission. Too often auxiliaries are perceived as inexhaustible revenue sources that can be tapped for larger and larger subsidies of campus operations. What becomes overlooked is that most auxiliaries operate under substantial market conditions that require them to reinvest and continually upgrade the presentation and quality of their services to remain viable against competitors. Complicating the matter further, few of those private sector competitors are burdened by the educational components and subsequent operational costs that are core to student affairs auxiliary services and programs. Outsourcing to competitors often involves abandoning the educational components central to current auxiliary services.

With such changes, there is an emerging motivation for functional areas within and across institutional divisions to be more willing to partner and work cooperatively on projects and initiatives, and to combine similar functions and staff. Auxiliary and business-related services exemplify the potential for doing so. Divisions, units, and departments are becoming more willing and in fact often have little if any choice but to give up sole control to realize financial savings and staff efficiencies. Given current economic trends, and the increased focus on transparency and efficiency in higher education organization, centralization of similar functions and positions and greater partnerships are likely if not inevitably going to increase.

While joining similar functions under more centralized leadership can appear at first to offer great financial savings and efficiencies, significant planning must take place before making such decisions. To ensure that efficiencies and savings are realized and the planning is not shortsighted, a solid strategic planning outline should be followed (Freeman & Wilmes, 2009). A broad group of representative staff should be involved in planning and organizing such changes. Doing so will better assure that desired goals are achieved and will better guard against student or institution services being negatively affected. In addition, it is sure to increase buy-in from staff affected by the changes. Imposing decisions on centralizing leadership and functions can result in staff distrusting the decisions and leadership and, ultimately, causing a good decision to fail.

The organizational frames of structural, symbolic, political, and human resources identified by Bolman and Deal (1997), as discussed later in this work, provide a helpful mechanism for evaluating changes and how they might affect higher education organizations. When merging functions, structural aspects are often well analyzed, but other frames are not given adequate consideration. Bolman and Deal's frames provide a simple mechanism for structuring examination and evaluation of potential changes.

As with most large and complex organizations, individual units often exhibit and operate as distinct subcultures reflecting specific academic and experiential preparation, orientation, and priorities. Leaders who appreciate those differences and are adept at bridging them must be in place if such changes are to be effective and productive. It is critical that organizational changes be communicated both within affected units and to the campus community in a thoughtful, careful, and respectful manner. It is also invaluable to monitor the changes closely for a few years to ensure that proper molding of functions is occurring and leadership is following the direction and vision that accompany the changes. This often determines the success or failure of decisions to centralize.

When creating a broad-based student affairs auxiliary services position, it is important to ensure that appropriate relationships are fostered, not just within the student affairs organization but across the institution as well. When reducing administrative redundancy, the implications for failing to maintain cross-institutional networks increase. The goal should be not only to strengthen the division or the specific functions, but also to coordinate and deliver overall institutional services to students and the broader campus community.

That can best be done with a focused, shared vision and a clearly communicated top-down priority across the institution to partner and work effectively rather than in functional area silos. The specialized and often hybrid roles described in this book highlight the need for units to remove barriers between one another and install a culture of trust and respect so the institution can operate as a large collective unit rather than as separate and only marginally connected entities.

Higher Education Versus the Private Sector

As the size and complexity of organizations grows, so too do the inherent nuances and challenges of reporting lines (Brinkman & Leslie, 1986; Hall, Hass, & Johnson 1967). Structuring of higher education has not been particularly different from that of other large production organizations in terms of distinct but similar features being grouped together in functional areas, with those functional areas reciprocally grouped together and reporting up through increasingly narrow organizational bands.

Emerging models in both the private and public sectors have resisted those trends and sought to "flatten" traditional organizational pyramids. Overlapping responsibilities and cross-training are at the basic levels of that orientation. As efforts mature they lead to a more organic orientation of shared responsibility and the blending and shifting of skills and related staff in a dynamic rather than traditional static orientation. Doing so seeks to take advantage of better matching staff skills and abilities throughout an organization to meet shifting challenges as they arise. Such models have been particularly visible and effective in fast-moving and highly competitive private sector commercial ventures, but are still largely untested in contemporary higher education settings.

It is important to note, however, that while it is attractive to assume that successful practices in one arena are applicable to another, that is not necessarily the case. Commercial enterprises have traditionally been driven by one simple priority: that of profit and shareholder return on investment. Social sector enterprises, however, are driven by the expectation to provide more and better services over time, and that is often in almost total absence of a profit or efficiency motive.

Differentiation of success in delivering social goods such as higher education is dramatically more subjective in definition than the simple profit motive driving the organization and behavior of private commercial enterprises. The former often tends to be as much art as science in terms of meeting social needs and expectations with the resources available. Only in times of economic distress do social sector organizations find priority in seeking efficiency mechanisms to meet demands placed on them. They generally return to past organization and practices as soon as the given economic distress passes.

Concluding Thoughts

Although commonly compared to private sector commercial organizations, particularly when examining auxiliary services and programs, it is attractive to ponder why successful models of the former are not employed more commonly in the latter. As this premise implies, however, there are dramatically different dynamics at play in providing public goods, and particularly keeping in mind the historic and cultural complexities of higher education.

Auxiliary services should not be confused with common business services, even though they share many features and call for similar skills and expertise from those delivering them. However, auxiliary services in higher education have a distinct educational mission, and productive subcultures have matured around enhancement and delivery of those services. That process continues today and is resulting in more and better educationally complementing services than ever previously realized as a result of increasing breadth of preparation for those in the field. To be successful, steps to bring increased efficiencies from the staff and resourcing of such services are to be commended but approached thoughtfully and judiciously if desired goals are to be reached.

References

Bolman, L. G., & Deal, T. E. (1997). *Reframing organizations: Artistry, choice and leadership* (2nd ed.). San Francisco: Jossey-Bass.

Brinkman, P. T., & Leslie, L. L. (1986). Economies of scale in higher education: Sixty years of research. *The Review of Higher Education, 10,* 1–28.

Chandler, E. M. (1973). Student affairs administration in transition. In G. L. Saddlemire & A. L. Rentz (Eds.), *Student affairs—a profession's heritage: Significant articles, authors, issues and documents* (pp. 320–331). American College Personnel

Association Media Publication No. 35. Carbondale, IL: Southern Illinois University Press.

Freeman, J. P., & Wilmes, D. (2009, Fall/Winter). Facilitating change through integrated strategic planning. *Planning and Changing, 40*(3), 1–13.

Hall, R. H., Hass, J. E., & Johnson, N. J. (1967). Organizational size, complexity, and formalization. *American Sociological Review, 32,* 903–912.

Nuss, E. M. (2003). The development of student affairs. In S. R. Komives, D. B. Woodard Jr., & Associates (Eds.), *Student services: A handbook for the profession* (4th ed., pp. 65–88). San Francisco: Jossey-Bass.

Knock, G. H. (1988). The philosophical heritage of student affairs. In G. L. Saddlemire & A. L. Rentz (Eds.), *Student affairs functions in higher education* (pp. 3–20). Springfield, IL: Charles C. Thomas.

Shaffer, R. H. (1973). An emerging role of student personnel: Contributing to organizational effectiveness. In G. L. Saddlemire & A. L. Rentz (Eds.), *Student affairs—a profession's heritage: Significant articles, authors, issues and documents* (pp. 332–342). American College Personnel Association Media Publication No. 35. Carbondale, IL: Southern Illinois University Press.

Trow, M. (2000). *From mass higher education to universal access: The American advantage.* Berkeley, CA: Center for Study of Higher Education, University of California.

Young, R. B. (2003). Philosophies and values guiding the student affairs profession. In S. R. Komives, D. B. Woodard Jr., & Associates (Eds.), *Student services: A handbook for the profession* (4th ed., pp. 89–106). San Francisco: Jossey-Bass.

11

CHANGING ROLES AND RESPONSIBILITIES IN STUDENT AFFAIRS RESEARCH AND ASSESSMENT

Marilee J. Bresciani

O ver the decades, institutional research and assessment has seen an ebb and flow to its perceived importance as a practice in higher education (Astin, 1993). The role student affairs professionals have played in the emphasis on research and assessment has also fluctuated (Love & Estanek, 2004; Sandeen & Barr, 2006; Upcraft & Schuh, 1996). This chapter explores a brief history of research and assessment within higher education and illustrates how student affairs professionals have played a role in that history. In addition, it describes some current trends that are influencing the roles and responsibilities of all student affairs professionals as they engage in research and assessment. Finally, after describing some competencies desired in student affairs professionals, the chapter posits some considerations for professionals to explore as they look to future practice.

A Brief Review of the History of Research and Assessment in Student Affairs

It is always challenging to summarize the historical practices of a segment of a profession in a few paragraphs. Often, to do so would be to ignore many of the nuances that are significant to the emerging practices. However, to not give a brief history before exploring current trends and potential emerging issues renders a discussion about the future uninformed. Thus, readers are encouraged to seek additional information about the history of research and assessment in student affairs in other resources (Astin, 1993; Banta & Associates, 2002; Bresciani, 2006; Bresciani, Moore-Gardner, & Hickmott, 2009; Ewell, 1991, 2002, 2003; Kuh, Gonyea, & Rodriguez, 2002; Kuh, Kinzie, Buckley, Bridges, & Hayek, 2006; Palomba & Banta, 1999; Pascarella & Terenzini, 2005; Upcraft & Schuh, 1996).

A brief summary drawn from these detailed resources (Astin, 1993; Banta & Associates, 2002; Bresciani, 2006; Bresciani et al., 2009; Ewell, 1991, 2002, 2003; Kuh et al., 2002; Kuh et al., 2006; Palomba & Banta, 1999; Pascarella & Terenzini, 2005; Upcraft & Schuh, 1996) illustrates that institutional research or the notion of understanding how students can be more successful in their learning and development processes has a long history in the United States. The outcomes-based assessment movement reaches as far back as the educational and development psychology work of the 1930s and 1940s (Bresciani et al., 2009; Ewell, 1991, 2002, 2003; Kuh et al., 2002). Research to generate new knowledge, of course, extends even further back than that.

The role of student affairs professionals in the development of institutional research and outcomes-based assessment is significant. Upcraft and Schuh (1996), as well as Pascarella and Terenzini (2005), illustrate many examples of how student affairs/higher education scholars and practitioners historically brought awareness of a need to understand the student experience better. As such, research of student affairs and higher education scholars allowed student affairs practitioners to play a significant role in institutional decision making. Student affairs professionals' use of research and other assessment data meant that these professionals were involved in planning programs and facilities, designing interventions and support services, and informing policies and administrative practices. The extent of influence by student affairs professionals skilled in the ability to interpret evaluation and research data has been far-reaching.

While student affairs professionals have enjoyed a history of assessment and evaluation, exploration of outcomes-based assessment has been a more recent phenomenon. The evaluation, research, and assessment practices of student affairs professionals are directly applicable to the outcomes-based assessment practice, student affairs professionals are making strong contributions to their institutional leadership teams in this area. Practitioners also continue to draw on scholars' research to present the underlying theories of their practice and to further interpret outcomes data that inform decisions for improvement, resource allocation, and refined strategic plans. Responsible use of results generated from outcomes-based assessment depends on knowledge of the research in the field being evaluated; the two are inextricably intertwined.

Current Trends Influencing the Role and Responsibilities

As we experience the generation and application of research and assessment today in the student affairs profession, we can't move very far without recognizing the importance of accountability for general learning. In the United States, accountability for what can be termed general learning (e.g., writing, speaking, civic engagement, critical thinking, information literacy, quantitative reasoning, etc.) is ever-increasing (Astin, 1993; Banta & Associates, 2002; Bresciani, 2006; Bresciani et al., 2009; Ewell, 1991, 2002, 2003; Kuh et al., 2002; Kuh et al., 2006; Palomba & Banta, 1999; Suskie, 2009; Upcraft & Schuh, 1996). As such, student affairs professionals are encouraged to think about the general learning research available to them as they design programs that foster students' success. In addition, they would be wise to consider how their programs and collaborative relationships contribute to general learning outcomes. For example, if you work in a Hispanic-serving institution, how does the research on underrepresented populations' ability to access opportunities to learn and subsequently succeed in learning higher-order quantitative reasoning skills influence the design of your recruitment and orientation materials and seminars? How well does this research inform the design of first- and second-year success programs as well as how you structure learning communities and living environments? Have you included quantitative reasoning learning outcomes in those programs? If not, why not?

While this example may seem a little out of the scope of the student affairs professional's work, we must remember that we have moved well beyond the time when we can afford to think that our work does not contribute to students' ability to learn what they are expected to learn, regardless of their major or their general learning competency. We are there right now. We are well into the time when general learning is at a premium, when funding for higher education continues to dwindle, so we want to be mindful of how we can all contribute to generally expected learning by all students. It is helpful to consider what research and which outcomes-based assessment practices can further our understanding of how to collaboratively design opportunities for students to successfully be introduced to, reinforced in, or demonstrate their general learning knowledge and skills (Banta & Associates, 2002; Bresciani, 2006; Bresciani et al., 2009; Ewell, 1991, 2002, 2003; Kuh et al., 2002; Kuh et al., 2006; Palomba & Banta, 1999; Suskie, 2009; Upcraft & Schuh, 1996).

Regional institutional accreditation currently provides the motivation for higher education leaders to pay attention to the research that informs good practice design of learning opportunities. Regional accreditation also encourages institutional leadership to engage in systematic outcomes-based program review processes to identify how well students are learning what they are expected to learn (Banta & Associates, 2002; Bresciani, 2006; Bresciani et al., 2009; Ewell, 1991, 2002, 2003; Suskie, 2009; Upcraft & Schuh, 1996). In the past, one could argue that regional accreditation has been moderately successful in changing institutional leaderships' ability to improve student learning. However, all one has to do now is read any article in either the *Chronicle of Higher Education* or *Inside Higher Education* to discover how many disagree about regional accreditors' ability to transform student learning and development.

When I wrote this chapter, opinions about the effectiveness or sustainability of regional accreditation didn't matter. Regional accreditation exists now, and most regional accreditors in the United States expect that student affairs professionals are assessing student learning and development using outcomes-based assessment. The intent of many of these regional accreditors is to motivate everyone (including cocurricular professionals and student services) within the academy to focus on how they can help to the improve student learning and development (Banta & Associates, 2002; Bresciani, 2006; Bresciani et al., 2009; Ewell, 2003; Kuh et al., 2006; Palomba & Banta, 1999; Suskie, 2009). Even if regional accreditors no longer motivate institutional leadership to demonstrate accountability for student learning and development in the future, organizations such as the New Leadership Alliance for Student Learning and Accountability (http://www.newleadershipalliance.org/) and its institutional certification program may. This well-supported organization, while still early in its development, is unveiling a certification program similar to the Leadership in Energy and Environmental Design (LEED) project run by the U.S. Green Building Council. The certification program is intended to motivate as many institutions as possible to meet high standards for systematically evaluating and improving student learning and development, including that in the cocurricular.

The accountability conversations around general learning have also created a public that desires to see evidence of student leaning and development in a format they can digest, understand, and perhaps even compare with other institutions' (Banta & Associates, 2002; Bresciani, 2006; Bresciani et al., 2009; Ewell, 2003; Kuh et al., 2006; Suskie, 2009). The implications of this public demand for student affairs professionals to reveal how they contribute to the improvement of student learning and development begins with the practitioners themselves. Many student affairs professionals find humor in the notion that they cannot explain what they do in a manner that their parents or partners can understand. While I made these same comments a few years ago and laughed aloud at myself, I find myself no longer laughing. The importance of our ability to translate our research- and outcomes-based assessment results into terminology that those outside the profession can understand grows increasingly more every day.

Technological tools to support our ability to share research- and outcomes-based findings and decisions are available; however, none of them is close to perfect. Regardless of electronic tool availability—which may help us articulate shared outcomes, synthesize results, and collaborate electronically on decision-making processes—the ability to communicate what we know about how our students learn and develop so that the general public can understand is ours to determine. Therefore, we must do better at (a) explaining what we do as it aligns with the research in our field and the values of our constituents; (b) evaluating how well we do what we intend to do using outcomes-based assessment; and (c) connecting the results and needed resources for improvement to the presence of or lack of research within our profession and the decision makers' values in ways the public can truly understand.

Competencies and Skills Needed

The use of research and assessment, whether we are generating it or applying it in practice, requires us to reflect. In a profession that values *doing*, reallocating time from *doing* to *reflecting on our doing* is pertinent to the success of all student affairs professionals (Bresciani, 2006; Bresciani et al., 2009). The use of "all student affairs professionals" is not used incorrectly here. The roles and responsibilities of research and assessment in the student affairs profession belong to every single member of the profession. In taking the time to paint a picture of the current situation, I trust you can see the importance of ensuring that all student affairs professionals are competent in assessment and research. Yet, Hoffman and Bresciani (2010) found that we have a ways to go with regard to communication expectations for these competencies when hiring student affairs professionals.

Nonetheless, if you are looking for specific skills, knowledge, and attitudes that are needed to consider a student affairs professional "competent" in assessment and research, you need look no farther than two publications: the American College Personnel Association's (ACPA) *Assessment Skills and Knowledge (ASK) Content Standards for Student Affairs Practitioners and Scholars* and ACPA's and the National Association for Student Personnel Administrators' (NASPA) *Professional Competency Areas for Student Affairs Practitioners*, both of which are full of specific knowledge, skills, and attitudes practitioners need to engage in research and/or assessment successfully. The knowledge, skills, and attitudes are articulated at three levels (beginning, intermedi and advanced)—so those professionals who want to know a little about assessment and research can study the beginning level of expected learning outcomes, and those professionals who desire to become resident experts in research and assessment can study the advanced levels.

ACPA and NASPA, whose members wrote both publications, also sponsor annual assessment and research conferences and offer research and assessment learning opportunities at their annual conference and convention. In addition to the professional development opportunities at these annual conferences and conventions, both associations have print and online resources to educate student affairs practitioners regardless of what level of learning they desire.

Sample Job Descriptions for Director of Student Affairs Research and Assessment

[Editors' Note: Book editors have included two sample job descriptions to complement the content in this chapter. These can be found as Appendix 1 and Appendix 2 at the end of this chapter.]

Future Possibilities

As we explore future possibilities that may emerge in the roles and responsibilities of student affairs practitioners, I can't help but reemphasize the importance of our tending to what was outlined in the current trends section.

Our ability to develop the knowledge, skills, and abilities in every student affairs practitioner so we can tend to these issues will allow us to move into the future as leaders in evidence-based decision making. Consider, then, how you can collaborate better with colleagues in your current organizational structure and across other organizational structures to better align processes and administrative models so your organization systematizes reflection and the use of evidence to inform all types of decisions, particularly those that enhance improvements in students' general learning. How do you provide information on the theories that inform your practice, the outcomes of your practice, the results from your assessment, and the resulting decisions to all members of the public so they will better understand what you do and want to partner with you in promoting students' success? How do you leverage technology so it helps you connect your outcomes to constituents' values, collect the information you need in the way you need it, and communicate key items to those who need to make decisions? How do you reallocate your staff's duties and responsibilities so that reflection becomes a part of day-to-day activity, rather than something that gets added on only if there is time?

If we can address these questions strategically, then as savvy consumers of research and assessment data, we will be able to design more efficient and affordable student learning and development opportunities while maintaining learning effectiveness for all types of students. We will be able to use comparable data collected from standardized instruments while keeping education accessible to all because we will know the limits of each and have tools to fill in the missing gaps of information, allowing for access, equity, and student success to stay at the forefront of the design of general learning and the resource reallocations that finance it. We will engage in collaborative design of solutions and creative yet solid methods to evaluate them, and foster the generation of new knowledge that will inform creative reorganizations, systems, and policies that will enhance general learning and student development.

Finally, I hope that as we reengage in elevating the role of evidence-based decision making, we do not lose sight of the role that intuition plays in decision-making processes. We understand very little about how the ability to sense intuitively (as opposed to using experiences that inform the conscience or subconscious recall of memory) informs the interpretation and use of evidence in decision-making processes. It seems most appropriate for student affairs practitioners and scholars to develop models that help us better understand this so we can incorporate creativity into the design and evaluation of learning opportunities for all students.

Conclusion

This chapter briefly discussed the history of research and assessment within higher education and the role student affairs professionals have played, and introduced current trends that influence the research and assessment roles and responsibilities of all student affairs professionals. Finally, after directing the reader to knowledge, skills, and attitudes desired in student affairs professionals, considerations for professionals to explore as they look to future practice were posited. If only one learning outcome is taken from this chapter, I hope readers will be able to explain why it is so important for all student affairs professionals to demonstrate at least a beginning level of knowledge and skills in assessment and research. We are all accountable for the general learning of all students; we had best get about improving it in ways that ensure higher general learning remains accessible and equitable to all.

References

American College Personnel Association (ACPA). (2006). *Assessment skills and knowledge content standards for student affairs practitioners and scholars.* Washington, DC: Author.

American College Personnel Association (ACPA) & National Association for Student Personnel Administrators (NASPA). (2010). *Professional competency areas for student affairs practitioners.* Washington, DC: Author

Astin, A. W. (1993). *Assessment for excellence: The philosophy of assessment and evaluation in higher education.* New York: Macmillan.

Banta, T. W., & Associates. (2002). *Building a scholarship of assessment.* San Francisco: Jossey-Bass.

Bresciani, M. J. (2006). *Outcomes-based academic and co-curricular program review: A compilation of institutional good practices.* Sterling, VA: Stylus.

Bresciani, M. J., Moore-Gardner, M., & Hickmott, J. (2009). *Demonstrating student success.* Sterling, VA: Stylus.

Ewell, P. T. (1991). Assessment and public accountability: Back to the future. *Change, 23*(6), 12–17.

Ewell, P. T. (2002). An emerging scholarship: A brief history of assessment. In T. W. Banta (Ed.), *Building a scholarship of assessment.* San Francisco: Jossey-Bass.

Ewell, P. T. (2003, October). *Specific roles of assessment within this larger vision.* Presentation given at the Assessment Institute at IUPUI. Indianapolis, IN.

Hoffman, J., & Bresciani, M. J. (2010). Student affairs professional competencies: An analysis job description data. *Journal of Student Affairs Research and Practice, 47*(4), 495–512.

Kuh, G. D., Gonyea, R., & Rodriguez, D. (2002). The scholarly assessment of student development. In T. W. Banta, *Hallmarks of effective outcomes assessment* (pp. 100–128). San Francisco: Jossey-Bass.

Kuh, G. D., Kinzie, J., Buckley, J., Bridges, B., & Hayek, J. C. (2006). *What matters to student success: A review of the literature.* Final report for the National Postsecondary Education Cooperative and National Center for Education Statistics. Bloomington, IN: Indiana University Center for Postsecondary Research.

Love, P. G., & Estanek, S. M. (2004). *Rethinking student affairs practice.* San Francisco: Jossey-Bass.

Palomba, C. A., & Banta, T. W. (1999). *Assessment essentials: Planning, implementing, and improving assessment in higher education.* San Francisco: Jossey-Bass.

Pascarella, E. T., & Terenzini, P. T. (2005). *How college affects students, Vol. 2. A third decade of research.* San Francisco: Jossey-Bass.

Sandeen, A., & Barr, M. J. (2006). *Critical issues for student affairs: Challenges and opportunities.* San Francisco: Jossey-Bass.

Suskie, L. (2009). *Assessing student learning: A common sense guide* (2nd ed.). Bolton, MA: Jossey-Bass.

Upcraft, M. L., & Schuh, J. H. (1996). *Assessment in student affairs: A guide for practitioners.* San Francisco: Jossey-Bass.

Sample Job Description #1: Director of Student Life Research and Assessment, Division of Student Affairs, The Ohio State University

- Direct, manage, and supervise student life research and assessment.
- Recommend and conduct quantitative and qualitative research investigating factors that affect student involvement and student achievement, retention, and graduation.
- Provide consulting services to departments within student affairs and to other administrative and academic offices within the university.
- Collaborate and coordinate with other institutional research units on campus.
- Initiate and implement core assessment projects.
- Consult with senior leadership within student affairs and with other university offices in determining priorities and strategies.
- Organize and manage activities related to implementation of a rapid-response polling operation.
- Prepare and coordinate dissemination of research findings for use by the campus community, publish studies in professional journals, and present findings at professional meetings.
- Supervise staff, graduate students, and office work flow.
- Direct and monitor the budget.
- Provide training on research projects.
- Participate as core member of student affairs strategic planning team.
- Oversee student affairs assessment planning committee.
- Supervise associate director, research associates, research analysts, and student assistants.

The individual who fills this position should have at least a master's degree in higher education, student affairs administration, quantitative methods, or related field or a combination of education and experience; a PhD is preferable. Applicants should also have:

- considerable supervisory, strategic planning, and project management skills;

- knowledge of research methodology, statistical analysis, and database management
- understanding of student development theory and its application to student affairs practice;
- knowledge and experience in conducting both quantitative and qualitative research;
- experience using relevant statistical software packages, developing and measuring learning outcomes, making recommendations, and preparing and giving effective presentations; and
  prior assessment experience in applied educational research.

Sample Job Description #2: Director of Student Affairs Assessment Evaluation and Research, Division of Student Affairs, University of Utah

The responsibilities of this position include:

- Develop, coordinate, and oversee student affairs assessment, evaluation and research agenda and strategic planning.
- Provide assessment to student affairs departments and supervise technical aspects of assessment such as research design (quantitative and qualitative), instrument development, data collection and analysis.
- Operationalize learning outcomes for division.

The requirements for this position include:

- Master's degree in a related field or equivalency, although PhD in a related field and proven related experience are preferred;
- Five years' experience in research design, statistical analysis, and/or related responsibilities (or educational equivalent); and
- Outstanding verbal and written communication skills and strong interpersonal and collaboration skills.

PART THREE

INSTITUTIONAL AND ORGANIZATIONAL IMPLICATIONS OF EMERGING SPECIALIST ROLES AND STRUCTURES IN STUDENT AFFAIRS ORGANIZATIONS

The preceding chapters in Part Two described several emerging and changing specialist roles and structures. In many cases these specialist roles and structures existed within larger student affairs organizations or on larger campuses. The editors wanted to present a fuller picture with regard to institutional type, so this final section seeks to address more specifically emerging roles and structures based on institutional and organizational contexts.

Chapters 12–16 on the institutional and organizational implications of emerging roles and structures in student affairs organizations specifically include: (1) facilitating organizational change to incorporate the use of specialist roles and structures in student affairs; (2) emerging and changing specialist roles and structures at small colleges and universities; (3) emerging and changing specialist roles and structures at community colleges; (4) preparing and training for emerging and changing roles for those not trained in traditional methods; and (5) concluding thoughts and recommendations. The editors intentionally present perspectives for both small colleges and universities and community colleges. While many of the challenges facing student affairs and higher education exist at all types of institutions, each of these has its own set of unique challenges and was worth including.

Each of these, as you will read, is important on the institutional and organizational level for those charged with leading student affairs and the administrators who are or are seeking to be in these roles.

12

FACILITATING ORGANIZATIONAL CHANGE TO INCORPORATE SPECIALIST ROLES AND MATRIX STRUCTURES IN STUDENT AFFAIRS ORGANIZATIONS

Kathy Cavins-Tull

The 2020 Commission on the Future of Postsecondary Education (1998) in Washington State warned that by 2020, higher education in that state will serve 100,000 more learners than it did in 1998. Likewise, in California, student enrollment in higher education was expected to increase from 1.8 million in 1994 to 2.7 million in 2010 (Lerner, 1999). Many states have had similar patterns of growth over the last two decades, but increasing enrollment is simply one factor affecting higher education.

Greater access to higher education, the changing characteristics and needs of learners, and the way higher education has been delivered to accommodate access have transformed the industry. The list of transforming forces in higher education has become so common that Kezar (2003) notes they are almost unnecessary to name:

> technology, new teaching and learning approaches, such as community service or collaborative learning, cost constraints, changing demographics, international competition, assessment, accountability, diversity/multiculturalism, and other challenges create a complex climate. (p. 1)

Changing economic conditions over the last 40 years and the shift in funding sources for higher education, the move toward globalization, greater diversity, and increasing reliance on technology have caused higher education to reconsider how it delivers services to students (Leslie & Fretwell, 1996; Woodard, Love, & Komives, 2000).

The inundation of students and diversity of needs, coupled with declining support from state and federal agencies, is creating a demand on academic and support services that cannot be met with current structures. In this environment, colleges and universities are compelled to reexamine organizational structure, clarify priorities, create new partnerships, and design policies and practices that respond to a more fragmented and complex environment while at the same time promoting innovation and reducing costs (Bergquist, 1998; Woodard et al., 2000).

As higher education goes, so goes the role of student affairs. External social, economic, and political forces have changed the nature of student affairs divisions as well. Federal legislation affecting access to higher education, student learning imperatives, and calls for accountability has expanded and reshaped the roles and functions of student affairs units over the last three decades (Manning, Kinzie, & Schuh, 2006). At their onset, student affairs units were organized and developed to meet specific needs of students, and as student needs grew, programs and services grew in function and hierarchy. Departmental roles and functions became more specialized and complex. In some cases units became their own cost centers, lending to the entrepreneurial and insular culture of student affairs departments and divisions.

But siloed structures are challenged by cost, access, quality, and accountability issues, and student affairs divisions must reshape their practices to meet changing needs. Divisions of student affairs have been challenged to create change that will transform their organizations and test their assumptions about how services are delivered to students and how their organizations contribute to the university's effectiveness and efficiency.

This chapter addresses application of organizational change theories. How can those charged with leading student affairs organizations encourage planned and adaptive strategies for change? How do student affairs leaders assess the needs of their organizations, facilitate change, and evaluate the outcomes of their organizational change? How can those responsible for highly specialized, siloed, and vertical organizations prepare their organizations for the use of hybrid and matrix structures or specialist positions that work laterally through an organization? This chapter focuses on change issues, planned and adaptive models of change, strategies for facilitating change, and methods of assessing organizational change.

Defining Change

Organizational development specialists define change as altering structures, processes, or behaviors in a system or introducing something new to create a difference in an organization (Bess & Dee, 2008; Flamholtz & Randle, 2008). Organizational change can be incremental or transformational, small or radical, and can affect an organization in simple ways or facilitate a metamorphosis. As stated in chapter 1, change in higher education and student affairs organizations has often come in the form of adaptive change, meaning that as student characteristics and environments shift, organizations respond by making appropriate adjustments to meet needs. On the other hand, some colleges and universities have been transformed as they have redefined their organizational missions and have refocused efforts to meet the needs of online, part-time, or adult learners.

Creating or enhancing a service for students is often incremental in nature. For example, as access to higher education has grown, student affairs organizations have added services to address student needs, such as offices that administer Americans with Disabilities Act policies and practices, learning centers, and services for nontraditional students. Similarly, many universities have individual offices that address either a specific function (student housing, judicial affairs, leadership programs) or a specified population (students with disabilities, first-year experience, women's centers), and these offices may have grown and become more hierarchical with population shifts, yet the changes within the departments or the division of student affairs have not resulted in a shift of mission or culture. Adding a specialist position to the student affairs division to manage assessment, divisional communication, or fund-raising probably results in incremental change for an organization. Keller (1983) states that when higher education institutions change, they often do so incrementally and in an adaptive and unplanned way. He also argues that incremental change is not likely to be guided by vision and is sometimes only loosely connected to institutional goals, but more often it is an adaptation to environmental shifts.

Overhauling an organization's mission, structure, or strategy creates organizational transformation. Moving a student affairs organization from a hierarchical structure to a matrix structure may be more transformational mental and may require some attention to strategies of planned change. Matrix structures enable the organization to have cross-unit communication, coordination, and collaboration, which may challenge the culture and practices of vertically oriented organizations. While lateral structures allow for greater responsibility in decision making and more effective use of resources, they may also challenge traditional methods of organizing and budgeting and the vertical orientation of work. Although the mission of the organization remains intact, the structures and strategies used to achieve organizational goals may be very unfamiliar to the traditional student affairs organization. Facilitating a planned approach to change may help such organizations center on mission, develop strategy and vision, and engage in the changes needed to adopt more matrix structures.

Types of Change

To address the challenge of organizational change, student affairs can borrow from the work of organizational development researchers. While there is a growing body of research that advocates for scholars to use social, political, and cultural theories to interpret organizational change in higher education (Kezar, 2003), long-held theories of planned and adaptive change create a framework for understanding and facilitating change in student affairs organizations. Bess and Dee (2008) conceptualized planned change as an "intentional effort to improve organizational processes through the implementation of new ideas based on scientific knowledge" (p. 797). Models of planned change, while initiated internally and generally managed by senior administrators, are often guided by external forces and feedback. Feedback from an external review or accreditation process, new federal or state mandates or regulations, or certification changes could be the impetus for a planned strategy for change.

Adaptive change is characterized by local, decentralized, grassroots efforts that have been occurring on college campuses for many years. Adaptive change in higher education organizations is frequently a result of changing student needs, research and grant opportunities, and local faculty and staff initiatives. The cumulative effect of adaptive change can have a significant impact on a college or university, but it is decentralized in nature and sometimes loosely coupled with the institution's mission. Bess and Dee (2008) suggest that in adaptive change strategies, leaders do not become irrelevant but instead become facilitators of creativity and innovation in organizations.

Rather than articulate an agenda for change and attempt to persuade or coerce others "to buy in" to that agenda, organizational leadership can pay attention to local-level changes, make sense of the patterns that emerge from those changes, and then articulate a vision that reflects common strengths across multiple adaptations. (p. 809)

The authors warn of mission drift when adaptive change occurs across a wide range of decentralized initiatives and suggest that a compelling, unifying organizational identity, shared values, and understanding of organizational commitments can help focus decentralized efforts.

Planned versus adaptive change strategies have been grist for the debate mill about organizational change (Burnes, 2004, Nadler & Tushman, 1989). Planned change efforts are often perceived as top-down and generally envisioned at the executive level, while employees of all levels of the organization execute the strategies that accompany that change, which often lead to diffusion of the original vision (Bess & Dee, 2008). Adaptive change, on the other hand, can be fragmented and disconnected from the organization's mission. Planned change can be considered too linear and rational, ignoring the political and human resource needs of the organization, while adaptive change can be creative and innovative, but also disconnected from the political and structural needs of the organization.

Bess and Dee (2008) suggest a framework for use of both planned and adaptive change processes for human resource development and organizational effectiveness in higher education. They propose that the complexity of higher education requires leaders to employ a complementary approach that incorporates centralized and decentralized models of change. They identify five contingencies to consider when choosing a change model: "The structure for action; leadership capabilities; the culture of trust; financial slack; and external environment constraints and opportunities" (pp. 813–814). Highly interdependent, tightly structured organizations respond better to planned change strategies, whereas loosely structured organizations with multiple projects respond better to adaptive models of change.

Whether change is planned and top-down or adaptive and grassroots depends on the leadership skills of all members of an organization. Effective training and development at all levels is necessary for each model of change. Communication of organizational mission and direction is necessary to keep planned change on track and attract grassroots efforts that support the direction of the student affairs division. Likewise, the culture and level of trust in an organization will either support or stifle planned or adaptive change.

Leaders and organizations that value transparency and participation in leadership may be more likely to develop a culture of trust among those in the organization.

Organizations experiencing financial strength can support creative and innovative efforts and local-level change. On the other hand, when organizations are struggling financially, planned change can focus efforts and create a unifying identity and mission, sometimes attracting additional resources. Large, diverse environments have a tendency to tolerate adaptive strategies to change, whereas small, focused environments may require a more centralized, planned approach to change. Student affairs leaders need to become skilled at facilitating both planned and adaptive change strategies to help their organizations be innovative and responsive to the varying needs of those they serve.

Resistance to Change

Moving people from what is familiar to what is unfamiliar and sometimes uncomfortable can cause resistance to change. Flamholtz and Randle (2008) identify several factors that lead organizations to resist change. One factor consists of the values and norms an organization has formed over the years that influence how individuals within the organization act. Many colleges and universities are steeped in tradition developed and supported by generations of students, members of the faculty, and staff. Change in these organizations can be very difficult when either individuals or groups within the organization feel threatened by what is different.

Other factors that affect an organization's ability to change are the processes and practices that have formed over time to support the work of an organization. Significant investments of time or other resources in organizational processes can create an unwillingness to change. Likewise, for some organizations, unless a process or practice is considered "broken," impetus for change may be weak. Addressing individual and organizational motivation for change is an important part of the process for organizational leaders.

Van de Ven (1986) also studied change in organizations and found four central problems to managing change:

1. *A human problem of managing attention.* When an organization is perceived as successful, the efforts of its staff members are used to protect existing practices instead of developing new ideas.

2. *A process problem in managing new ideas.* Organizational change requires adoption and shepherding good ideas through organizational resistance, political processes, and competing interests of individuals and units. Good ideas need strong support from organizational coalitions and extended energy to move an idea to an innovation and then through organizational processes.

3. *A structural problem of managing part-whole relationships.* Change requires attention to individuals and units as well as to organizations' overall goals. Individuals or units may have difficulty supporting the end goal if the change to the individual or unit appears to be disruptive to or disconnected from the units.

4. *A strategic problem of institutional leadership.* Sometimes it is difficult to move beyond status quo for organizations, especially when an organization is functioning reasonably effectively. Institutional leadership that gives credence to continuous improvement, best practices, structural flexibility, and other outside influences can help overcome strategic resistance to change.

Moving an organization from the familiar to the unfamiliar and working to make the uncomfortable comfortable is a significant undertaking in transition and change. Change agents need to assess their organization's readiness for change, envision a strategy for change, and imagine outcomes for the organizational effort.

Assessing Readiness for Change

Woodard et al. (2000) outlined the American Council on Education (ACE)-Kellogg principles for assessing preparedness of an organization to adopt change and develop new approaches to meeting the challenges of a changing environment, adapted from *Taking Charge of Change: A Primer for Colleges and Universities* (Eckel, Green, Hill, & Mallon, 1998). They suggest that assessment of the concepts be done honestly and with integrity so that a process of change adopted by an organization is grounded in reality for that organization.

Woodard et al. (2000) suggest that change agents be "reflective and intentional about the principles espoused by the division and align divisional actions, processes and operations with professed principles" (p. 65). They recommend that organizations be self-reflective and self-critical as a means of becoming conscious of organizational values and priorities and acting on them. The authors of the principles advocate being clear about the agenda for social improvement and being intentional about outcomes, giving learning the highest priority and fostering inclusiveness and civility in the process. Finally, taking responsibility for decisions and actions and fostering information sharing and openness in decision making are seen as critical for effective organizational change.

Whether using the ACE-Kellogg principles to assess readiness for change or to guide a change process, Woodard et al. (2000) encourage leaders to conduct a healthy assessment of their division, seek advice from others, encourage civil discourse, and listen to their constituents. Change in an organization is often met with resistance, and change agents need to know when to persist through the resistance and when to diagnose failure and redirect an organization to action that reflects organizational goals and mission.

Models of Change

The seminal work of Kurt Lewin set the stage for theories of applied behavioral science, action research, and planned change in organizations (Schein, 1988). Although often dismissed as simplistic and outdated (Burnes, 2000; Dawson, 1994; Kanter, Stein, & Jick, 1994), nearly every theory of planned organizational change uses in some way Lewin's model of unfreezing, moving, and refreezing organizational culture (Burnes, 2006).

Lewin suggested that human behavior is controlled by a force field of driving and restraining forces and that changing behavior requires an "unfreezing" or destabilization of that force field before new behaviors can be learned. Step two involves the process of "moving" or learning new behaviors, and step three requires a "refreezing" or a restabilization of the group's equilibrium, or a new normal. Refreezing involves reestablishment of organizational cultures and norms, policies, and practices that support new behaviors (Burnes, 2006).

The Congruence Model of Change (Nadler, 2006) leads organizational change agents through the process of analyzing organizational fit in an effort to lead change. First, an organization assesses its "inputs," including external environment, organizational resources, and history that have influenced how the organization works. The change agents then assess the "strategy" or set of decisions made about the market, organization's offerings, competitive base, and performance objectives. Finally, the "output" or performance measures of the organization are evaluated.

Central to the Congruence Model is the notion of the "operating nization," which includes the organization's work, its people, and its formal and informal organization. The key to the Congruence Model is the concept of "fit." The more closely aligned the individual and organization fit, the greater their effectiveness. The more tightly linked the strategy is with its formal structures, the more productive an organization. A lack of fit between an organization's formal and informal environments, between people and their work requirements, or between the environment and an organization's strategy results in an ineffective and unproductive organization. Nadler (2006) indicates that changing one or two components will not necessarily cause the others to fit neatly into place. Change requires attention to inputs, strategy, and outputs as well as an organization's operating structure.

Bolman and Deal (2008) suggest reframing change in organizations by using a versatile approach to understanding and facilitating change. They argue that changes conceived and implemented from the top-down usually fail because leadership does not often completely understand the organization's environment. The authors examined organizations through four frames: human resource, structural, political, and symbolic lenses to understand organizational needs and lead change.

Bolman and Deal (2008) describe the human resource frame as centered on the needs, skills, and participation of an organization's membership. They suggest that people resist change when they feel anxious, powerless, and lacking skills and confidence to perform roles or duties that are new to them. They feel anxious and insecure when they have had no involvement in the process or decision making and sometimes they resist change when they think decisions made by management may be taking the organization in the wrong direction. Bolman and Deal advise that "training, psychological support and participation all increase the likelihood that people will understand and feel comfortable with the new methods" (p. 382).

Bolman and Deal (2008) explain that change can undermine the structure of an organization, causing confusion and role ambiguity for its members. Van de Ven (1986) also explains that resistance to change sometimes comes from role conflict and the competing interests of what is known and what is envisioned. Bolman and Deal advise change agents to anticipate structural issues with change and address them by redefining and communicating changes in organizational roles and relationships. To make room for new ideas and innovation, organizations need to have flexible structures or processes.

Student affairs organizations that want to incorporate some matrix structures into their traditional structures may attempt some project groups that span several departments but are focused on a common problem or issue. Considering a matrix structure using the structural lens might entail imagining a project group centered on an issue that engages the interest of several offices, perhaps a topic like the influx of war veterans on campus. Leaders from enrollment management are probably interested in the process of admission, financial aid, and advising; while leaders in student support may want to define appropriate counseling, health and wellness, and learning support; and others may want to examine appropriate living arrangements and opportunities for involvement and creative expression. Creating a problem-centered group to explore options, educate itself and others, and propose a unified approach to support for returning veterans allows for communication across many units and promotes a culture of collaboration.

The political nature of change almost always spurs conflict. Organizations often comprise traditionalists and change agents, which ensures that some individuals and groups will oppose change and others will support it (Bolman & Deal, 2008). Change naturally affects some in positive ways and others in negative ways, and people are unsurprisingly opposed to change that has a negative effect on them as individuals or members of a group. Bolman and Deal recommend that to build successful change, leaders need to frame issues politically, build coalitions, and establish arenas and opportunities for disagreements to be discussed and solutions to be negotiated.

A task in student affairs that sometimes meets with political resistance is assessment. While assessment has been a value of student personnel work for several years, many practitioners still lack the skills and motivation to develop measurable outcomes and assessments for student affairs programs and units. A common response has been to hire a specialist to lead the student affairs division in effective evaluation and assessment. A specialist undoubtedly understands how to create and carry out a plan for assessment, but must also help the organization build a culture of assessment and openness to gathering data and feedback about programs and units. Organizational leaders must persuade members to envision the value and benefits of assessment and create opportunities for unit or program leaders to be recognized for participating in evaluation.

With change comes loss—loss of symbols and rituals known to individuals and organizations, loss of meaning and purpose, loss of that which may be comforting and comfortable. "Any significant change in an organization may trigger two conflicting symbolic responses. The first is to keep things as they were, to replay the past. The second is to ignore the loss and plunge into the future" (Bolman & Deal, 2008, p. 390). Attention to ritual is essential to the process of change. Well-designed ritual allows individuals to let go of the past, deal with the present, and embrace the future. Innovation or leadership awards, physical adjustments to offices to encourage communication and collaboration, or an event that welcomes a new staff member or celebrates new structures can be meaningful symbols for individual and organizational change.

Several organizations have recognized individual and group performance for years that demonstrates support of organizational mission. These acknowledgements take the form of top performer, outstanding group, or department awards. Although recognizing individual and group performance supportive of desired direction of an organization seems simple and obvious, it is sometimes overlooked in daily life in student affairs. Finding ways to recognize those who imagine and work toward divisional change is important.

Making space for specialists or matrix structures requires individuals and the organization to envision the organization as different from and better than its current structure. Spending time and energy to introduce change and motivate both individuals and the organization to leave what they know for a different organization is critical for change to be successful. For student affairs professionals, opportunities to contribute to planning new structures, effective training and development that support new structures, appropriate reinforcement and authority for the agents of change, rituals that allow individuals to transition to the desired structure, and recognition for performance are critical to achieve and sustain change.

Processes for Change

The Eight-Stage Process of Creating Major Change

Kotter (1996) offers an eight-stage model to move an organization away from its status quo, introduce new practices, and ground the new practices in organizational culture. He advises that all stages are important and should be undertaken in sequence, although some stages may take place simultaneously. He warns against getting ahead of the process and not allowing an organization to experience the "defrosting" stages before adding new practices and then working to "make them stick" (p. 23).

Stage one begins with the process of *establishing a sense of urgency.* Kotter (1996) opines that in many organizations, complacency is high and few people are interested in working on a change problem. Creating a sense of urgency requires bold moves by leadership to adjust expectations and reset performance targets, eliminate signs of excess, increase the amount of external feedback to the organization, or significantly adjust pay and reward systems. It requires leaders to talk broadly and openly about future opportunities for individuals and the organization and engage members' attention and energy for change.

To student affairs professionals, it may seem that the nature of their work is driven by urgency. In just the last few years, student affairs professionals have dealt with planning for pandemic flu, the increase of students with special needs, the influx of nontraditional students, the return of war veterans to campuses, the expectations for technology, and the growing need for security changes, to name just a few. Capturing the attention of a diversified student affairs division requires strong leadership and a broad-based plan to address several needs.

Stage two, *creating the guiding coalition*, requires that a group of powerful, single-minded individuals come together to champion the change. An effective member of a guiding coalition has position power, expertise, credibility in the organization and leadership. The coalition needs to be built on trust, able to transcend departmental or personal interests, and able to agree on common and shared objectives (Kotter, 1996). Effective leaders come from all positions and levels in student affairs organizations. Many guiding coalitions in higher education intentionally include staff at all levels, faculty members, and students as a means of getting direct input and support for unit and program change.

Developing a shared vision and strategy is stage three in this model. Kotter (1996) defines vision as "a picture of the future with some implicit or explicit commentary on why people should strive to create that future" (p. 68). Vision clarifies a direction for change, motivates people to want to work toward that change, and organizes the efforts and actions of individuals and groups. Kotter suggests that a strong vision is an "exercise of both the head and the heart" (p. 79), usually developed in a first draft by an individual in leadership and worked on by the guiding coalition over time. He urges leadership teams to spend the requisite time and energy on an appropriate and inspired vision and strategy, noting that not giving this stage its due will have severe consequences for any process of change.

Stage four continues with developing a plan to *communicate the change vision.* Gaining an understanding of and commitment to a new future requires an enormous communication effort. Kotter (1996) explains that coalition members spend hours researching options; making decisions about opportunities; letting go of other choices; and figuring out how options will affect them as individuals, departments, and as an organization. It stands to reason that members of an organization not privy to the decision-making conversations will go through similar cognitive and emotional processes when they hear the vision and strategy for change. However, organizations do not always allow the time or space for its workers to process the change, thereby causing resistance to the change. Kotter suggests that those communicating change keep their message simple, communicate using different formats, lead by example to avoid inconsistencies in message, and listen to the members of the organization.

Student affairs organizations are often some of the most diverse subgroups in colleges and universities. They employ professionals at every stage of their careers who are diverse in gender, race, and thought and interest. Not unlike their academic counterparts, they need transparency and involvement in decision making. It stands to reason then that no change process in the culture of student affairs will be successful without careful attention to communication and input. Finding a variety of ways to communicate and ask for feedback throughout a process is a critical process and value for change in student affairs.

Stage five requires *empowering employees for broad-based action.* In this stage, employees have accepted the vision and strategy and want to work toward that end, but may face the barriers of structures, skills, system, and supervisors. Kotter (1996) suggests aligning structures and systems with the vision, providing training to address skill deficiencies, and addressing behaviors that undercut the needed change. The use of matrix structures in student affairs may meet with structural or systemic barriers because organizations have been primarily hierarchical and vertical. Encouraging matrix structures may require the use of project money, allowing time and resources for cross-departmental projects and communication, and an adjustment to the reward structure for these efforts.

Stage six involves *generating short-term wins.* Creating opportunities to evaluate performance measures and benchmarks, show progress toward the larger vision, and understand that the strategy is effective is as important to the morale and support of change as it is to the actual change. According to Kotter (1996) "short-term wins are visible, unambiguous and relate directly to the change effort" (pp. 121–122). Short-term wins keep people interested and committed to change, they affirm strategy, and they help build momentum for organizational change.

For student affairs organizations, short-term wins that require low risk or small behavior changes may create momentum for greater change. A common cause of student frustration focuses on the many offices designed to serve them but structured in a way that confuses them. For some campuses, students have common ways of describing their experiences when it comes to these service offices, such as "shuffle," "runaround," and "hassle." An organization may use a matrix structure to streamline some services for students by creating a one-stop student center. This matrix structure might employ a coordinator but rotate staff members from several high-traffic student services (i.e., financial aid, parking services, billing and receivables, registrar, student ID card office) into the center. Staff members begin to work together and learn common answers to student questions and needs.

The small wins come from providing an efficient service location for students and an increase in satisfaction from students. Other wins come when high-traffic offices become lower-traffic offices and require students to wait less and get more attention for complicated problems. Yet other wins come for student affairs staff members when the cross-training process builds a more educated and better-trained work force. As the student affairs organization experiences wins in the one-stop center for students, it begins to imagine possibilities for collaboration in other areas, perhaps leading to greater cross-unit structures. Stage seven *consolidates gains* and produces more change. Kotter (1996) warns that in celebrating short-term wins, organizations sometimes get the notion that taking a break from change is earned. He explains that giving up effort before the job is done may lose critical momentum. Instead of slowing down, Kotter suggests creating more change. He recommends revisiting the sense of urgency or establishing additional groups or teams that may help implement change at the departmental level.

Stage eight requires *anchoring new approaches into the culture*. Kotter (1996) describes this process: "in many transformation efforts, the core of the old culture is not incompatible with the new vision, although some specific norms will be. In that case, the challenge is to graft the new practices onto the old roots while killing off the inconsistent pieces" (p. 151). He advises that changes in culture come last, not first, and they are generally accepted only if there are clear signs that they work. Often with change comes turnover of key staff people, and he suggests organizations pay attention to succession plans and promotions for those who support the new culture.

Even some great ideas and important programs championed by bright scholars and wise leaders have difficulty becoming anchored into college and university campuses. Programs such as faculty mentors, living-learning communities, and faculty-in-residence have been beneficial but unsustainable on many campuses. Residence halls designed for interaction between students have given way to apartments that provide market-driven amenities. Organizational change is a journey that involves continual assessment; constant visioning and clarification of mission; consistent broad-based action; and recognition of progress, more assessment, and more change.

Bryson's Ten Steps to Change

Bryson (1995) created a process for planned change in nonprofit organizations often used to guide university strategic planning processes. His process outlines 10 steps for organizations to strengthen and sustain their achievement. It begins with an organization agreeing on the process it will use for planning and continues with identifying organizational mandates that the planning team must understand. Bryson prescribes that planning teams clarify the organizational mission and then assess internal and external environments to determine strengths, weaknesses, opportunities, and threats. Following the strategic assessment, organizations must determine strategic issues and then determine appropriate strategies for addressing them. The planning team adopts a strategic plan for the organization and creates an effective and compelling vision. Finally, the team develops a tactic to implement its plan and reassess its strategies and process.

Bryson's (1995) work provides a linear approach to facilitating an organization through a change process. Student affairs organizations can benefit by using this work to facilitate discussion and assessment of organizational environments. Using Bryson's work to discuss and agree on a vision for a student affairs division allows individuals and groups to envision something greater for their organization. Establishing a mission as a group creates a spine that pulls individual and group efforts to a central purpose, while also allowing units to develop unique tactics that contribute to the mission and vision of the larger organization. Some believe that the process in many of these planning strategies is as important as the outcome—and for very diverse divisions of student affairs, this may be the case.

Restructuring Resources for Planned and Adaptive Change

If one wants to understand the goals of a university, follow the money. Budgets become the mechanisms for advancing organizational plans and priorities. The principal goal of any planning process is to link planning and budgeting. While there are a number of methods used to allocate resources within colleges and universities and student affairs units, the key to moving an organization in the direction of desired change is to fund the areas and projects that support organizational goals.

Student affairs organizations often use a variety of budget models, including cost-centered or responsibility-centered budgeting for units that are revenue-producing or those funded through a designated fee, incremental for those funded through the general fund, and program budgeting in some cases. Both cost-centered and responsibility-centered budgeting require units to develop their own revenues and be responsible for their own expenses. Cost- and responsibility-centered models tend to encourage entrepreneurism on the upside, but can also spark boundary building and competition between units.

Incremental budgeting is the most common approach to budgeting for colleges and universities. Student affairs divisions at small colleges and universities are often subject to incremental budgeting as all revenues go into a general fund and are distributed to department and division budgets. It essentially uses the same budget from year to year with slight changes in revenue levels and resource distribution (Lasher & Greene, 2001). Incremental budgeting makes planned or incremental change difficult when resources are needed to accomplish new or different outcomes because those resources stay relatively stable.

Program budgeting was one of the first attempts to link activity with outcomes. In this model, budgets are created for programs or activities instead of departments or units (Lasher & Greene, 2001). The process requires a program plan, program budget, and cost-benefit analysis. The federal government and some universities used this budget model, best known as Planning, Programming, and Budgeting Systems (PPBS), for a short time in the 1960s. While proponents of the model laud its outcome orientation and its ability to provide a sense of direction for universities, others find it impractical or impossible to manage due to the structural confines of universities.

Whatever the model, establishing a funding source for supporting the change an organization wishes to create is critical. Securing funds for matrix or lateral projects will help to avoid the politics of project ownership and the pitfalls that come with funding bifurcation within student affairs units. Addressing Van de Ven's (1986) structural and process barriers to change, and establishing a common funding source to support planned strategies for change may encourage greater buy-in to the process and desired outcomes from individuals and units.

For many innovative projects in student affairs, grant opportunities may also be available. Projects that address the changing student population, create greater access and retention for traditionally underserved populations, or have a meaningful impact on student learning or civic leadership may be eligible for local or national grant funds. Student affairs change agents should explore these opportunities with institutional partners and grant offices on their campuses.

Measuring the Results of Change

Viable organizational change efforts also include a plan for evaluating progress toward divisional goals and mission. Continuous evaluation and implementation of a plan is often referred to as *strategic management*, or the process that links planning and decision making to the day-to-day efforts of enacting a strategic plan (Dooris & Lozier, 1990). The planning part of change involves making decisions about mission, goals, vision, strategy for achieving goals, resource allocation, and structural and systemic alignment. The day-to-day management of that plan requires a coordinated communication effort and collaboration, while keeping organizational units focused on mission, vision, and goals. Rowley, Herman, and Dolence (1998) state that the greatest resistance to change often emerges at implementation, when the strategic planning process shifts toward the process of management. Without a plan for monitoring, evaluating, and communicating progress, plans at the point of implementation are subject to failure, especially in organizations that have policies and practices that create barriers to change. For example, sometimes budget policies and practices can prevent change in organizations. Take the earlier example of using a matrix structure to design a program to support the influx of war veterans to campus. If the planning group decides on change in staffing patterns or program money to serve this population effectively, but budget flexibility does not follow, implementation of this program may fall short. Shepherding planning efforts through implementation, assessment, and continual change requires strategic management of planning efforts.

In an adaptive environment, evaluation identifies projects that need to be supported or enhanced based on their centrality to mission. Likewise, regular evaluation also serves to bring attention to those projects that may contribute to mission drift. Chance and Williams (2009) cite the work of Hunt, Oosting, Stevens, Loudon, and Migliore (1997) as particularly helpful in creating a framework for control and evaluation of organizational plans for change. They indicate that evaluation plans should be linked to strategy, be simple and economical to use, measure both activities and results, flag the exceptions, focus on key success factors, be timely, be flexible as strategy changes with environmental demands, and be reality-based and followed up in written and face-to-face communication (p. 44). The use of specific measures, such as performance indicators (Barnetson, 2001), benchmarking (Upcraft & Schuh, 1996), scorecards, or dashboards, provides an organization with frequent snapshots of progress and allows its members to adjust the plan based on new information, changes in environment, and organizational learning.

Conclusion

Colleges and universities are growing less immune to the economic, technological, and global issues that affect our society and have been challenged to respond to the call for greater access, diversity, and accountability in the industry. Student affairs organizations are expected to do their part to make their organizations more effective for students with greater needs, more collaborative, and more efficient. To meet the needs of these complex organizations, student affairs divisions are looking to those outside the field of student personnel who specialize in communication, research, technology, and fund-raising to assist with meeting new organizational needs and mandates. To become more effective, student affairs organizations are beginning to shift from vertically oriented organizations to lateral or matrix organizations.

Change in organizational personnel and growth or reduction of units within the division of student affairs reflects incremental change in the organization, whereas structural and systemic shifts signal more transformational change. Given the changing environment, student affairs leaders are challenged to facilitate both planned and adaptive approaches to organizational change. Regardless of method used, change agents need to encourage a readiness for organizational change and innovation, work to overcome barriers and resistance to change, encourage and facilitate innovation, and adopt a plan for organizational assessment and learning.

References

2020 Commission on the Future of Postsecondary Education. (1998). Retrieved from http://www.digitalarchives.wa.gov/governorlocke/taskcomm/2020/lea rning.htm

Barnetson, B. (2001). Performance indicators and chaos theory. In M. Cutright (Ed.), *Chaos theory and higher education: Leadership, planning, and policy* (pp. 145–158). Baltimore: Peter Lang.

Bergquist, W. (1998). The postmodern challenge: Changing our community colleges. *New Directions for Community Colleges, 102,* 87–98.

Bess, J. L., & Dee, J. R. (2008). *Understanding college and university organization: Theories for effective policy and practice. Volume II: Dynamics of the system.* Sterling, VA: Stylus.

Bolman, L. G., & Deal, T. E. (2008). *Reframing organizations: Artistry, choice, and leadership* (4th ed.). San Francisco: Jossey-Bass.

Bryson, J. M. (1995). *Strategic planning for public and nonprofit organizations: A guide to strengthening and sustaining organizational achievement.* San Francisco: Jossey-Bass.

Burnes, B. (2000). *Managing change* (3rd ed.). London: Pearson Education.

Burnes, B. (2004). Emergent change and planned change: Competitors or allies? The case of XYZ construction. *International Journal of Operations and Production Management, 24* (9–10), 886–902.

Burnes, B. (2006). Kurt Lewin and the planned approach to change: A reappraisal. In J. V. Gallos (Ed.), *Organizational development: A Jossey-Bass reader* (pp. 133–157). San Francisco: Jossey-Bass.

Chance, S., & Williams, B. T. (2009). Assessing university strategic plans: A tool for consideration. *Educational Planning, 18*(1), 38–54.

Dawson, P. (1994). *Organizational change. A processual approach.* London: Paul Chapman.

Dooris, M. J., & Lozier, G. G. (1990). Adapting formal planning approaches: The Pennsylvania State University. *New Directions for Institutional Research,* 1990: 5–21. doi: 10.1002/ir.37019906703

Eckel, P., Green, M., Hill, B., & Mallon, W. (1999). *Taking charge of change: A primer for colleges and universities.* Washington, DC: American Council on Education.

Flamholtz, E., & Randle, Y. (2008). *Leading strategic change: Bridging theory and practice.* New York: Cambridge University Press.

Hunt, C., Oosting, K. W., Stevens, R., Loudon, D., & Migliore, R. H. (1997). *Strategic planning for private higher education.* Florence, KY: Psychology Press.

Kanter, R. M., Stein, B. A., & Jick, T. D. (1994). *The challenge of organizational change: How companies experience it and leaders guide it.* New York: Free Press.

Keller, G. (1983). *Academic strategy: The management revolution in American higher education.* Baltimore: Johns Hopkins University Press.

Kezar, A. J. (2003). Understanding and facilitating organizational change in the 21st century. *ASHE-ERIC Higher Education Report, 28*(4). San Francisco: Jossey-Bass.

Kotter, J. P. (1996). *Leading change.* Boston: Harvard Business School Press.

Lasher, W. F., & Greene, D. L. (2001). College and university budgeting: What do we know? What do we need to know? In J. L. Yeager, G. M. Nelson, E. A. Potter, J. C. Weidman, & T. G. Zullo (Eds.), *ASHE reader on finance in higher education* (2nd ed., pp. 475–502). Boston: Pearson.

Lerner, A. L. (1999). A strategic planning primer for higher education. Retrieved August 28, 2010, from http://www.sonoma.edu/aa/planning/Strategic Planning Primer.pdf

Leslie, D. W., & Fretwell, E. K., Jr. (1996). *Wise moves in hard times: Creating and managing resilient colleges and universities.* San Francisco: Jossey-Bass.

Manning, K., Kinzie, J., & Schuh, K. (2006*). One size does not fit all: Traditional and innovative models of student affairs practice.* San Francisco: Jossey-Bass.

Nadler, D. A. (2006). The congruence model of change. In J. A. Gallos (Ed.), *Organizational development: A Jossey-Bass reader* (pp. 252–266). San Francisco: Jossey-Bass.

Nadler, D. A., & Tushman, M. L. (1989). Organizational frame bending: Principles for managing reorientation. *The Academy of Management Executive, 3*(3), 194–204.

Rowley, D. J., Herman, D. L., & Dolence, M. G. (1998). *Strategic choices for the academy: How demand for lifelong learning will re-create higher education.* San Francisco: Jossey-Bass.

Schein, E. H. (1988). *Organizational psychology* (3rd ed.). London, UK: Prentice-Hall.

Upcraft, M. L., & Schuh, J. H. (1996). *Assessment in student affairs: A guide to practitioners.* San Francisco: Jossey-Bass.

Van de Ven, A. H. (1986). Central problems in the management of innovation. *Management Science, 32*(5), 590–607.

Woodard, D. B., Jr., Love, P., & Komives, S. R. (eds.). (2000). *Leadership and management issues for a new century.* New Directions for Student Services, 92. San Francisco: Jossey-Bass.

13

EMERGING ROLES AND STRUCTURES IN STUDENT AFFAIRS ORGANIZATIONS AT SMALLER COLLEGES AND UNIVERSITIES

Frank P. Ardaiolo and Kathleen M. Callahan

These are extraordinary times across the nation for all institutions as they seek ways to cope with shrinking allocations, shrinking endowments, and the shrinking capability of many students to find the funds to enroll in the institutions of their choice. The "Great Recession" lingers, and employment and economic growth rates seem to be improving only in small, incremental stages and the situation may be with us for a number of years. Smaller institutions may be more vulnerable because they often do not have the economies of scale and endowment dividends of larger institutions that may soften such economic downturns. Shrinking resources are causing institutions to raise their fees to met previous budget allocations while examining many processes and mechanisms to either increase revenue flows or decrease expenditures. The *new normal* of higher education economics may best be characterized as the constant reallocation of increasingly scarce resources.

Coping with cuts in budgets, funding, resources, and staff and increasing demands from students, parents, faculty, and administration, student affairs organizations have been forced to make changes and find flexibility on all fronts, literally examining all operations from every angle (Varlotta & Jones,

2010). Already with small staffs, cutting them can be the most effective quick fix fiscally for institutions since salary-intensive budgets comprise the major portions of these budgets. Smaller colleges and universities feel the cuts deeply because their individual student affairs staff members often perform multiple roles and functions. Confounding this situation, staffing needs in technology, development, research and assessment, communications, and human resources are changing rapidly. These are functions that student affairs has not traditionally had to maintain.

Student affairs staffs at smaller institutions are demonstrating vital roles by accomplishing specialized functions within their organizations, in many cases, without dedicated professionals serving solely in specialized roles. How do smaller colleges and universities accomplish specialized functions within their student affairs responsibilities while employing fewer full-time professionals? How do student affairs organizations deploy mechanisms that encourage professionals to be the best they can be while asking them to do more with less? How is morale maintained and how are careers advanced? Many emerging and changing roles and responsibilities within student affairs have been explained in previous chapters. How do smaller colleges and universities compare with larger institutions that have larger budgets and more resources? What are the best practices that, when fully deployed, ensure that students at smaller institutions are getting the best services?

"The effective student affairs manager cannot work in isolation. Student affairs programs are an integral part of the institution and are influenced by the role, mission, policies, and procedures of that institution" (Upcraft & Barr, 1988, p. 79). Throughout this volume are best practices for specialized functional roles; however, in this chapter we offer more information on how smaller colleges and universities creatively manage these specialized roles even in difficult fiscal climates and how, specifically, one smaller institution in the southeast United States manages these roles and responsibilities effectively.

Bottom line, to maintain state-of-the-art practices within the student affairs professional curve while coping with the new normal of less funding, smaller institutions' student affairs staffs must do everything they can to fulfill and even survive their missions on these campuses. Collaborating, condensing, and combining become paramount. Collaborate with everyone to share responsibilities across the institution. Condense resources and staffing within the typical student affairs functions. Combine positions and creatively give employees additional roles and responsibilities.

Historical Development and Influences

Shaffer (1993) asserts:

> Student personnel work in the next 50 years will be called upon to perform even more significant functions than it has for the past 50. If it responds with creativity, ingenuity, and flexibility, there is no doubt of its future. If, however, it becomes the agent of the status quo and mere tradition, other fields will assume its work, and it will be reduced to performing mere housekeeping functions. (p. 167)

With ever-changing functions and added services, student affairs has become more than what it was in the immediate past. Demands from everyone have increased and student affairs organizations have faced many challenges. Still, at smaller colleges and universities, staffing and funding do not increase just because the demand for them does. These colleges must fit the new normal where work must continue, even increase, while coping with budget cuts and changing roles.

At smaller colleges and universities, student affairs organizations seek to condense and combine roles when facing budget cuts rather than eliminating specialized functional roles. They do this by creating a more fluid and dynamic division of student affairs, both structurally and organizationally. Such divisions maintain formal line-staff organizational charts but portray an organizational structure and culture that reflects nimbleness and flexibility by forming partnerships within the student affairs division itself.

An example is a functional area such as the career services office's assuming responsibility for an aspect of the new student orientation program by running the welcome fair, instead of the orientation staff being responsible for running the entire program. Second, students affairs continually seeks similar arrangements in partnership focused on student learning with other major divisions of the university, especially academic affairs—for instance, residential learning coordinators in housing assisting academic advisement during new student summer orientation.

The idea of budget cuts and changing roles is not new. As seen in the literature, professionals have been alluding to combining skills for years. In Garland and Grace's (1993) *New Perspectives for Student Affairs Professionals: Evolving Realities, Responsibilities and Roles*, one can see the new normal:

> To assume a more central position of leadership in the institution, student affairs professionals must possess a wider repertoire of skills. Traditional

skills required in the promotion of student development must be matched with the skills needed to help the student affairs professional serve as environmental scanner, milieu manager, market analyst, legal adviser, development officer, researcher, and quality assurance specialist. In short, student affairs professionals must continue to build their repertoire of skills to enable them to lead an institution's efforts to develop comprehensive responses to changing conditions. (p. 7)

This state of flux requires professionals to look to best practices. However, best practice in today's world of shrinking budgets demand that individual student affairs staff members fill more than one specialized functional role.

In smaller colleges and universities these roles have evolved just as at any other institution. Assessment of student needs drives these new roles and responsibilities, along with the needs of the institution. When these needs arise, or when they are seen in a trend elsewhere, student affairs designates different offices and individuals to explore new arrangements to fulfill these needs. In response, this evolution adapting to new roles sometimes relates within the office as it currently is organized and functions, and at other times it may be delegated to someone, regardless of that person's home department, who has an interest in that topic or is seen to be an expert in the making.

It Begins at the Beginning

Recruiting the right type of new staff is critical in allowing the smaller institution's student affairs organization to survive and even thrive among today's higher education institutions. Finding the right person has to move beyond allowing just the university's human resources office to fill any staff vacancy. There must be a complete vetting of all candidates' credentials and minimum basic qualifications for a specific position and the HR office does this well. However, the intangibles associated with institutional fit and student affairs organizations professional expertise must be assessed and teased out. It is much better to invest time and effort on the front end of the hiring process than on the back end, especially if much time must be spent on separating an unproductive or unhappy employee later.

Efforts on the front end of hiring are especially important at smaller institutions where new roles are emerging, exacerbated by shrinking personnel budgets. This is especially true because a majority of entry-level master's candidates come from larger, more complex universities. While internships and practica attempt to expose nascent student affairs professionals to smaller campuses, a rich understanding of the multiple roles that staff must play often are not achieved. Newly hired staff members often join smaller institutions falsely thinking they will be responsible solely for their functional expertise. They often initially fail to grasp that every individual staff member at smaller institutions is also responsible for recruitment activities; retention initiatives; and superior customer service interfacing with all actors entering and already in the institution's arena, including the public, visitors, donors, faculty, staff in other organizational divisions, and students. A confounding circumstance is that first impressions can often set the tone of how one is perceived initially and received subsequently in all of the interactions that start from the first day of employment. This contrasts with larger-scale institutions that often insulate new student affairs employees from many interactions beyond their immediate job descriptions' functions.

The need for quick acculturation activities for new employees at smaller institutions is thus critical. This is especially true at a smaller institution where the current culture allows student affairs professionals to be considered partners with faculty, not just service providers. The following steps should be followed during the hiring processes associated with any position that requires a master's degree because the person holding the job is also considered an educator:

1. The department head or hiring authority forms a search committee in consultation with the SSAO that comprises the hiring department staff, a staff member from another department within student affairs, a full-time faculty member, and students, when possible.

2. The SSAO approves the search committee and requires search parameters that ensure a wide net is cast within the student affairs professional field nationally while also making every effort to find candidates from minority pools.

3. All finalists are invited for multiple campus interviews that involve a heavy cross-section of the campus community, especially those who regularly intersect with the position's responsibilities.

4. Every candidate has an interview with the SSAO who ensures all candidates that he or she will not be the person who decides whether the candidate will be offered the position. Rather, this is an opportunity for the candidate to interview "the institution" in a way and to gain perspectives on the institution's mission and the role of student

affairs in that mission. Candidates' questions often can be answered from a much broader knowledge base than the search committee. The SSAO typically pays attention to the theoretical knowledge base of the candidate, assessing whether the individual sees him or herself as an educator and why. The SSAO also asks the same two questions of each candidate: "How do you answer a faculty member who demands to know why you should be hired in this position when the faculty member's own department has had to eliminate a position?" and "Why is what you do more important than my faculty member teaching a content course in a class?"

After hiring the successful candidate, the SSAO, working with the hiring authority, selects a coach outside the employing functional area but in the student affairs organization. The coach assists new full-time staff members (both professional and administrative support) in assimilating into and adjusting to the university community and the division of student affairs specifically. The primary responsibility of the selected coach is to give personal attention and serve as a source of information to the new staff member.

The coach should be an established student affairs staff member who works in a different department from that of the new staff member, and should be a peer who is at an equivalent professional level or close as possible. The assigned coach is responsible for contacting the new staff member as soon as possible to welcome him or her to campus, and if possible, contact the new staff member before she or he arrives on campus to help with any moving or adjustment concerns. The coach will also have the checklist of required and optional orientation activities and job description of the coach role. The level of involvement beyond that minimally required in the coach's suggested activities is at the discretion of the coach, but one hopes that a meaningful relationship will be established, and the coach will continue to serve as a resource person for the new staff member even after the initial orientation process is completed.

In addition to the university's human resource department's daylong orientation that is given twice a year at our institution and thus may not be timely, the coach assures an immediate orientation by ensuring that the new employee completes the following checklist within 30 days of the first day of work:

- Review orientation packet and orientation checklist with immediate supervisor.

- Meet with your coach.
- Tour campus with your coach.
- View three archival films made before the 1960s on DVD: *One Hundred Years of Winthrop History*, *Winthrop Day by Day*, and *The Winthrop Girl*.
- Review the university's primary annual planning document, *Vision of Distinction*, and your department's planned learning outcomes and learning objectives.
- Meet with the vice president for student life (VPSL).
- Meet with the president of the university if he or she is available.
- Arrange to attend the next life division leadership meeting conducted by the VPSL.

Following such a systematic and rigorous approach in selecting and orienting new staff has resulted in a remarkable team approach at one university. These methods involve staff in a meaningful way so they feel vested in the institution's success and the potential contribution they will make even before being hired and as they begin their new jobs. Although hundreds of new staff have come and gone over the two decades these methods have been used, not one professional student affairs staff member has ever been terminated involuntarily or dismissed for cause.

Using such approaches can also support the emerging philosophical framework and roles on many campuses where institutions focus on the entire meaning-making apparatus and all of the developmental domains of traditional age students, including cognitive, personal, and interpersonal growth and development (Ardaiolo, 2007). Hiring and orienting processes such as these quickly incorporate new student affairs staff members into the fabric of the smaller institution where student affairs staff members hold pivotal roles in partnering with faculty to advance the institution's mission.

Background and Experiences in Developing New Roles and Responsibilities for Student Affairs Staff

The trend of having specialized knowledge is crucial in discharging functional responsibilities for serving all student populations, especially as the needs of student subpopulations have emerged. This is coupled with an expanding content-based knowledge of how certain functions should be handled as our professional practice standards have emerged the last few decades. When this SSAO first arrived at Winthrop University over two decades ago, the president directed the student affairs division to discharge its various functions in a state-of-the-art manner. An evaluation according to the CAS Standards (*CAS Professional Standards for Higher Education*, 2009) was used to document what was done well and what still needed to be done to comply with these standards fully. Only one department at that time had the level of staffing CAS recommended. Conducting a staffing pattern survey with 10 peer institutions revealed that the student affairs division was understaffed in all departments! Yet at this state-supported institution, it soon became clear there would be no new funds coming to the university, certainly not to student affairs, which was viewed at that time as not central to the mission of the institution. In fact, there was no articulated mission for the entire student affairs organization. Over the next 20 years since that initial assessment, state appropriations dropped almost yearly, from providing 41% of the institutional budget in 1990 to just 12% in 2010 and now 9.6% in 2011. The division rapidly learned that any growth in staff would be incremental at best.

Given this never-ending, budget-cutting scenario, the student affairs organization set out to create some rituals and mutual understandings to help mitigate the depressing environment. These notions are encapsulated in a small ritual carried on for more than 17 years. At the conclusion of the student affairs orientation program outlined previously, each new staff member is invited to a private meeting with the SSAO. The goal of this meeting is simply to learn how things are going and whether new employees' expectations are being met. They are asked in particular whether any surprises arose. At the conclusion of the informal meeting, the new staff member is asked to read *The Covenant*, written by staff in the mid-1990s. The SSAO asks whether the new employee agrees (and they always have), and then the SSAO and the new employee jointly sign and date the document with the following words: "This now gives you license to come see me if this is not happening." To date, no one has needed to take the SSAO up on the offer. The document, suitable for framing and signed by the new staff member and the SSAO, says:

> In order to create a more perfect union within the Division of Student Life at Winthrop University; and, in order to provide the university community with the tools to reach its greatest potential, THE STUDENT LIFE TEAM WILL:
>
> • Understand each other's role, responsibilities and activities in an effort to support all of our endeavors. This will in essence allow us to complement each other's efforts, avoid duplication of programs and services,

and encourage each other to take risks and not fear change; creating an atmosphere of respect for each other's differences.

- Recognize our prejudices and accept change while maintaining an open mind to new concepts and ideas.
- Strive to be visionary and not be consumed by shorter-term problems; whereby we will remain cognitive of our long-range goals versus immediate gratification.
- Encourage and nurture each other in our personal goals as well as our professional ones.
- Respect and recognize each other as professionals and as individuals. We will make sincere, genuine recognition an ongoing process and not just a one-time program that will heighten sensitivity of one another's accomplishments and dedication.
- Utilize constructive criticism with positive interaction; realizing that we unite for a common purpose and that we understand that we are all different. Our feelings are neither right nor wrong, only the facts affecting those feelings are.
- Have the courage to be honest with our feelings and hold each other accountable for the continued development of the whole person.
- Create and develop life-long friendships.

Winthrop University's budget cuts over many years foreshadowed what most institutions are now experiencing with the current recession. Following the above rituals has inculcated in new staff a sense of belonging and commitment to achieving the goals of the student affairs division. More important, staff have come to view themselves from their first day of employment as willing partners with key actors across the university working as a team, especially with academic affairs. Staff members also learned to cope with budget cuts and embraced the emerging trends in technology, development, research, assessment, human resources, auxiliary services, and professional development. Embracing them meant, as with smaller colleges and universities across the nation with limited funding sources, that it was impossible to have so many specialized individual roles within the student affairs organization. Staff members learned to work with limited means. Our keys to accomplishment included setting the tone for student affairs staff from the beginning of any search process through an orientation and socialization process that emphasized collaboration among ourselves and campus partnerships with other key players who also need to be focused on student engagement, learning, and success.

Changing Our Student Affairs Roles and Responsibilities to Become Central to the University Mission

Perhaps the best aspect of working at a smaller institution is the smaller scale, which allows meaningful interactions with other key actors resulting in real and lasting change. At Winthrop the five executive officers meet with the president weekly (with the SSAO literally being at the table for over 20 years). University-wide decisions are reached here, which has allowed student affairs perspectives to result in new roles that are woven into the institutional fabric as higher-level decisions are contemplated as trends emerged.

The key interactions among and within the student affairs functional departments also mimic top leadership's style. This style has been coupled with constant encouragement for professional development for all student affairs staff members even during the leanest of fiscal times. The result has been that every student affairs professional becomes a force multiplier influencing others on campus, as outlined below.

These efforts are given prominence in the university's annual planning document, *The Vision of Distinction (2010–2011)*, which highlights the institution's core values—a value set that explicitly frames all conversations as the Board of Trustees and the administration makes all decisions. The following commitment statements from this document reflect those core values:

- We center the Winthrop experience on student development inspired by our commitment to the liberal arts traditions, to national-caliber professional education, and to developing leadership and civic responsibility;
- We nurture collective and individual growth, enlightenment, and transformation;
- We value the search for truth through reasoned and disciplined inquiry, innovation, and free expression;
- We embrace multiculturalism and the broadest possible diversity of people and perspectives;
- We share a strong sense of place—a beautiful, historic campus with a collegial and caring atmosphere; and
- We fulfill and enhance the nature and character of the university through policies and resources that reflect and advance these ideals and aspirations. (p. 2)

At first read, it may seem that core values have little to do with emerging roles and structures concerning staffing; but at an institution where such planning matters, these are taken seriously so the institution stays on point. This is what is important; it allows the executive officers to talk from the same playbook ensuring a constancy and consistency that allows and even encourages staff to be flexible and hard working. This core values statement, which emphasizes conceptual educational goals such as student development, leadership, civic responsibility, caring atmosphere, and multiculturalism, has resonated repeatedly during the most difficult times. These values are the linchpins that have created new student affairs roles and positions that are often restructured from existing ones to deliver the institution's promise. For example, a single student affairs position devoted to orientation and multiculturalism simultaneously was split into two positions, one for orientation and the other for multicultural programming. The orientation position then added a peer mentoring program that worked in conjunction with the required new student academic seminar. Now peer mentors also provide peer academic counseling to students reportedly doing poorly academically. The multicultural programming position was then changed to advise the minority voice newspaper. Also added was responsibility for commuter student affairs, and now the person holding the position is also a key player in the division's assessment program and is working as part of the institution's Southern Association's Quality Enhancement Plan team. All of these changes were adopted willingly because of the demand for emerging roles to be filled, but were the initial acculturation processes and the ongoing staff development program encouraged their adoption.

Providing Human Resources at Smaller Institutions

When professionals are working toward the same vision and mission of both the institution and the division, they are more likely to focus on and be committed to their roles while at the same time remaining open to new possibilities. Having a central mission for the division and similar messages through each department shows students, faculty, staff, and parents one consistent message; this is important in smaller institutions with smaller staffs whose individual impact potential is greater. This message conveys to outsiders that all staff work in support of each other and toward the same goal and precludes allowing silo thinking or approaches to emerge.

Cross-training staff is vital to work between departments or functional areas in a division of student affairs at smaller institutions. To work toward a goal and to understand each other's work, student affairs organizations must provide professional development opportunities for staff. Beyond sending staff to professional workshops sponsored by national professional associations, a primary method for meeting the growth and development needs of staff is to create your own staff development series. For example, at our institution, tasking two mid-level managers to create such a program as part of their own personal professional development has resulted in a remarkable array of presentations and opportunities over the past few years. These staff were not given a budget but were simply told to use available resources. The presentations of the student affairs professional committee have included topics on conflict mediation, student affairs law and policy, embracing new technology, understanding the business of university development, coping with difficult students, grant writing, how to be hip and trendy, career paths, critical incident management, and transition skills for young professionals. These have resulted in an informed staff while developing mutually beneficial relationships across campus. These were realized simply by tapping fellow colleagues, including faculty, for their expertise.

Many are familiar with the ancient Chinese proverb, "Give a man a fish and you feed him for a day; teach a man to fish and you feed him for a lifetime." This principle holds true in student affairs as well. To further assist smaller staffs providing professional development, resources, support and assistance, efforts should be focused. One suggestion supporting this might be to provide a professional student development resource center. Books, journals, newspapers, and magazines from all functional areas in student affairs can be collected or donated so that all staff can find materials on just about any subject in the field. Such a collection is very important at smaller institutions where library periodicals, serials, and book budgets must be maintained for the broadest institutional audience.

Outside student affairs, the university's teaching and learning center also provides professional development opportunities for all faculty and staff institution-wide. Sessions include how to connect better with students, teaching methods, gardening, sustainability, and even how to understand your own health screening results provided by wellness services in the student health center.

Without expert training, student affairs professionals cannot be expected to have certain specialized functions often found in large university student affairs divisions. Needed expertise for dealing with the media, raising thousands of dollars, or fixing the heating and Internet in residence halls comes to mind. Other offices on campus that specialize in development, public relations, technology, and other auxiliary services must also be willing to assist student affairs in its daily work. Having strong relationships with these offices is crucial to functioning smoothly. Obviously, having employees "in house" would be the easiest solution; but where does the money come from? The instrumental relationships with institutional technical support, publicists, development officers, custodial staff, and facilities workers will determine how often and how well things get done. Partnership with these offices serves everyone. Members of these departments have been encouraged to join student affairs committees, have presented professional development sessions, and have worked closely on campus projects with student affairs staff resulting in authentic professional collaboration across university divisions.

In addition to this instrumental collaboration, smaller institutions should have university-wide committees or task groups to help our students educationally while providing services and cross-cutting campus-wide events and initiatives.

Assessment is a word that may cause professionals trepidation on a day-to-day basis if one does not constantly keep up with how to do it. At smaller institutions, different departments have their own assessment committees to assess their programs, student learning, and day-to-day functions. These departmental committees typically are chaired by one who has more expertise. Using these distributed staff with some assessment expertise in addition to their primary roles, smaller institutions can have members from some of these assessment committees serve on a larger campus assessment committee as well to help others learn and acknowledge what is occurring division-and campus-wide. Representative task forces and such distributed committees also help provide vital programs and services at smaller institutions that cross divisional responsibilities. Such initiatives that could be campus-wide collaborations may include the Safe Zones program for assisting LGBT students, diversity training, critical incident management, new student recruitment and orientation, and campus-wide events such as Homecoming and family weekend.

Staffing in a student affairs division to fill the aforementioned roles can be spread out across departments when provided with individually focused staff development opportunities that add more to an individual's initial skill set. When acculturated and encouraged through staff development, professional staff can add small duties to their current positions to fill other specialized needs or sit on division or university committees that fill a need.

An Innovative Approach to Staffing

Following the aforementioned mechanisms of recruiting, orienting, and collaboration are necessary, but they may not be sufficient for our changing times on smaller campuses when it comes to sustaining student affairs staff members as individuals. As Manning, Kinzie, and Schuh (2006) ask:

> How can a student affairs division be crafted in such a way that high-quality staff are recruited and retained within the university? How can student affairs educators be professionally motivated and developed through the course of their life-long career? How can the human resources of the profession be nurtured within the context of a healthy student affairs field? (p. 154)

One approach to sustaining staff is to create individual project managers who cross functional lines and responsibilities within a student affairs organization. This is a good opportunity for professional development while encouraging staff to "step out" into an uncomfortable zone that is not part of their written job descriptions. It is especially stimulating for those whose student affairs career is a "calling" where they are committed to a lifelong career. Another reason for establishing a project manager initiative is because the SSAO office at a smaller university may consist of just one other person, an administrative assistant. Stated simply, there just may be too many things going on for the SSAO to attend to all in a high-quality manner.

The project manager initiative asks for professional staff volunteers on matters that cut across many functional specialties in a division's professional practice. Objectives for such an initiative are:

- Continue to sustain a division in a new, innovative way not previously provided or performed well.
- Provide professional staff involvement in matters that cut across typical functional organizational arrangements.
- Provide the SSAO with some needed professional assistance.
- Allow volunteers to learn new things, to renew themselves, and to find fulfillment in doing new things.

It must be understood that such an initiative is not trying to add more work to anyone's already overcommitted or busy work schedule. The following guidelines prevail if a staff member applies and is selected to be a project manager:

- You are a volunteer essentially taking on more work; your current responsibilities cannot suffer.
- As soon as you find a project becoming burdensome, you may leave at any time.
- Some group and individual meetings with the SSAO will be required to establish mutually agreed-upon time frames for a volunteer's extra work.
- The supervising department head must endorse an application to become a project manager.
- A volunteer's performance as project manager will not be considered in an annual evaluation.
- The volunteer will do meaningful work that assists student life at the institution and for his or her future career.

At Winthrop University, where this project manager initiative was conceived, volunteer applicants were sought for the following emerging roles:

- public relations (telling the division's and students' stories);
- online delivery of student services;
- data collection;
- assessment of learning outcomes;
- student retention;
- legal issues;
- human resources;
- credit bearing courses for students;
- SACS reaffirmation visit preparation; and
- division-wide staff development and events.

Volunteers were told that if they were not selected for a role, they should not take it personally. The SSAO making the selection decisions promised to work with them individually to find something else that needed to be done.

The project manager program, which continues today, has had remarkable results, such as the university relations office adopting the student success stories motif that are now told constantly for recruitment purposes; a very knowledgeable staff member in learning assessment techniques became so well respected by faculty in the university's small assessment office that she was made a standing member of the institution's reaccreditation team and now leads the division's assessment efforts; the aforementioned approach to division-wide staff development programming; an excellent study on staff salary inequities that the regular human resources office could not undertake; systematic and rigorous data collection on the impact students who reside in the residence halls on retention and academic achievement; and new credit-bearing courses for students holding resident assistant, peer mentor, and orientation leader responsibilities taught for the first time by regular student affairs staff.

Mining Student Talent

Unlike at larger institutions, student affairs professionals at smaller institutions are expected to take on extra roles beyond their job descriptions' specific responsibilities by serving as advisors to student organizations, teaching classes beyond the freshman seminar, and helping students develop outside their offices and specific functional job assignment. The expectation for student affairs professionals at a smaller university is not to do the required minimum but to do everything within reason to serve the mission and vision of their department, division, and university. While doing this they work with volunteer or hourly student employees and leaders to carry out many significant responsibilities. Student leaders are trained by professionals to strive for the same personal excellence they expect from themselves and their professional colleagues. Accordingly, it is not uncommon to find large student staffs (at Winthrop University, an institution with more than 6,000 headcount enrollment, student affairs employs some 450 students). Students receive programs and services from their peers for such matters as mentoring, residential learning, tutoring, wellness advising, orienting, multicultural programming, career assistance, personal fitness coaching, recreational programming, social programming, and facilities operations for the resident halls, recreation and campus centers. Students are given wide latitude, and the great majority perform their specific responsibilities quite well.

Student employees soon come to understand that doing their jobs alone is necessary but not sufficient. They see that professional staff supervisors are relying on them while looking out for their student employees' personal growth and development. Accordingly, the departments in student affairs are expected to carry out employee development programs for their student workers. Programming includes dealing with difficult situations, their role in promoting civility, what freshmen students need to learn, emotional intelligence, leadership styles, and so on. Winthrop University's student life division also conducts half-day workshops that all of its student employees must attend each semester. This programming usually focuses on the work habits their current and future employers will look for. Approaching student employees in these ways stimulates students' personal growth and development while giving them the requisite skills to fill many roles and structures that are necessarily abbreviated by the scale of smaller institutions.

A Significant New Reporting Structure With New Roles and Responsibilities for the Future

Winthrop University's Division of Student Life (2010) has a long-standing mission statement directly aligned with the vision and core values of the university:

> The Division of Student Life provides opportunities and services to foster student development along cognitive, personal, and interpersonal dimensions. As educators, we work with our faculty colleagues to nurture and stimulate student learning and success within a pluralistic campus community. We accomplish this by delivering primary services that provide for the out-of-classroom caring for students, the foundation upon which classroom growth occurs.

Many of the professional student life staff (orientation, peer mentors, residence life, wellness, leadership, service learning, etc.) are linked structurally and are involved in emerging ways with Winthrop's University College whose

> purpose is to increase and enhance student achievement, responsibility, and engagement throughout the Winthrop Experience. University College coordinates curricular and co-curricular programs enabling faculty and staff to work across disciplines. This type of collaboration ensures that every Winthrop student, regardless of his or her ultimate degree goal, has a common academic foundation and a commitment to lifelong learning, leadership, and service. (Winthrop University, University College, 2010)

Student affairs staff members in these programs are now considered part of the college's faculty assembly. As such, they interact continually with full-time faculty across all disciplines and have taken on new roles that help inform and shape this emerging college's structure, programming, and initiatives.

For example, a project manager in the student affairs program mentioned previously conducted a data analysis that demonstrated students living in residence halls correlated to a higher collective GPA for resident students. Additionally, first- and second-year resident students were retained at higher rates than were off-campus students. Much of this success was attributed to a newer staffing arrangement at the university that placed a full-time, master's-level, live-in professional staff member in each residence hall. These staff members were directly responsible for developing academic success communities on each floor that reinforced the Winthrop experience promised in recruitment literature. Their presence allowed for quicker intervention with students exhibiting troubled behavior and created a seamless environment between students' in-class and out-of-class experiences. Their working with University College led to a hybrid evolution of their positions, which resulted in an eventual natural extension to add the title of "academic associate" in University College to "residential learning coordinator." This formal link prompted revision of the job descriptions and gave these staffers responsibilities for teaching a section of the freshman seminar course (something they did without extra compensation). It also provided University College (which has no full-time dedicated faculty to teach its courses) with a cadre of instructors who had student development expertise. In two years, these residential learning coordinators and academic associates have become involved in designing extra academic counseling for pre-majors, assisting with planning the common book program, providing direct academic advising for new students, and assisting with the development of a newly established Academic Success Center for new students.

These results give full testimony to what was stated in the *Student Learning Imperative* (American College Personnel Association [ACPA], 1996): "The choice for student affairs is simple: We can pursue a course that engages us in the central mission of our institutions or retreat to the margins in the hope that we will avoid the inconvenience of change" (p. 1). The context of the results also frames a future where students do not distinguish between faculty and staff because students and fiscally constrained institutions look to all of them to assist in their students' education (Ardaiolo, 2007).

Successes and Challenges of Emerging and Changing Roles

At smaller colleges and universities benefits emerging from changing roles and responsibilities include opportunities from the cross-training that professional staff engage in. Professionals have the ability to wear multiple hats, try out new roles, and train for job functions they never thought of. Upcraft and Barr (1988) presaged this more than 20 years ago: "Effective managers in student affairs understand the unpredictability of their work environment and acquire skills and competencies to increase their effectiveness in the management role" (p. 79). This benefits their futures, especially those of new professionals trying to comprehend and adjust for their best fit and future roles in student affairs. With so many roles in student affairs today, working at a smaller institution actually can give professionals an advantage in the job market.

However, a major challenge when balancing multiple roles and cross-training employees is to keep a sense of personal harmony. It is important for professionals to feel a sense of equality and stability in these complex roles. Do the benefits outweigh the negatives, or vice versa? Keeping staff focused on the overall goals of student success, retention, and development rather than on the workload can help young staff especially stay focused on reaching harmony in their own personal and professional lives because they can see that their responsibilities as educators do transcend their functional roles at any given time.

Collaboration and partnerships means more relationships. It is easy to get lost in a silo in departments at larger institutions, but when cross-campus partnerships are developed, staff create relationships to which they normally would not have access. These relationships retain staff and keep their morale high. The student affairs profession is a relational field. The more partnerships and collaborations individuals have, along with the opportunity to create strategies to fill emerging needs and roles, the more connected they will feel to the institution and to their jobs.

In *Managing Student Affairs Effectively*, Upcraft and Barr (1988) outlined 12 general rules for managers that still resonate today, especially for all student affairs professionals working at smaller colleges and universities. While language may have changed, these general rules are simple, direct, and very instructive in the smaller campus setting: "hire an excellent assistant, plan for the unexpected, invest time in people, be clear about expectations, make a commitment to get organized, learn to move the paper, avoid procrastination whenever possible, learn to delegate, break up large projects, use a tickle file, acquire the skills you need, and, finally, the most important rule that many cannot afford to forget, maintain your sense of humor" (pp. 16–19). Hard-hitting times are ahead with higher expectations and more emerging roles to meet evolving student needs. Professionals must remember the underlying purpose of student affairs work and realize that the arenas provided for that work are manageable and particularly exciting at smaller colleges and universities because of the many personally rewarding relationships that allow them to be true educators in collaborative roles with faculty and fellow staff members.

References

American College Personnel Association (ACPA). (1996). *The student learning imperative: Implications for student affairs.* Retrieved February 24, 2011, from http://www.acpa.nche.edu/sli/sli.htm

Ardaiolo, F. P. (2007). The once and future collaboration of academic and student affairs. In J. H. Cook & C. A. Lewis (Eds.), *Student and academic affairs collaboration, the divine comity.* Washington, DC: NASPA.

CAS professional standards for higher education (7th ed.). (2009). Washington, DC: Council for the Advancement of Standards in Higher Education.

Garland, P. H., & Grace. T. W. (1993). New perspectives for student affairs professionals: Evolving realities, responsibilities and roles. *ASHE-ERIC Higher Education Report*, 7. Washington, DC: The George Washington University, School of Education and Human Development.

Manning, K., Kinzie, J., & Schuh, J. (2006). *One size does not fit all—Traditional and innovative models of student affairs practice.* New York: Routledge.

Shaffer, R. H. (1993). Whither student personnel work from 1968 to 2018? A 1993 retrospective. *NASPA Journal, 30,* 162–168.

Upcraft, M. L., & Barr, M. J. (Eds.). (1988). *Managing student affairs effectively.* San Francisco: Jossey-Bass Inc.

Varlotta, L. E., & Jones, B. C. (Eds.) (2010, Spring). *Student affairs budgeting and financial management in the midst of fiscal crisis.* New Directions for Student Services, 129. San Francisco: Jossey-Bass.

Winthrop University. *Vision of distinction, 2010–2011.* Retrieved November 15, 2010, from http://www.winthrop.edu/uploadedFiles/president/2010–11_VoD_color.pdf

Winthrop University, Division of Student Life. *Mission statement.* Retrieved November 15, 2010, from http://www.winthrop.edu/student-life/default.aspx?id = 11590

Winthrop University, University College. *Mission statement.* Retrieved November 15, 2010, from http://www.winthrop.edu/uc/

14

EMERGING SPECIALIST ROLES AND STRUCTURES IN STUDENT AFFAIRS ORGANIZATIONS AT COMMUNITY COLLEGES

Bette M. Simmons

The traditional community college was founded on the mission of open access, affordability, and innovation in its reach to educate thousands of students, some of whom might never have pursued higher education. The current federal-level attention being given to community colleges, as a means to revitalize the economy, focuses on providing even more students with access to higher education. With this challenge, community colleges must maintain fluid organizational structures that will deliberately target, engage, and support the students they serve—and seek to serve.

As a result of changing demographics and workforce needs, community colleges have grown and become more diverse. They have broadened their programs and course offerings to respond to societal changes. Student populations have changed dramatically as well, with a wider range of students, including high school students taking college courses, larger pools of traditional-age college students, more mature students looking to retool or prepare for a different career path, and senior citizens pursuing educational enrichment. Students' needs and expectations have changed along with these demographic shifts as students present with greater mental health challenges, weaker developmental education preparation, and particular "customer service" mentalities.

A part of the community college mission has always been to reach out to many diverse student cohorts and provide them with support services they need to achieve their goals. Student affairs professionals need to be more flexible, quicker to respond to student needs and expectations, and better able to provide comprehensive support services within more tightly organized structures. These support services require individuals in different kinds of positions who are capable of providing a wide array of support services to students. Staff in student affairs divisions at community colleges are no longer segmented into traditional roles. To that end, the roles and structures in community colleges are emerging into something much different from what was witnessed previously, but that may set the stage for similar organizational designs in other higher educational sectors.

It is to be expected that the role and function of student affairs professionals in these institutions has undergone a fundamental change. By moving beyond the traditional responsibilities of maintaining student records, financial aid administration, and student advocacy, student affairs professionals have been urged to expand their roles in response to changing enrollment patterns, focusing on recruitment, enrollment, and retention, and developing programs that attract new markets to the community college. These professionals are becoming more tightly linked to the institution's strategic academic and economic objectives. Student affairs professionals, in partnership with academic officers, are emphasizing higher-value activities, such as student retention and graduation rates, enrollment management, resources management, revenue generation, academic planning, marketing, and performance assessment, for both students and the institution (Kvavkik & Handberg, 2000).

While student affairs positions within four-year institutions have been studied periodically, this is not necessarily the case with similar positions in community colleges (Helfgot & McGann Culp, 1995). Literature reports that expectations and responsibilities have changed over time, thus requiring different competencies, but does not report whether these changes have actually occurred at community colleges (Hernandez, 1989). And, more important, many community colleges, faced with shrinking financial support and greater dependence on college enrollments to manage budgets more effectively, have come to depend on staff assuming multiple responsibilities to get work done. The mantra, "do more with less," is a stark reality for those employed at community colleges, and the possibility of being a "specialist" at one's job is not necessarily a given. To achieve educational enrollment, retention, and completion goals, student affairs professionals find themselves having to become masters of many tasks, while maintaining a competency level in specific areas.

This chapter addresses how community colleges may be designing student affairs organizational structures to meet the demands on them. Changes to roles, responsibilities, and ways in which student affairs professionals must perform required tasks will be addressed. In addition, the chapter identifies specific student affairs roles in community colleges and discusses the issues student affairs professionals currently face, the models proposed to address them, and practical application of these models.

Student Affairs Models

According to Kuk and Banning (2009), today's student affairs organizations constitute a wide variety of operating units, programs, and services within nearly every higher educational institution in the United States. This growth and complexity was propelled initially by tremendous growth in the number, diversity, and needs of students accessing higher education after World War II. From the late 1950s into the mid-1970s, higher educational institutions created separate student affairs structures to address the needs of students more specifically (Barr, 1993). Student affairs professionals were viewed as surrogate parents, ensuring students' welfare and proper behavior. Campus unrest, civil rights, and court cases challenging institutional *in loco parentis* and First Amendment speech issues led student affairs to take on additional responsibilities and services and increase in organizational complexity (Manning, Kinzie, & Schuh, 2006). In recent decades this growth and complexity has been sustained by the demands of consumer-oriented students and their families for greater access, greater educational and service amenities, and more individualized programs and services. To compete, higher education institutions have added services, programs, and facilities to lure and retain students and to maintain and enhance the organizations' educational reputations (Kvavkik & Handberg, 2000).

With this growth and complexity, the mission of community colleges changed and expanded, and they made adjustments to the roles and functions of student affairs professionals. However, the models providing a theoretical framework for the profession have remained relatively unchanged. While there is no singular organizational model that is used by, or "fits," all student affairs operations (Ambler, 2000; Barr, 1993; Sandeen & Barr, 2006), some organizational theories and research can be universally applicable to one's understanding of how student affairs organizations must rethink their organizational structures to enhance their role and effectiveness. And these models affected the development of most community college student affairs organizations as they did for those of other colleges and universities.

There is agreement that student affairs structures are designed based on certain types of theoretical models. For example, Kuh (1989) indicates that there are four conventional approaches to organizing the work of most colleges and universities. These include (1) the rational model, (2) the bureaucratic model, (3) the collegial model, and (4) the political model.

In 1937, the American Council on Education published the *Student Personnel Point of View Statement*, the first national guideline for student development practice. The statement declared that student affairs professionals were to facilitate students' intellectual, personal, social, and moral development (Leach, 1989). Since then, a number of theoretical models have evolved as student affairs professionals attempted to integrate theory and practice.

The Human Development Facilitator

In 1972, O'Banion and Thurston proposed a model of the student personnel worker as committed to positive human development and possessing the skills and expertise needed to implement programs for the realization of human potential. Other aspects of the model included the involvement of student affairs professionals in community outreach, promotion of student participation in campus life and the education of their peers, and guardianship against oppressive institutional regulations.

The Maintenance Model

This model reduced the student affairs function to a segregated set of services available through various offices of the college, including admissions, registration, financial assistance, orientation, and counseling. McConnell's 1965 report to the Carnegie Foundation listed 36 different student affairs functions as essential to the community college. As well, a taxonomy of student services developed for California community colleges identified 106 core activities (O'Banion, 1989).

The American College Personnel Association Model

In 1975, the ACPA released a position paper, "A Student Development Model for Student Affairs in Tomorrow's Higher Education." that significantly influenced the development of the student affairs function. As applied in the Dallas County Community College District, this model emphasized the intentional and systematic use of adult development theories in carrying out assigned functions; development of the skills and attitudes needed for lifelong learning; creation of an environment conducive to student development; and integration of learning experiences (O'Banion, 1989).

The League for Innovation in the Community College Model

In 1986, the League developed a statement, "Assuring Student Success in the Community College: The Role of Student Development Professionals," to provide a framework for further evolution of the student affairs profession (Doucette & Dayton, 1989). The statement reaffirmed the principles of student development established in previous years and recommended minimum requirements for ensuring student success. It asserted that community colleges must monitor student intake, progress, and outcome; encourage student involvement with the campus; coordinate their programs with other secondary schools, business, and industry; and implement staff development programs to ensure that all staff possess an organizational culture and ethic that supports the institutional mission. This statement listed specific activities that student affairs professionals must undertake to achieve these goals.

According to a study by Kuk and Banning (2009), student affairs structures continue to be organized and essentially operate as hierarchical, functional units across all institutional types. There was no indication that any student affairs units were predominantly organized under any other structural models, although there were elements of other structural models operating in some organizations.

When asked about the possibility of redesigning their organizational structures, SSAOs responded that they would do so to address financial concerns, meet strategic priorities, enhance efficiencies and effectiveness, promote teamwork and collaboration, and reduce hierarchical approaches to decision making. When looking at restructured or redesigned student affairs organizations, some changes may include 1) moving enrollment services units out of student affairs to either academic affairs or a separate division of enrollment services; 2) moving the entire division of student affairs within academic affairs; 3) merging health and counseling services; 4) moving multicultural programs to a vice president for institutional diversity, and 5) moving the access office into student affairs. There was no mention of any changes that would provide a different approach to organizing resources, or structuring them differently other than traditional functional units moved to report to other existing units (Kuk & Banning, 2009).

Most community college organizational charts demonstrate how the basic functions that provide assistance and support to students often transcend formal organizational lines. Student affairs staff must understand that to accomplish their goals they must collaborate with their colleagues in academic affairs, business, and development. The relationship of the student affairs organization to the institutional organization as a whole is very important, but it is not as critical to the success of student affairs as are the relationships, coalitions, and cooperative programs that can be developed.

The Challenge of Reform

Over the last 30 years, several challenges have influenced the future direction of the nation's community colleges and the philosophical and theoretical framework of the student affairs profession. Student affairs professionals have had to stay abreast of these challenges to continue to play an important role in promoting the mission and goals of their institutions. This required them to respond with the development of innovative strategies and practices to address the requirements of the future (Hernandez, 1989). Thus, since the 1990s, student affairs professionals, even in community colleges, had to deal with the challenge of forging new models for delivering student services, well grounded in theory and appropriate in practice.

The Quality Reformation

During the 1980s, several national commissions offered a variety of criticisms of and recommendations for higher education that have clear implications for student affairs, including those urging community colleges to increase their expectations of students, become more directive, provide more information to students, and uphold high academic standards (Creamer, 1989).

Educational Technology

McCabe (1989) suggests that student affairs should depend heavily on information technology for accurate and timely information to offer good advice and direction to students, monitor their progress accurately, give continual feedback, and provide the correct intervention strategy based on accurate information.

Financial Constraints

Commonly, student affairs functions feel budget cuts earlier and more strongly than do other college programs and services. Some community college student affairs professionals have been addressing financial problems by implementing fee-based services, differential staffing, cooperative programs with community groups, and efforts to explore alternative funding sources (O'Banion, 1989).

Changes in Institutional Mission

A number of external forces influenced the community college's mission (Hernandez, 1989). The federal government and several state governments have stressed the role of community colleges in economic development and vocational training. Florida dealt with the question of the appropriateness of remedial education as a community college function, and California virtually eliminated public funding for community service courses. If the mission of community colleges changes, so too will the mission of student affairs.

Enrollment Management

McCabe (1989) predicted a significant role for student affairs in the following aspects of enrollment management: (1) data collection about the place of the college within the community, the interests of students, influences on college choice, and student perceptions of the strengths and weaknesses of the college; (2) a comprehensive plan for the college's interaction with students from the time they first inquire about the college until they register; and (3) monitoring students' responses to the college's programs and services.

Transforming Student Affairs

The League for Innovation in the Community College issued a set of concepts regarding student affairs (Cohen & Brawer, 1996). Included were 31 directives organized under seven major headings instructing community college student affairs professionals to design processes that would smooth student entry and placement, enhance student interaction with college staff and functions, assist students in gaining support from all types of college services, ensure student learning and development, coordinate with other organizations, maintain student records, and assist in selecting college staff members (Doucette & Dayton, 1989). In 1990, the Board of Governors of the California Community Colleges listed seven categorical responsibilities of student affairs incorporated in matriculation services: admissions, orientation, academic assessment, counseling and advising, follow-up on academic progress, research and evaluation, and coordination and training of staff (Helfgot & McGann Culp, 1995).

Today, centralized, departmentally delivered services are giving way to decentralized, learner-oriented services. This shift includes numerous opportunities for self-help as well as student and faculty access to information and services. Services are being provided electronically—at any time from any place—and without the intermediation of student affairs staff. Community college student affairs professionals have become generalists who serve as facilitators and navigators in an information-rich environment as opposed to directly delivering services (Kvavkik & Handberg, 2000).

Due to the need to demonstrate cost savings, downsizing/rightsizing, and restructuring, while at the same time enhancing productivity, student affairs offices now are required to do more than register students for classes, report grades, schedule classrooms, print transcripts, and award financial aid in the form of scholarships, need-based grants, work-study, and loans. Staff need cross-training so they can answer a broader array of questions; this was the genesis of the one-stop shopping concept. The generalist role challenged the "silo" structure of student affairs, which fostered decisions by specialists who controlled functional domains. To respond to an avoidance of overspecialized student services in tight financial times, community colleges provided the right kind of training and incentives for employees, so staff could provide a broader range of services.

While there is no universal administrative model all institutions use, most community colleges designate senior student affairs officers or SSAOs (Sandeen, 1996). The responsibilities of the SSAO may vary from one campus to another, depending on the problems facing the institution, the president's priorities, the ability of the SSAO, or the traditions and history of the institution. The SSAO often reports directly to the president, but in some cases may report to the provost or senior academic affairs officer. It is rare for all student affairs functions to fall under the administrative direction of the student affairs division at any given institution; at most institutions, other departments administer some of the functions (Helfgot & McGann Culp, 1995). For example, admissions and registration may be part of academic affairs, financial aid may be responsible to the business affairs division, and career and placement services might be part of the development program.

Regardless of the reporting structures, under the SSAO is a variety of practitioners organized either rigidly into departments or loosely into teams. Housed in a central student affairs area or scattered throughout the college to support specific programs, these practitioners traditionally report to middle managers who report to the SSAO (Kvavkik & Handberg, 2000). Occasionally, practitioners—particularly those who function as counselors or recruiters—find themselves reporting to two supervisors: one in academics, the other in student affairs. A few two-year colleges are flattening their reporting structures, eliminating middle managers, and asking all staff to report directly to the SSAO.

At some community colleges, size alone may dictate that extensive, separate departments be established, especially in registration and financial aid. When such large and relatively autonomous departments exist, the distance between student affairs and other campus programs can increase. Typical community college student affairs tasks can be compartmentalized in the areas described next.

Admissions, Recruitment, and Marketing

These services inform prospective students about the institution and its programs and solicit, accept, and screen applicants (Sandeen, 1996). Admissions officers maintain active communications with high schools, community agencies, local businesses, professional testing associations, parents, and others interested in the institution's admissions requirements. Due to the open admissions philosophy at most community colleges, admissions officers tend to be information specialists who promote the institutions' programs and services and communicate about areas of interests and needs of community members. Recently, with the implementation of different interactive recruitment and enrollment solutions, the typical process of analyzing students' applications for acceptance has become one of cultivating applications received and processing these applicants into actual registrants.

Services in the community college admissions office begin even before students arrive on campus. Because community colleges try to serve as many members of the community as feasible, they frequently engage in extensive recruitment activities. These activities, which have accelerated and diversified as the population of 18-year-olds declined after peaking in the late 1970s, have been especially vigorous in communities where the percentage of high school students beginning college has decreased, and continue to alter as technology infiltrates the enrollment processes (Cohen & Brawer, 1996). Such activities in which admissions personnel engage include:

- Linking recruitment procedures with surrounding high schools, local agencies, business, and corporations.

- Responsibility for all general recruitment practices and recruitment promotions.
- Administering tests to high school students, and then helping them to interpret the results. This includes cooperating with the instructional staff in using test results to place students in appropriate courses.
- Providing campus facilities for activities attracting prospective students.
- Offering advanced placement classes to qualified students.
- Disseminating information to potential students, regardless of whether they are high school students or members of the broader community, advising them of campus events.
- Ultimately, admissions personnel process applications for admission, offer orientation and pre-orientation services for students, deliver assessment and counseling at the time of enrollment, counsel students regarding their academic and career objectives, assess study and learning skills, advise on course selection, and conduct postenrollment evaluations of students' performance.

Finally, because the economy tends to affect community college enrollments, admissions personnel must be cognizant of economic trends, how community members' needs change as a result of a positive or poor economy, and what career opportunities will drive enrollment increases in certain academic programs. Interacting with community development agencies is essential to admissions personnel having the pulse of what's happening that could affect enrollment trends.

Records and Registration

The office of the registrar is charged with keeping the official academic records of current and former students. Also, this office usually conducts the process by which students enroll for their academic courses and publishes the official schedules of courses for the institution (Sandeen, 1996). At times, the registrar's office is linked administratively with admissions and, in some cases, with orientation or student financial aid.

Due to the movement toward self-service processes as well as more paperless systems, the role of the registrar has become more technical in nature (Kvavkik & Handberg, 2000). The registrar's tasks broadly affect other areas of community colleges and include responsibility for providing institutions with more information related to student demographics. While typically linked to other enrollment management areas, now the registrar must interact with almost all segments of the college community, faculty, academic departments, institutional researchers, athletics, and so on. In the community college environment, the level of processing is much less, while registrar staff members spend more time validating student information, providing support to students as they transact any number of self-processes, working more to maintain the integrity and confidentiality of student information, and working with academic colleagues to ensure courses to meet student needs.

Financial Aid

Most colleges and universities provide a financial aid office to help students with their educational expenses (Sandeen, 1996). Staff in community college financial aid offices work closely with government agencies, banks, loan guarantee agencies, parents, corporate and individual donors, and, of course, student recipients. In addition to assessing student financial needs and making decisions about student aid packages, financial aid staff also assist students with financial planning while in college. While the role of financial aid staff is dictated by federal and state guidelines, the roles can be institutional-specific depending on priorities; for example, managing institutional scholarships, work-study programs, and so on. Financial aid staff need to be familiar with academic programs, other community financial resources available to students, and how out-of-pocket costs can be reduced. Again, due to the advent of paperless systems and electronic processes, financial aid professionals spend more time validating information and eligibility compliance than they do actually processing.

International Student Services

With large numbers of international students in the United States, most community colleges have established special offices to meet their needs (Sandeen, 1996). These offices help international students with travel, orientation, financial assistance, registration, housing, counseling, and successful adjustment to the campus and community. In many cases international student affairs offices are responsible for study-abroad programs, foreign visitors, and the many international student organizations on campuses.

Staff working with international students need to be cognizant of requirements for visa eligibility as well as alternative financial resources to support these students' academic pursuits and personal needs. Staff roles also expanded to include monitoring the status of international students to make sure that federal enrollment, transfer, and active visa status requirements are maintained.

Student Activities Offices

On most community college campuses, the student activities office is responsible for developing and supervising activities that complement the educational programs and goals of the institution (Sandeen, 1996). This is a critical component for community college student activities as most community college students spend little time on-campus outside the classroom taking advantage of campus life programs and activities. To enrich students' experiences, student activities advance the political, social, religious, academic, and recreational interests of students, and they are often linked to leadership and community service programs. Student activities professionals at community colleges work diligently to coordinate parts of their programs with the curriculum, especially the general education core curriculum, in an effort to attract students, make their involvement meaningful, and engage them in quality-of-campus-life programs. The staff work closely with colleagues in academic affairs to develop programs that relate to classroom discussions and enhance in-class learning with out-of-class experiences.

Community college student activities staff assume responsibility for the development of orientation programs that help students learn the institutions' history, traditions, educational programs, academic requirements, support services, and student life. In recent years, these programs have become extensive, involving parents, community leaders, faculty, and student leaders. Because the community college student population spends little time on campus, student activities staff must create programs that focus on enrollment functions, student affairs offerings that enhance students' first year experiences, academic support services, and links to academic programs.

As most community colleges do not have a formal office dedicated to community service and leadership development, many conduct such programs through student activities offices. Not only are students encouraged to participate in a variety of community service programs or service-learning activities connected to their academic course work, but responsibilities fall on student activities staff to engage students in activities and programs that promote leadership development. Frequent cooperation with academic programs, community organizations, and corporate and community agencies is required in this area, demanding student activities staff to be aware of community issues, trends, and opportunities that will lead to meaningful community activities for students.

Counseling Services

Community colleges expend substantial effort to help students with their personal development and everyday problems. Usually, this is accomplished through a counseling services office that is staffed with professionals trained to provide assistance to students in a variety of areas, including mental health and psychological services and educational, career, academic, and personal matters (Sandeen, 1996). Because community college students spend little time on campus and have access to a wealth of human services in the community, counselors must be knowledgeable about the various community service agencies that support student needs. Many counseling services now engage in outreach activities with other campus offices and with various community agencies. On occasion, the counseling office may also provide services to persons in crisis, but they tend to make this more of an intervention service that connects students to the appropriate agency in the community.

Typically, community college students are uncertain about their educational and career goals, and, in most cases, they are forced into making decisions too quickly since their enrollment in the community college is short term. As a result, they require effective support services to give them clear direction. The core of counseling services includes comprehensive academic, career, and educational planning, personal and mental health services; and services for specialized student groups. In addition to crisis management, behavioral assessment interventions, transfer services, and student success programs, community college counselors

- provide academic guidance that matches students to programs best suited to their own goals and abilities, and help them recognize their academic abilities and limitations in an organized and caring manner;
- provide all entering and continuing students direction about their future and develop plans to achieve their goals;
- integrate with other campus activities to the extent that they maximize students' chances to reach their potential—for example, academic advisement, tutorial services, services for students with disabilities, etc.; and

- provide comprehensive counseling that includes goal-setting, personal assessment, identification of strategies, and problem-solving techniques.

Academic Advising and Support Services

Depending on institutional size, special offices have been established to assist students in making decisions about their course of study (Sandeen, 1996). Often, staff specially trained for this responsibility are hired for tasks that traditionally were assumed by faculty members. The academic advising professional often includes special academic support services to address the needs of students who may need any type of academic assistance that promotes student success and program completion.

Transfer and Articulation

Program matriculation refers to the movement of students—or, more precisely, the students' academic credits—from one point to another (Sandeen, 1996). *Matriculation* covers students going from high school to college; from two-year colleges to universities and vice versa; double-reverse transfer students who go from two-year colleges to university and then back again; and people seeking credit for experiential learning as a basis for college or university credit. Typically, community college counselors are responsible for assisting students with transfer activities and aiding the institution in maintaining and disseminating articulation information. Interacting frequently with representatives from four-year institutions is essential to these individuals' ability to provide these services. The concept includes admission, readmission, advising, counseling, planning curriculum, and course and credit evaluation as well as the following:

- Work with students to plan curriculum transfer strategies and financial aid arrangements, and introduce them to senior institutions to which they might transfer.
- Coordinate on-site instant decision days that provide opportunities for students to apply to four-year institutions on-site and receive admissions and transfer of credit decisions instantly.
- Maintain agreements on course equivalencies, transfer credits, legislative and state policies regarding transfer, and statistics on student transfer rates.
- Facilitate the design of transfer programs with the assistance of faculty from community colleges and senior institutions who define course requirements, course content, and academic expectations.

Career Services

While some community colleges embed career development into counseling services as they look to treating the whole person, more and more of them have specialized career services offices that offer a breadth of career development services. For many years, this service was known as the *placement office*, as its primary function was considered to be helping students obtain jobs after graduation (Sandeen, 1996). Now the purposes of this office include helping students learn about their own interests and skills and developing plans that fit students' career and personal needs. Staff work closely with students, faculty, corporations, and community and government agencies to uncover employment opportunities. The community college career services program often includes an emphasis on career planning, assessment, cooperative education, internships, placement, and alumni support.

Sports and Recreational Programs

Community college student affairs divisions often have responsibility for directing a wide variety of programs in intercollegiate athletics, intramural sports, fitness, and recreation. These programs enable students to participate in athletic competition in a variety of sports; engage in recreation and fitness programs that promote good health, teach physical skills, and encourage health and wellness; and offer intramural and informal activities such as sports clubs to compete outside official intercollegiate programs (Sandeen, 1996). These diverse athletic programs address issues of sportsmanship, training, nutrition, safety, gender equity, financial support, and institutional representation.

Student Health Services

Some community colleges provide some form of health care for their students, whether directly through a service on-campus or in conjunction with a community agency or hospital. The purpose of student health services is to provide medical assistance to students who are ill or injured, encourage good health, and help prevent illness or injury. Community college health services staff often work closely with community health organizations to increase emphasis on wellness. On some campuses coverage extends to faculty and staff as well as students. Addressing current health-related issues in an effort to better educate students about those issues and what they need to do to remain cognizant of them, is a major focus of community college health office staff.

Dean of Students

This office, which often has responsibility for several of the functions listed in this section, has traditionally carried with it the expectation of helping to establish and enforce the institution's community standards (Sandeen, 1996). The primary educational role within student affairs is assumed by the dean of students and is expressed most frequently through policy, links with academic departments, and campus leadership. At some community colleges the dean of students assumes the undefined but significant role of *conscience of the campus*, responding to the general concerns of students, faculty, staff, parents, and community members, and organizing and directing the institution's responses to student crises.

Additionally, staff in the community college dean of students office are responsible for ensuring that the academic integrity and behavioral standards of the institution are maintained. Deans of students typically have responsibility for student judicial matters that develop, interpret, and enforce campus rules and regulations. In this role, a representative of the dean of students office conducts student hearings, publishes rules and regulations, and encourages student learning through direct participation in the judicial system.

Special Student Populations

Many community college campuses have student affairs professionals to address the special needs of at-risk student populations, such as women, minority students, students with disabilities, veterans, student-athletes, and so on (Sandeen, 1996). As opposed to having individual offices that address the unique needs of each of these groups (e.g., disability services, multicultural affairs, women's center, etc.), community colleges must employ a cadre of individuals, typically in a general student affairs office or a counseling services office, who are on hand to provide a wealth of services to these special groups. Special efforts are usually made to respond to the educational and social concerns of these student populations. Individuals in these offices are trained and capable of providing help to these students so they have a successful college experience, and assisting faculty, students, and staff in becoming more knowledgeable about particular needs.

Staff in this office work to improve physical conditions and understanding on the campus and in the community. Typically, they find themselves in an advocacy role, serving as a catalyst in discussions of academic policies and procedures that affect students with special needs and discussing with faculty how they can provide reasonable accommodations to support students' ability to be successful.

Conclusion

The future of American community college education is changing. Along with President Obama's challenge to graduate an additional five million students by 2020, there is increasing pressure for institutional accountability and a change in emphasis from access to one of access *and* success. Community colleges are increasingly viewed as the postsecondary institutions most capable of strengthening the U.S. economy by equipping students with leadership and workforce skills for today's rapidly changing, competitive global economy. Student affairs organizations within the community college will play a vital role in this renewed direction of educating and guiding our students to completion, and this presents an opportunity for student affairs professionals to analyze organizational structures, programs, and services to serve students effectively.

In response to diminishing resources, changing demographics, growing demand, and fast-paced technology, community college student affairs professionals need to choose what programs and services remain intact, which need to be redesigned or eliminated, and what staffing patterns will support all. Student affairs professionals will need to prioritize goals that demonstrate efficiency, innovations, creativity, and strategic planning. In addition, they will need to develop more community partnerships, investigate entrepreneurial ventures, engage in educational collaborations with schools at all levels, establish alliances with business and industry for additional resources, and look at ways of maximizing technology to deliver services.

These demands will affect staffing and roles of community college student affairs professionals as well. Now more than ever student affairs professionals will have to get out of their offices and into classrooms—or online—to connect with students. But they will also have to tailor services to students' specific academic needs and partner with academic colleagues in the process. Our organizations need to become more customer service-oriented, less bureaucratic, and more creative. And, most important, we need to take advantage of more staff development that prepare staff to find new ways to support today's college students, especially if we are to take a greater leadership role in responding to the Obama administration's challenge of preparing students for the world of the 21st century.

References

Ambler, D. A. (2000). Organizational and administrative models. In M. J. Barr & Associates. *The handbook of student affairs administration* (2nd ed., pp. 121–133). San Francisco: Jossey-Bass.

Barr, M. J. (1993). Organizational and administrative models. In M. J. Barr & Associates. *The handbook of student affairs administration* (pp. 95–106). San Francisco: Jossey-Bass.

Cohen, A. M., & Brawer, F. B. (1996). *The American community college* (3rd ed.). San Francisco: Jossey-Bass.

Creamer, D. (1989). Changing internal conditions: impact on student development. In W. L. Deegan & T. O'Banion, *Perspectives on student development.* San Francisco: Jossey-Bass.

Doucette, D., & Dayton, L. L. (1989). A framework for student development practices: A statement of the league for innovation in the community college. In W. L. Deegan & T. O'Banion, *Perspectives on student development* (pp. 61–72). San Francisco: Jossey-Bass.

Helfgot, S. R., & McGann Culp, M. (1995, Spring). Organizing for student success. *Promoting Student Success in the Community College* (69).

Hernandez, K. R. (1989). *Are new models of student development needed?* Los Angeles: ERIC Clearinghouse.

Kuh, G. D. (1989). Organizational concepts and influences. In U. Delworth, G. R. Hanson, & Associates, *Student services: A handbook for the profession* (2nd ed., pp. 209–242). San Francisco: Jossey-Bass.

Kuk, L., & Banning, J. H. (2009). Designing student affairs organizational structures: Perceptions of senior student affairs officers. *NASPA Journal, 46*(1).

Kvavkik, M., & Handberg, M. (2000, November 2). Transforming student services. *EDUCAUSE Quarterly.*

Leach, E. (1989). Student development and college services: A focus on consumers. In W. L. Deegan & T. O'Banion, *Perspectives on student development* (pp. 45–60). San Francisco: Jossey-Bass.

Manning, K., Kinzie, J., & Schuh, J. (2006). *One size does not fit all: Traditional and innovative models of student affairs practice.* New York: Routledge.

McCabe, R. (1989). Future directions for student services: A view from the top. In W. L. Deegan & T. O'Banion, *Perspectives on student development* (pp. 85–92). San Francisco: Jossey-Bass.

McConnell, T. E. (1965). Junior college student personnel programs—Appraisal and development. *Report to the Carnegie Corporation.* Washington, DC: American Association of Junior Colleges.

O'Banion, T. (1989). Student development philosophy: A perspective on the past and future. In W.L. Deegan & T. O'Banion, *Perspectives on student development* (pp. 5–18). San Francisco: Jossey-Bass.

O'Banion, T., & Thurston, A. (1972). *Student development programs in the community junior college.* Englewood Cliffs, NJ: Prentice-Hall.

Sandeen, A. (1996). Organization, functions, and standards of practice. In S. Komives, D. B. Woodard Jr., & Associates, *Student services: A handbook for the profession* (3rd ed., pp. 433–457). San Francisco: Jossey-Bass.

Sandeen, A., & Barr, M. J. (2006). *Critical issues for student affairs: Challenges and opportunities.* San Francisco: Jossey-Bass.

15

PREPARATION FOR NEW AND EMERGING ROLES AND RESPONSIBILITIES

Linda Kuk

A s student affairs organizations face new challenges and begin to adapt their organizations to meet them, they are also faced with the reality of how to prepare and train their staff in new knowledge and competencies. This reality is complicated by the fact that student affairs professionals enter student affairs organizations through a number of professional preparation channels and may not receive part or all of their professional education through student affairs' graduate preparation programs. Second, graduate preparation programs have not always built solid connections to the changing needs of student affairs practice, so they may not be current in their awareness of changing needs that in the field of student affairs or designed to adapt easily to changing needs. Third, professionals who have been in the field for some time are not likely to have been exposed to newly required knowledge and competencies in either their preparation or through existing professional development opportunities—thus, they may require ongoing training in a new set of knowledge and skills to be able to address new challenges effectively. Fourth, student affairs organizational roles are shifting to require skill sets not traditionally acquired through traditional preparation programs. At the same time, new staff also need to be trained to specifically address the needs of students and should receive training in some of the traditional areas of student affairs preparation. Fifth, the responsibility of professional preparation and professional development is not the singular role of any one entity within the profession of student affairs, and more integrated, collaborative approaches may be needed to provide effective staff development for student affairs practitioners.

This chapter explores some of the dynamics associated with these complex issues and the role graduate professional preparation and ongoing professional development play in preparing and adapting student affairs practitioners for the changing nature of student affairs roles and responsibilities. It also presents some ideas on how graduate preparation programs can be more systematic and intentional about preparing practitioners to assume these new and changing roles. Finally, it explores the realities of how collaboration among preparation programs, professional associations, and student affairs organizations can prepare those who come into student affairs from both inside and outside student affairs graduate preparation to be better equipped to address the changing needs of student affairs organizations and the students they serve.

The Complexity of Professional Development in the Midst of Changing Roles and Responsibilities

Professional development has long been an important issue within the field of student affairs. Because student affairs is an intensively human interaction profession, the organization's human resources and their ongoing professional development are most critical to its success and to the learning and development of the students they serve. "It may be argued that the most important function of any administrative level [student affairs] professional is to select, assign, supervise and develop the people who staff the division's units" (Winston & Creamer, 1997, p. 6). The student affairs profession has historically treated professional development as consisting of two fairly distinct parts, professional preparation prior to entry, and ongoing professional development. However, both of these efforts taken as complementary sets of professional development strategies need to be considered systematically. Together they are critical to ensuring professional competencies in the changing nature of student affairs work. This is especially true as roles change and new roles and responsibilities emerge and student affairs organizations become increasingly complex and face seriously diminished resources.

In the initial development of student affairs, professional preparation and ongoing professional development consisted of on-the-job training. With the establishment of professional associations in early in the 20th century the role of ongoing professional development was partially assumed by these organizations, and this has continued to become an essential part of their role. Today these organizations continue professional development efforts by offering national conferences and distance-delivery and regional professional workshops, and publishing professional journals and textbooks. Over the years, professional development efforts have become more organized to consider professional development at varying stages of professional need, and have taken on the increasing complexity of the multifaceted functional nature of student affairs roles. With diminishing resources for professional development activity on individual campuses, the varied professional associations' professional development offerings may be one of a few sources of ongoing development for practitioners.

However, professional associations generally view their role in professional development from a competitive perspective, often trying to gain a competitive advantage or to be the leaders in professional development for their members. While there are some efforts to collaborate with other professional associations and with for-profit consulting businesses, there has not been much effort to collaborate with professional preparation programs as a collective group or to provide a systemic approach to professional development across all constituencies within the profession.

Professional development beyond formal master's and doctoral programs has not really engaged professional preparation programs systematically. Some preparation program faculty may be involved in professional development activities within professional associations or serve as consultants to individual student affairs organizations, but they have not parlayed their expertise in a collaborative and inclusive strategic plan for ongoing professional development in student affairs. (We return to discuss this issue in more detail later in the chapter.)

For many current practitioners the initial source of professional development and socialization came from their student affairs professional preparation program. These programs can be traced to the establishment of Teachers College at Columbia University, which in 1913 established "a program of special training, exclusively on the graduate level, designed to train 'deans and advisors of women'" (Lloyd-Jones, 1949, p. 262).

Today there are well over a hundred master's-level student affairs preparation programs throughout the United States. Over the last 50 years or more these programs have developed as a primary entry point for professionals into student affairs organizations in higher education institutions. The number of professionals with master's degrees from such programs has greatly increased over the past few decades, and many in the field have come to view the advanced degree as a necessary credential in many areas of student affairs. These programs serve as a major source of professional socialization for master's-level graduate students preparing to enter the student affairs profession and also as a major source for developing professional knowledge and competencies at the entry level (Kuk & Cujet, 2009; McEwen & Talbot, 2008). Through these programs practitioners gain exposure to professional standards and develop entry-level competencies that serve as a baseline for future development and form ties with professional associations and colleagues that will support their professional development throughout their career.

However, unlike many other professions, a professional preparation master's degree is not a requirement for entry into student affairs, and many professional staff are hired into student affairs roles without professional training. In fact, many roles in student affairs divisions require skills and competencies that are not included in student affairs preparation, nor have they ever been. For example, health care, counseling, and recreation personnel have rarely had student affairs professional training before being hired by student affairs organizations. With the shifting nature of some roles in these organizations, this phenomenon may be increasing, with student affairs organizations seeking and hiring more people with nontraditional knowledge and skills and no professional training. For example, fund-raising, marketing, grant-writing, and functional technology competencies are not generally taught in traditional student affairs preparation programs, yet these types of professionals are joining the ranks of other non-preparation-trained professionals within student affairs organizations.

This reality creates distinct challenges for student affairs organizations' professional development efforts as well as for professional associations. How do student affairs organizations serve the professional development needs of their staff when so many staff have not been professionally trained and socialized within the field? Second, student affairs organizations have no assurance that those who have been professionally trained have been trained adequately in the knowledge and competencies needed to assume emerging roles and responsibilities. Rarely do student affairs organizations have the resources or time to create professional development efforts that systematically enable current staff to gain the professional development and cross-training they need to assume new and emerging roles within their organization. Third, student affairs organizations are increasingly hiring staff with professional task competencies to perform emerging student affairs roles and responsibilities, but these professionals may not be trained adequately in the knowledge and skills—for example, student development theory or student group facilitation—needed to serve students or the student affairs organization successfully. As a result, student affairs organizations face a challenging future with a need for ongoing comprehensive professional development, and at the same time, not having the expertise or the resources to manage the complexity and array of professional development needs on their own.

Professional associations have traditionally been a major, if not the main, source for professional development among student affairs practitioners beyond formal degree education. These organizations increasingly provide a variety of professional development activities for their members. These efforts have become even more complex and plentiful given professional associations' desire to expand membership and provide cutting-edge training and professional development on emerging issues within student affairs areas. However, professional associations generally are not equipped with the depth of, or the technological, expertise to develop and deliver extensive professional development activities in a systematic and comprehensive fashion that serves the needs of student affairs organizations. They are also not accredited to provide credit courses or certifications. In some cases, professional associations have turned to for-profit organizations to create professional development opportunities for student affairs practitioners.

Over the last decade an entire new for-profit cottage industry has emerged to address ongoing training needs of student affairs practitioners. Some of these efforts partner with professional associations, and others are simply profit-motivated professional development activities conducted face-to-face and through distance technology. Given the number of these events that are posted online each day or solicited through the mail, they clearly produce great streams of revenue and appear to be filling a growing need for professional development in a rapidly changing environment. For-profit organizations would not be in the business if these activities were not profitable.

Despite the plethora of these professional development activities, they are hampered by two major concerns, regardless of whether they are hosted by professional associations or for-profit training and consulting firms. The first issue has to do with who is doing the professional development training. What are their professional credentials, and how do consumers know they have the expertise to provide training in a given area? The second has to do with the credibility and reliability of what is being discussed/presented. How do consumers know that the content of the presentation or training is accurate and reliable or that the process being promoted actually works? At present, there are no standards or professional expectations for the expertise or credentialing of people and organizations providing the educational/training experience. There is also no process for validation of the extent to which these activities provide honest and reliable information or that they have been proven to work. In some cases, the only thing recipients have to go by is the reputation of someone fronting or marketing the training program and the perceived value of the experience verses the cost. In all of these cases no professional standards are in place to guide such efforts. In this age of an accumulating potpourri of increasingly competitive professional development activities, the fox is often in the midst of the henhouse with no one to oversee or regulate what is going on, to determine what is quality and accurate, or to decide who is qualified as an expert to deliver the educational product.

Second, these efforts are not organized systemically to provide anything but ad hoc professional information, and they add little to solving the need for a systemic plan to provide ongoing professional development. Most of these efforts, whether part of a conference or an isolated training event, focus on a specific topic or rarely part of a more comprehensive professional development program or anything beyond the singular event. Rarely are the results of these efforts infused or transferred into professional accountability or demonstrations of gained competencies. As a result, these activities do little to ensure a student affairs organization that their staff are being systematically developed and appropriately prepared and enabled to perform emerging roles and responsibilities or even understand the rapidly changing dynamics occurring in the organization's work environment.

Given the changing needs within student affairs organizations for ongoing professional preparation and development, it may be time to change the professional paradigm that separates preparation and professional development within student affairs and to use the skills and expertise of all segments of the profession more effectively, including professional preparation programs. What is called for is a more systemic focus across the spectrum of professional development needs that creates a more seamless professional development process. Student affairs preparation programs bring expertise, resources, and educational delivery mechanisms to the process in ways that student affairs organizations and professional associations acting alone cannot deliver. Adding their expertise to comprehensive professional development as an extension of preparation may help address many of the complex issues facing professional development for student affairs practitioners. How might professional preparation programs fit more effectively into a more comprehensive professional development effort for the student affairs profession?

A Changing Role for Student Affairs Professional Preparation

Woodward and Komives (1990) stress the importance of determining both specific and general preparation requirements and posit systematic professional development programs for practitioners as critical to the future of student affairs. In 1998, Evans, Phelps Tobin, and associates examined the state of preparation programs in light of future needs and discussed the need for programs to be more attentive to changing needs in the profession. They outlined a number of important changes that had been occurring in the field, in research associated with the field, and in the external environment in which the profession existed. They concluded that student affairs preparation programs must adjust their curriculum to address these changes and that "in light of the rapid changes occurring in higher education, the need for continuing education for student affairs practitioners is greater than ever before" (p. viii).

Over the last decade the changes and challenges affecting student affairs organizations and their work has continued and in many cases have accelerated. It is not known to what extent preparation programs are attending to the profession's changing needs and, if they are, how they are adapting their programs to address these needs so they are also future-oriented. Second, how might they change the systemic way they engage in preparation and ongoing professional development to be quicker and more adaptive in addressing changing needs, and as a result, how might they more effectively use their expertise and an already existing educational delivery mechanism?

To better understand the focus and mission of graduate preparation programs, and to determine to what extent the programs appear to have a changing or future-oriented focus, the author reviewed the program and curricular descriptions of 90 of the student affairs preparation programs that were posted on the NASPA graduate program directory. A similar analysis had been done in 2007 with many of the same preparation programs to better understand the focus and content of student affairs preparation programs (Kuk & Cuyjet, 2009). At that time, the analysis found an array of preparation programs with a continuum of foci from administration and student development and learning to counseling. The programs appeared to have very different curricular offerings, and only about a third of them self-reported complying with the Council for the Advancement of Professional Standards in Higher Education (CAS) (Dean, 2006; Kuk & Cujet, 2009). These standards have become the professional standards for the student affairs profession to evaluate and benchmark acceptable practice and resource allocation in student affairs organizations and graduate professional education in student affairs.

This time, analysis of preparation programs sought to review the stated current focus of the programs and evaluate the language and descriptions of both the programs' mission statements and their curricular descriptions to determine whether there were any signs of a change or future orientation in their self-promotional materials.

The analysis asked the following questions:

- What was the self-reported focus of student affairs preparation programs?
- Did their mission statement contain any language or direction that would indicate a change or future orientation? If so what were these descriptions?
- Did the descriptions of their curriculum or of their delivery process indicate any future or change orientation? If so, what were these descriptions?

The analysis found that the foci of the various programs were fairly diverse, with the majority of programs stressing student learning and development and/or administration (67.5% of the total). The self-reported foci of the programs were 39% (35) on student learning and development; 28% (25) on administration, and .5% (five) on both student learning and development and administration. Only .7 % (seven) indicated they had a counseling focus; .88 % (eight) indicated they had a leadership focus; and 1% (nine) indicated a more general focus such as student affairs, higher education, and higher education organizations. Only one indicated it had a policy focus. The programs vary in required credit hours, from 30 to 52 credits, and length of completion, from one to two or more years.

It is not clear whether these preparation programs are actually shifting their focus or just providing a clearer statement of the various programs' overall foci. In either case, it does appear that fewer programs identified with a predominant counseling focus than in the past, and student learning and development appears to be emerging as the most frequently sighted focus of preparation programs, closely followed by administration. Nearly all of the programs now state that they comply with the CAS standards for professional preparation (CAS Professional Standard for Higher Education, 2010). Both of these findings also support the assumption that preparation programs are continuing to evolve and adapt, and they are increasingly attending to the emerging values and role of professional standards in shaping professional practice.

In reviewing the self-reported mission statement of student affairs preparation programs, about two-thirds of them have a fairly traditionally focused preparation mission statement. These statements stress preparing practitioners or scholar practitioners for traditional roles (functional roles) and entry-level positions in student affairs organizations. They also often include a focus on research and assessment, and other traditional student affairs skills and competencies, among them multicultural competencies. Nearly all of the programs stated that their missions focused on diversity, multiculturalism, or social justice. Few of the statements contained any language or indication that the program was preparing students for the future or signaled any attention to adaptive change or innovation skills or competencies as part of their program's mission.

A third of the mission statements contained language or descriptions that emphasized either a change or future orientation focus of varying degrees. Some implied that they are preparing students to have collaborative or community-focused relationships and or partnerships; others said they prepared students to become generalists in a changing environment or to be successful in a wide range of circumstances. Still others commented that students were developing skills for the 21st-century college/university. A number stated that they were preparing students to be change agents, to effect system change, or to effect positive change in individuals and organizations. Some identified skill sets such as developing entrepreneurial skills, improving decision making, and/or skills needed to interact with the local and global community. A few stated that they were preparing students for traditional student affairs roles as well as other roles, such as alumni relations and development, that have not been traditional student affairs concerns in the past. And a few mentioned that they were preparing students to be able to facilitate effective group interaction and work as part of a team.

In trying to get a sense of a future focus or orientation of the programs that might be found in course or curriculum descriptions or their pedagogy or delivery processes, researchers made some interesting observations. First, the overall curriculum and individual course descriptions were pretty uniform across all programs. While the course descriptions varied, they were traditional and appeared to follow CAS standards recommendations. There did not appear to be any real differences across the programs, even for the third that had some future- or change-focused descriptors as part of their mission statements. In other words, administrative-focused curricula looked similar across programs, and counseling-focused curricula looked similar across counseling-focused programs. There were no indications that new courses that focused on nontraditional student affairs skills or competencies, such as grant writing, marketing or fund-raising, were offered. There was also no evidence that courses had a future-oriented focus in terms of the development of adaptive or innovative skills or competencies.

Most of the programs were attended predominantly by full-time resident students, and only a few offered nonresident, blended, or distance instruction delivery options. Many of the programs did state that they were attracting a more diverse student population, and a small number were clearly focused on providing student affairs preparation for a nontraditional student population, including an international perspective.

So while some programs appear to have a mission statement that has a change or future focus that was different from traditional student affairs preparation practices, curriculum descriptions did not indicate any signal that change or a future orientation was portrayed. It is important to point out that curricular changes may be more adaptive in that they are occurring more subtly and are readily not apparent in mission or course descriptions. Most of the organizations did offer student development theory, assessment, and or organizational, administration, and leadership courses that may have a future orientation built into their content; however, the descriptions did not indicate this fact. This analysis also did not indicate to what extent individual faculty challenge or provide learning experiences that support an orientation to change and development of future skills and competencies through these or other courses. It also did not reveal to what extent graduate students participate in a variety of practica [or assistantships that provide diverse student affairs experiences. The analysis did indicate a need for student affairs preparation programs to examine their curriculum and program focus more closely to ensure that they are preparing student affairs practitioners adequately for the roles and responsibilities that will be needed in the future.

Complying with the CAS standards is an important hurdle to achieve, but preparation programs also have to be forward-thinking if they are going to address the skill and competency needs of student affairs practitioners and their organizations. Shannon Ellis (2009) discusses the need for student affairs practitioners to develop a vision of the possible and to take a long look into the future. Preparation programs have a role to play in preparing student affairs professionals to attend to the development of these skills and competencies so they can adapt to changing needs as they engage their practice.

The task of being future-focused can be difficult and at times present a catch-22 for professional preparation. How can student affairs preparation programs better prepare students for roles and responsibilities that may not yet be known or fully understood? With the increasing levels of complexity and demands for greater knowledge and skill development on these programs, how can they effectively provide preparation for emerging skills and competencies on top of all the traditional expectations that currently exist? How can preparation programs become more attuned to changing needs within the field and be structured to respond more quickly to these changing dynamics so their students can have cutting-edge knowledge and competencies when they enter student affairs organizations, all in the face of already strained resources?

Some scholar practitioners have claimed that student affairs preparation programs are not as closely connected with practice as they need to be (Komives, 1998; Upcraft, 1998), which has resulted in some delays and disconnects from what is being taught in these programs and how emerging needs for training and development of practitioners in the field occur. Professional preparation faculty need to collaborate actively with student affairs practitioners in revising and refining their curriculum and program foci to ensure that they are attuned to the dynamic changes that are occurring and will continue to occur in student affairs practice. Many student affairs preparation programs currently have student affairs practitioners serving as adjunct instructors in their programs, and others have developed advisory boards that include student affairs practitioners.

This book has outlined a number of emerging and revised roles and responsibilities within student affairs organizations. To what extent might preparation programs better prepare their students to take on these new roles? How might they better prepare their students in the partnering, collaborating, and teaming skills that accompany a horizontal organizational orientation? Can they expose students to the skills and knowledge needed to work in a hybrid or matrix organization that requires knowledge and skill competencies and orientations that are both organizationally vertical and horizontal in reporting and operating? Can preparation program students learn how to be adaptive to changing work cultures so they can change roles and responsibilities on a regular basis, and so they are continuously engaged in learning new ways of doing things, where they work in teams and have a great deal of personal decision-making responsibility? Can they be trained to engage in double-loop learning and to be innovative in using their skills and competencies to envision news way of serving students and using existing resources more efficiently and effectively as a part of their everyday work life? Chris Argyris and Donald Schon (1978) use the concept of "double-loop learning" to describe the process of learning that occurs when the parameters or theory that govern learning are expanded beyond just understanding or discovering a solution to a problem. This type of learning results in a change in the theory or parameters of what is being learned or understood and creates a ripple effect that produces change throughout the system.

Focusing on traditional and adaptive, as well as collaborative and team–based, leadership skills and competencies, may enable student affairs organizations and preparation programs to ensure that students are able to adapt to changes without necessarily knowing exactly what specific skills might be needed. From this perspective students learn how to adapt and continue their professional development on the job within the context of their ongoing experiences. Rather than focusing on skills for a specific functional role, they learn how to expand their existing skills and knowledge in new directions and to value the change and professional growth that such processes can create. The mission and focus of professional preparation in these cases is not on being functional specialists but on being practitioner generalists who know what they need to learn for the present, how to engage in ongoing learning that enables them to continue to develop and be successful in other roles and circumstances, and how to be innovative and lead at all levels within the organization.

The roles and responsibilities outlined in this book provide only a glimpse of what is to come as the nature of student affairs work continues to shift and adapt to the demands placed on it. These changes will require professional preparation to have a future orientation and be able to develop new sets of the skills and competencies required to engage in new roles and responsibilities; they will also require programs to provide for acquisition of adaptive skills and innovative competencies that will enable practitioners to invent new ways of doing student affairs work as new needs arise. Training for specific functionality will still be needed, but that role may be in the hands of student affairs organizations. Through on-the-job training student affairs supervisors can help practitioners take on the specific roles and responsibilities needed to perform a specific job.

Most of the preparation programs studied say they are adhering to the CAS professional standards (Dean, 2006; CAS Professional Standards for Higher Education, 2010) and/or the *ACPA Professional Competencies Statement* (2007). In reviewing these standards, it was clear that these organizations have created professional preparation standards that highlight more uniform curricular foci as well as knowledge and skill competencies that provide sound guidance to preparation programs regarding curriculum, learning, and competency outcomes. Adherence to a common set of professional preparation standards is important if the profession wants to have a baseline of professional knowledge and skill competencies to build on and enhance as the profession changes.

These standards also provide some guidance about future trends and recognize the complexity of changing roles and responsibilities within the profession. Yet at this point, these standards predominantly focus on the knowledge and skills of traditional student affairs roles and responsibilities in traditional student affairs organizations. These standards largely fail to recognize the need for competencies that enable students to be able to adapt, innovate, and transcend traditional roles to take on new roles as needed. Professional associations and those responsible for developing preparation standards must take a leadership role in ensuring that the standards for professional preparation maintain and enhance their traditional focus and are attentive to the dynamic of change and the need for adaptive competencies that will be necessary in the future.

Such changes will also require professional preparation to be more strategic and systematic in the way it engages professional development across the life span of practitioners. It is increasingly clear that the complexity of student affairs work and the changing demands placed on practitioners require ongoing development and preparation that cannot be achieved through a two-year master's program or even doctoral education. Change requires ongoing learning, adapting, and professional development that enables practitioners and faculty to step in and out of the learning and development process as needs arise, skills and knowledge need retooling, and responsibilities need refocusing and realignment. The student affairs organizations of the future will require practitioners who are comfortable with change and who continuously engage in innovation and leadership. Given the needed resources and expertise to ensure this type of future–oriented, systematic approach to professional development, all sectors of the profession must be involved and must see professional development as a core collaborative responsibility.

A Comprehensive Approach to Preparation and Professional Development With a Future Orientation

Student affairs has come to think of preparation as the first step in professional socialization and development, but it is becoming increasingly clear that preparation for changing roles and responsibilities and new ways of engaging in student affairs work maybe an ongoing need. Given the nature and increasing needs emerging for graduate professional preparation and staff development within student affairs organizations, professional preparation programs also might want to consider expanding their role to serve the continuing professional development needs of alumni and other student affairs practitioners. This requires a shift in the professional development paradigm that has distinguished professional preparation from ongoing staff development within student affairs.

Such a shift in this paradigm suggests that preparation programs might take a leadership role in partnering with professional associations, and other student affairs organizations to provide ongoing professional development and curricular offerings to address the changing nature of student affairs practice beyond the formal degree-oriented role. Through the use of distance delivery mechanisms, these programs could provide graduate education certificates, ongoing professional development workshops, and consultations with student affairs organizations. These partnerships could ensure mutual exchange of information concerning the changing nature of student affairs practice and assist organizations to transfer theory to practice. Preparation programs and their faculty could become a primary source of expertise and serve as an established venue for professional associations and student affairs organizations to use in delivering ongoing professional development opportunities beyond formal education at the master's and doctoral levels. These efforts could be funded through continuing education operations and provide additional fiscal and faculty resources for maintaining both degree-based preparation and ongoing professional development.

Some professional development efforts beyond formal degrees are beginning to occur. A number of institutions have started to offer distance delivery certificate programs geared specifically to professional staff who are placebound and do not have formal preparation degrees. Others are offering specialty training and certificates in emerging areas where traditional training has not been easily accessible, such as emergency response, program evaluation and assessment, and alcohol intervention training. These efforts have been good sources of additional revenue for resource-strapped graduate programs, and they probably will be increased and expanded in the years ahead. However, these efforts are not yet organized in any formal way.

What is really needed in the dynamic, changing world of complex student affairs organizations is a professional development system that engages and provides for the development of student affairs professionals at all stages and levels of professional practice and across all types of roles. Some of this effort is the responsibility of student affairs organizations, but they do not have the individual resources or expertise to develop or manage such an effort alone. While professional associates should be actively engaged in this professional development effort and may serve in active leadership roles, they are not equipped to develop and execute such initiatives alone. They rarely have the professional staff depth or expertise, nor can they count on volunteers from their membership to execute such an effort on their behalf. Individual preparation programs also face strains on their resources and are as limited in their level of expertise and ability to deliver a broad, comprehensive, non-degree effort as individual programs.

But collectively, with planning, collaboration, systematic intra-organizational agreement of roles and responsibilities; gathering and identifying expertise, and adopting professional development standards, such a project could be realized. An organized, collaborative effort that involves student affairs organizations, professional associations, and a collective of professional preparation programs, as well as for-profit consulting companies working together, can develop a comprehensive, future-based staff development program for student affairs practitioners. Such an effort could include degree-based professional preparation and certificate programs as the base for professional practice. But it would also help professional preparation programs provide a more comprehensive life span approach to professional development as well.

This collaborative rather than competitive approach could create a comprehensive array of professional development trainings, tools, and processes across the spectrum of ongoing professional needs. These might include an array of performance and organizational assessment tools that can be integrated with professional development needs, with coaching to assist student affairs organizations in determining what type of development is needed within their organization and with their individual practitioners; feedback loops and processes that would guide organizations and professional training efforts in determining what types and levels of professional development are needed; coaching for effective supervision, performance assessment feedback and cross-unit training; and processes for helping organizations develop adaptive structures and processes that engage staff in their work. A comprehensive approach to professional development could enable student affairs organizations, professional associations, and preparation programs to use their resources and enable student affairs practitioners to grow, change, and adapt to the roles, responsibilities, and challenges that will become a part of their everyday future.

Conclusion

As student affairs organizations face new challenges and begin to adapt their organizations to meet them, they also face the reality of how to prepare and train their staff in new knowledge and competencies. This reality is complicated by the fact that student affairs professionals enter student affairs organizations through a number of professional preparation channels and may not receive part or all of their professional education through student affairs preparation programs. This reality creates distinct challenges for professional development efforts for student affairs organizations and for professional associations and preparation programs as well.

The student affairs profession has historically viewed professional development as consisting of two fairly distinct parts, professional preparation and ongoing professional development. However, both of these efforts, taken as complementary sets of professional development strategies, need to be considered systematically and individually as critical to ensuring professional competencies in the changing nature of student affairs work. Professional associations and those responsible for developing preparation standards must take the lead in ensuring that the standards for professional preparation maintain their traditional foci and are attentive to the dynamic of change and the need for adaptive competencies that will be necessary in the future.

Professional preparation faculty need to be actively involved in collaborating with student affairs practitioners in revising and refining their curriculum and program foci, to ensure that they are attuned to the dynamic changes that are occurring and will continue to do so within student affairs practice. Focusing on traditional and adaptive, as well as collaborative and team–based, leadership skills and competencies may enable both student affairs organizations and preparation programs to ensure that students are increasingly able to adapt to changes without knowing exactly what specific skills might be needed the future.

It is increasingly clear that the complexity of student affairs work and the changing demands placed on practitioners require ongoing development and preparation that cannot be achieved adequately through a two-year master's program or even doctoral education. These changes will require professional preparation to be more strategic and systematic in how it engages professional development across the life span of practitioners. Preparation programs and their faculty could become primary sources of expertise and serve as an established venue for professional associations and student affairs organizations to use in delivering ongoing professional development opportunities.

What is really needed for the changing reality of student affairs organizations is a professional development system that engages and provides for development of student affairs professionals at all stages and levels of professional practice as well as across all types of roles and organizations. A collaborative rather than competitive approach that engages professional associations; student affairs organizations; a collective of preparation programs; and, possibly, private consulting firms could create a comprehensive array of professional development trainings, tools, assessments, and process across the spectrum of ongoing professional needs resulting in a comprehensive, future-based staff development program for student affairs practitioners. Such a system would change the paradigm of professional development and focus collective resources on ensuring a future orientation for student affairs work and would enable the profession to prepare for and address emerging roles, responsibilities, and challenges.

References

ACPA Professional Competencies Statement: A report of the steering committee on professional competencies. (2007). Washington DC: American College Personnel Association.

Argyris, C., & Schon, D. (1978). *Organizational learning: A theory of action perspective.* Reading, MA: Addison-Wesley.

CAS professional standards for higher education (7th ed.). Washington DC: Council for the Advancement of Standards in Higher Education. Retrieved from http://www.cas.edu/index.php/index.php/index.php

Dean, L. A. (2006). Master's-level student affairs professional preparation programs. In L. A. Dean (Ed.), *CAS professional standards for higher education* (6th ed., pp.

349–358). Washington DC: Council for the Advancement of Standards in Higher Education.

Evans, N. J., & Phelps Tobin, C. E. (Eds.). (1998). *The state of the art of preparation and practice in student affairs*. Washington, DC: American College Personnel Association.

Ellis, S. (2009). Words of wisdom. In M. Amey & L. Reesor (Eds.), *Beginning your journey: A guide for new professionals in student affairs*. Washington, DC: National Association of Student Personnel Association, Inc.

Komives, S. R. (1998). Linking student affairs preparation to practice. In N. J. Evans & C. E. Phelps Tobin (Eds.), *The state of the art of preparation and practice in student affairs* (pp. 177–200). Washington, DC: American College Personnel Association.

Kuk, L., & Cuyjet, M. (2009). Graduate preparation programs: The first step in socialization. In A. Tull, J. B. Hurt, & S. A. Saunders, *Becoming socialized in student affairs administration: A guide for new professionals and their supervisors* (pp. 89–108). Sterling, VA: Stylus.

Lloyd-Jones, E. (1949). The beginning of our profession. In E. G. Williamson (Ed.), *Trends in student personnel work* (pp. 260–264). Minneapolis: University of Minnesota Press.

McEwen, M. K., & Talbot, D. M. (2008). Designing student affairs curriculum. In N. J. Evans & C. E. Phelps Tobin (Eds.), *The state of the art of preparation and practice in student affairs* (pp. 125–156). Washington DC: American College Personnel Association.

Upcraft, M. L. (1998). Do graduate preparation programs really prepare practitioners? In N. J. Evans & C. E. Phelps Tobin (Eds.), *The state of the art of preparation and practice in student affairs* (pp. 235–237). Washington DC: American College Personnel Association.

Winston, R. B., & Creamer, D. G. (1997). *Improving staffing practices in student affairs*. San Francisco: Jossey-Bass.

Woodward, D., & Komives, S. (1990). Ensuring staff competencies. In M. J. Barr & M. L. Upcraft (Eds.), *New futures for student affairs* (pp. 217–238.) San Francisco: Jossey Bass.

16

CONCLUSIONS AND RECOMMENDATIONS

Ashley Tull and Linda Kuk

This book has been about change that has occurred and continues to occur in student affairs organizations. The change we have presented, both transformational and adaptive, has come about as a response to new realities that have prompted existing and newly identified roles and structures in student affairs. Over the decades, student affairs organizations have sought adaptive ways to meet the new and changing demands of their work. More recently these challenges have included higher enrollment, declining resources, greater calls for accountability, emerging technologies, new methods of communication, and greater connection to external constituencies. We have discussed each of these, and many more.

The intent of this book has been to expose readers to the many and multidimensional challenges that have changed the nature of student affairs work. We have highlighted ways in which change has occurred and will continue to occur and have addressed change with regard to the contexts and current practices in specialist roles and emerging structures in student affairs organizations. While there is no one particular organizational model in student affairs organizations, the authors have presented examples of the use of specialist roles and hybrid organizational designs to demonstrate how some student affairs organizations are meeting today's challenges. Additionally, we have given attention to how student affairs leaders can facilitate organizational change while incorporating specialist roles and hybrid structures in their organizations. Finally, we have discussed how small colleges and universities as well as community colleges are currently meeting today's challenges through their unique approaches to using emerging roles and structures in their student affairs organizations.

This concluding chapter summarizes the major themes the chapter authors have covered, while exploring the need for student affairs practitioners to consider the development of specialist roles and structures to meet today's challenges in their work with constituencies, most important of which is the students on their campuses. We have included in this chapter several recommendations for student affairs leaders, mid- and entry-level student affairs administrators, graduate preparation program faculty, and professionals outside of student affairs. In many cases we refer to the collective body of these roles with the term *student affairs leaders*. These recommendations provide points to consider in the development of new specialist roles and emerging structures to use in their work.

Current and Emerging Challenges and Practices With the Use of Specialist Roles and Structures in Student Affairs Organizations

The changed nature of student affairs work presents several challenges. The ways in which student affairs organizations have addressed these are as broad and varied as the number of student affairs organizations themselves. Many student affairs organizations share many of these challenges, and others are unique and vary by state or institutional type. Student affairs administrators' ability to address these is often affected by their ability to identify and select trained personnel from within or outside their organizations. Their ability to do this often depends on the availability of resources and can hinge on institutional practices and policies. Some organizations, depending on the size and type of their institutions, may be forced to discover ways in which they can meet new demands with existing human and fiscal resources, which can place even greater strain on an already-taxed student affairs staff.

Student affairs leaders should strategically plan for and assemble resources in preparation for hiring professionals for specialist roles and structures. With many student affairs organizations and institutions facing budget shortfalls, student affairs leaders seeking to establish new roles and structures may have to be very creative. Many of these leaders have some flexibility because they manage multiple types of budgets and have some discretion over the use of particular funds, such as those garnered through auxiliary operations. Most important is ensuring that the reasons for creating such positions and structures have been carefully thought out and articulated to those who need to know them.

Those student affairs administrators and organizations that are able to create new roles and structures should carefully consider their own organizational and institutional characteristics. While some change occurs through a transformational change process, so it may be more strategic and extensive, much of the change in student affairs organizations has been adaptive, incremental, and sporadic in nature (see chapter 1). While many changes have occurred as adaptive shifts (Kuk & Banning, 2009), these should be designed as part of a larger review across the organization, with consideration of the overall systematic and collaborative impact they might have. This notion is particularly true in creating cross-organizational specialist roles that are meant to provide expertise on an organizational level, often in support of multiple departments within the organization.

Student affairs leaders should pay close attention to organizational and institutional characteristics that may support or hamper their efforts to hire professionals for specialist roles and structures. This may not always be an easy task and may take some time to explore depending on the nature of the student affairs organization and institutional characteristics. Student affairs leaders should carefully consider factors that may affect their ability to create specialist roles and hybrid organizational structures. Such factors might include use of resources, perceptions from other internal or external constituencies, centralization or decentralization of roles and structures, and reporting lines. They might also be strategic in looking at the skills and talents of existing staff in their organizations or institutions when making these changes.

Because all student affairs organizations are different, and assuming that change within organizations is inevitable (see chapter 2), student affairs leaders should consider the structural context that will influence roles and structures. Careful attention to the redesign of organizational structures will help administrators respond to changing internal and external demands. For example, through the creation of matrix or other hybrid structures, administrators may be able to address both the functions and processes of their work. Such organizational designs can lead to greater collaboration, more responsive service delivery, and overall efficiency. Each of the redesign processes described previously works best with greater organizational member participation at all levels. Inclusive engagement of staff throughout the student affairs organization becomes critical to the effectiveness of the organizational roles and structures that are formulated through a redesign process.

Student affairs leaders should adequately equip those they hire for specialist roles and structures to work effectively with multiple consistencies. As with any newly hired staff member in student affairs, specialists need orientation and training. This may be even more important for the specialist hired from outside student affairs or higher education. Specific time should be spent on organization and governance structures; campus politics; the nature and purpose of student affairs work, especially as it relates to the nature of student learning and development; and helping them to form relationships with multiple constituencies.

Current Practices With Specialist Roles, Responsibilities, and Structures

As discussed previously, the evolution of student affairs administration has not occurred overnight, but the need for new specialist roles and structures appears to be emerging more quickly. Many traditional functions and staffing practices continue unchanged; however, many student affairs organizations are responding in different ways to their environments, which include many constituencies and stakeholders (Manning, Kinzie, & Schuh, 2006).

Professionals from outside student affairs and higher education organizations should identify methods for operating within these unique systems to conduct their work as specialists. Performance goals should be developed with the SSAO or other administrators supervising the specialist. Professionals hired as specialists would be wise to spend some time reviewing annual reports or other institutional documents, conducting "informational interviews" with key administrators, attending meetings of various student affairs departments, and establishing networks with those who can contribute to their success. In many cases, specialists are the only ones conducting their type of work within the organization, and may be few in number on campus. Specialists should also form networks with those in similar roles at other local, regional, or national institutions.

Student affairs staff in entry- and mid-level positions should consider pursuing specialist roles and structures that will serve them well in their careers. Those staff already employed in student affairs organizations may be interested in serving the organization through a specialist role. Careful consideration should be given to long-term career goals of staff, as some may feel becoming a specialist will narrow their chances for advancement. This notion is complicated in that many specialists don't directly supervise other staff in their roles or manage larger budgets, tasks often viewed as critical to assuming a more senior position in student affairs. However, these roles can provide opportunities for experiencing and understanding the larger picture and cross-division and institution perspectives, which are also important for the move to senior roles and responsibilities. Some, on the other hand, may find more satisfaction in these roles.

Organizational Implications of Emerging Roles and Structures in Student Affairs

To best facilitate organizational change through the use of specialist roles and emerging or hybrid structures in student affairs organizations, senior student affairs leaders must first understand the forces in higher education and the eternal environment that present current and future challenges (Kezar, 2003). Student affairs administrators at all levels should know and understand the concept of change and be able to identify and use various change processes appropriately. As previously discussed, this is not always easy to do, particularly as adaptive change can be slow, subtle, and sporadic in nature, and transformational change can create fear in and resistance from organizational members. In chapter 12, Kathy Cavins-Tull presented methods for accessing readiness for change that included organizations' being self-reflective and self-critical when determining values and priorities for their work. Planned change processes have also been illuminated that provide specific examples applicable to student affairs organizations. These seek to help readers identify current challenges that prompt change in their organizations and describe how they might manage the needed change more effectively. In addition to understanding the nature and value of various change processes, Cavins-Tull provided budgetary considerations related to the change processes that were addressed.

Student affairs leaders might carefully craft their organizations so they can continually plan for and adapt to change as part of their day-to-day organizational life. When change becomes a component of the organizational culture, it can enable student affairs staff to see change as a positive, rewarding, and necessary part of what they do. They begin to learn and incorporate change into their work and to respond to challenges with the foresight to see what needs to be changed to make the organization work more effectively.

Finally, student affairs administrators should not overlook the importance of measuring the results and impact of any changes they implement. Building into a unit's evaluation and performance plans metrics that assess the organization's effectiveness, with specific attention to assessing the components and process of implementing and managing change, will enable the organization to continue to adapt and to focus efforts effectively and responsively. This will prove to be an important step as we are challenged with greater calls for accountability.

Student affairs administrators in entry- and mid-level positions might seek engagement in change processes for their own development and the development of the organizations that employ them. Some student affairs administrators have been change agents within their organizations and institutions. Those currently employed in student affairs would be well served to engage in organizational change processes for their own professional development. This will serve them well in their careers, particularly as they seek to advance to more senior positions. Their ability to adapt to meet the needs of multiple constituencies will help in their ability to stay current. In addition, their ability to craft change that can respond to environmental demands and foster new approaches to managing change will increasingly be a skill set effective organizational leaders will need. This may or may not involve taking on specialist roles or managing elements of hybrid structures in the process.

Graduate preparation program faculty at colleges and universities might consider engaging in change processes where appropriate or permitted in the student affairs organization, and in the ongoing development of preparation program curricula and experiences. Through such collaborations graduate preparation program faculty could gain insights into the changes that are occurring in student affairs organizations and so prepare program students more effectively to enter work in these organizational settings. Graduate preparation program faculty might also lend their expertise to student affairs organizations and higher educational institutions in connecting theory to practice and modeling best practices for maximum effectiveness in their work with students.

In chapter 13, Frank Ardaiolo and Kathleen Callahan addressed current and future challenges with emerging roles and structures in student affairs organizations at small college and universities. They described unique institutional characteristics that often affect how these types of institutions are able to address challenges using specific case analysis from their institution, Winthrop University. Small colleges and universities don't often have opportunities for developing specialist roles and hybrid structures as they operate with flatter staffing models and tighter resources. Through their examples, the authors provide context for how others at similar institutions might address current and future challenges through innovative staffing practices that allow for "cross-trainee" staff equipped to achieve multiple goals. Finally, the authors addressed positive benefits of collaborative partnerships and greater relationships at small colleges and universities, which are formed through the need to be more innovative in staffing practices to meet the challenges that come with student affairs work at small colleges and universities.

Graduate preparation program faculty at colleges and universities might pay close attention to the current challenges facing small colleges and universities as they prepare professionals to assume positions within this type of institution. As many graduate preparation programs in student affairs and higher education are located at large, public institutions, faculty members should pay close attention to what is occurring at small colleges and universities. This will aid them in portraying the challenges and successes of working in this particular type of institution more fully. This is particularly true of cross-training student affairs practitioners to carry out multiple functions, as discussed in chapter 13.

Much like the current and future challenges of emerging roles and structures in student affairs organizations at small college and universities, community colleges are similar in nature. Chapter 14 described the unique institutional characteristics that often affect how community colleges are able to address the challenges they face. Like small colleges and universities, community colleges often don't have the resources for creating specialist roles and structures. They, too, generally have flatter staffing models and tight resources. Community colleges, however, are more nimble and are used to adapting to their changing environments. Perhaps more than any institutional type, they must respond regularly to shifting demands from multiple constituencies. Community colleges have some traditional roles and structures that are not unlike their counterparts at other institutional types. As presented in chapter 14, student affairs leaders at community colleges are encouraged to be entrepreneurial and creative and to maximize their use of technology in providing services to their students. Student affairs professionals at any type of institution can learn from their ability to meet current and future challenges through unique and innovative practices.

Graduate preparation programs at colleges and universities have been preparing professionals for work in student affairs organizations for many years. Their focus has been primarily on preparing professionals for work in functional areas or population-specific types of positions, as discussed previously. With the emergence of specialist roles and structures, graduate preparation programs may soon have to rethink how they are preparing professionals for work in student affairs administration. Many students have entered graduate preparation programs directly from undergraduate programs of study. As Linda Kuk discussed in chapter 15, graduate preparation programs will need to be primed for professionals entering through multiple entry points, in some cases from more nontraditional backgrounds and ages. For example, a journalist may seek training in student affairs or higher education to prepare for entry as a communications officer in a student affairs organization. Some already employed in student affairs organizations may seek further training or skill development in a specialist capacity, perhaps to make an internal shift to this type of role within a student affairs organization or to take on additional responsibilities, as discussed in chapter 13. Others may simply seek additional training through professional development programs that does not result in a graduate degree, but better prepares existing student affairs staff to meet new challenges. Graduate preparation programs probably will become more complex as they are called on to provide more diverse and extensive training for student affairs professionals at all levels. Professional preparation program faculty might consider partnering with professional associations and student affairs organizations to provide professional development opportunities throughout the student affairs career.

Professionals from outside student affairs and higher education organizations should carefully consider pursuing graduate education in student affairs and higher education. While not required for some specialist roles and structures in student affairs organizations, graduate-level training, a certificate, or other training might be beneficial. Not only would the specialist gain valuable knowledge and insight into work in student affairs and higher education settings, a degree or further training would provide a credible credential that may serve the specialist well as he or she works inside and outside the organization or institution. Many institutions offer tuition assistance programs as a benefit of full-time employment. Those specialists hired by institutions with a graduate preparation program in student affairs and/or higher education may want to engage in graduate-level work in these settings.

Concluding Thoughts

Throughout this book we have discussed the creation and use of specialist roles and hybrid structures in student affairs organizations. Many of these have come about in response to the need for change brought on by new and challenging demands of student affairs work. While no commonly accepted practice exists for the use of specialist roles and hybrid structures in student affairs, the authors have provided examples of how some student affairs leaders and organizations are using these practices and redesigning strategies to address challenges in their work. We encourage you to review the recommendations provided and decide for yourselves how you can best use these insights, concepts, and examples in your work in student affairs organizations. We also encourage you to continue to develop best practices in the use of specialist roles and emerging organizational structures and to promote these through conference presentations, literature, and established networks.

Our purpose in crafting this book has been to capture the essence of recent practices in the use of specialist roles and emerging organizational structures, and offer insight to those considering the need for changes within their organizations. The challenges that student affairs faces will require ongoing adaptation and change to best serve the increasing and shifting demands of students and the external environment. We hope this work has provided some insights into how to face such challenges and will spark new ideas in continued development of organizational change within student affairs.

References

Kezar, A. J. (2003). Understanding and facilitating organizational change in the 21st century. *ASHE-ERIC Higher Education Report, 28*(4). San Francisco: Jossey-Bass.

Kuk, L., & Banning, J. H. (2009). Designing student affairs organizational structures: Perceptions of senior student affairs officers. *NASPA Journal, 46*(1), 94–117.

Manning, K., Kinzie, J., & Schuh, J. (2006). *One size does not fit all: Traditional and innovative models of student affairs practice.* New York: Routledge.

Dr. Ashley Tull is a visiting assistant professor in the Department of Educational Leadership and Policy Studies in the College of Education and Health Professions at the University of Texas at Arlington and most recently served as senior associate dean of students and adjunct assistant professor of higher education leadership at the University of Arkansas–Fayetteville. He previously held positions in student affairs at Florida State University, Georgia Highlands College, and Middle Georgia College. Dr. Tull earned a bachelor of science with honors in social and rehabilitation services and a master of education in college student personnel services from the University of Southern Mississippi. He also received a graduate certificate in human resource development and a doctorate of education in higher education administration from Florida State University, where he was a Hardee Scholar. Dr. Tull edited *Becoming Socialized in Student Affairs: A Guide for New Professionals and Their Supervisors*, with Joan Hirt and Sue Saunders, and he serves on the editorial boards of the *Community College Review*, *Oracle: The Research Journal of the Association of Fraternity Advisors*, *Journal of College and Character*, *Community College Journal of Research and Practice*, and the *Journal of Student Affairs Research and Practice*. His research has been published in *Net Results*, the *NASPA Journal*, the *College Student Affairs Journal*, the *Journal of College and Character*, and the *Journal of College Student Development*. His research interests emphasize management concepts and supervision in student affairs and higher education.

Dr. Linda Kuk is associate professor of education and chair for graduate programs in higher education leadership and counseling at Colorado State University as well as program chair for the College and University Leadership doctoral program. Prior to her faculty role, she served as vice president for student affairs at Colorado State University; the Rochester Institute of Technology, in Rochester, New York; and State University of New York at Cortland. She brings diverse experience to her post, from her consulting work in China and France, to sitting on boards of directors for a family counseling center and a women's sports advocate group, the YMCA, Funding Partners of Fort Collins, and EDUCO of northern Colorado. She has served on the National Association of Student Personnel Administrators (NASPA) Board of Directors as Region II vice president, the NASPA Foundation Board, *NASPA Journal* Board, and the American College Personnel Association (ACPA) Board of Directors as well as on the editorial board of the *Spectrum Journal*. In October 2003 she was named Alumni of the Year for the College of Education at Iowa State University, and in March 2004 she was named a Pillar of the Profession by the NASPA

Foundation. She also recently received the Outstanding Advisor Award from the College of Applied Human Studies at Colorado State. Dr. Kuk earned a PhD in professional studies at Iowa State University, and a master's in education and a bachelor's with distinction in social work from Colorado State University. She has written and presented on varied subjects in higher education administration, organizational behavior, leadership, gender studies, and career development, and serves as a student affairs organizational consultant.

ABOUT THE CONTRIBUTORS

Dr. Frank P. Ardaiolo has been vice president for student life at Winthrop University in Rock Hill, South Carolina, for the past 21 years overseeing a broad portfolio of student-related areas at this public comprehensive institution. He has been instrumental in shifting his institution's focus to student learning while creating cross-functional structures to bridge efforts between academic affairs and student affairs. He received his doctorate in higher education, student affairs, political science, and African studies from Indiana University and his bachelor's from Assumption College. Dr. Ardaiolo is also an associate professor in education and has taught undergraduate and graduate courses ranging from freshman seminars to African politics to college legal issues at varying institutions. He has published more than 25 monograph chapters, articles, and essays on legal issues, quality improvement, adult learners, student affairs/academic affairs collaboration, and African politics. His professional activities include serving as past national chair of ACPA's Commission XV on campus legal issues and NASPA's regional vice president for the Southeast. A frequent national consultant, he has given over 90 major presentations.

Dr. Cynthia Bonner is chief of staff and director of administration for the Division of Student Affairs at Virginia Tech. In this capacity she coordinates the human resources, finance, communications and marketing, strategic planning, professional development, emergency preparedness, and assessment functions of the division and serves as a liaison to administrative officers throughout the university. Dr. Bonner earner a PhD in higher education administration from Florida State University. Previously she served as associate vice president for faculty and staff resources as well as associate vice president for student services and special programs with the University of North Carolina General Administration. She was also director of housing and residence life and director of student affairs research at North Carolina State University. Her memberships in professional organizations include the National Association of Student Personnel Administrators (NASPA) and the Southern Association for College Student Affairs (SACSA).

Dr. Dean Bresciani is the president of North Dakota State University, where he is also a full professor in the College of Education. Dr. Bresciani received his doctorate in higher education finance with a doctoral minor in economics from the University of Arizona; a master's degree in college student personnel from Bowling

Green State University in Ohio; and a bachelor's degree in sociology from Humboldt State University in California. He was previously vice president for student affairs at Texas A&M University, where he was also a full professor of educational administration and HR development. He has also served in a variety of academic and student affairs roles at Humboldt State University, Bowling Green State University, University of Wisconsin–Stevens Point, University of Minnesota–Morris, University of Arizona, Arizona University System Board of Regents, University of Nebraska at Kearney, and the University of North Carolina at Chapel Hill. Dr. Bresciani's scholarship focuses on higher education finance and its relationship to higher education organization and behavior. He is a member of the Association of Public and Land Grant Universities, National Association of Student Personnel Administrators (NASPA), National Association of College and University Business Officers, Association for the Study of Higher Education, and Council for the Advancement and Support of Higher Education.

Dr. Marilee J. Bresciani is professor of postsecondary education leadership at San Diego State University, where she coordinates the master's and doctorate programs in community college leadership. The curriculum at San Diego State University emphasizes student-learning–centeredness; integration of the curricular and cocurricular learning paradigms; and analysis, planning, and responsible practice of leaders in a socially just and global environment. Dr. Bresciani's research focuses on the evaluation of student learning and development. She uses grounded theory to explore how systems and processes contribute to student-learning–centeredness, which includes the study of leaders' roles in these systems and processes. Dr. Bresciani has held faculty and higher education administration positions for more than 21 years during which time she has conducted enrollment management research, quantitative and qualitative institutional research, course-embedded assessment, and academic and administrative program assessment. As assistant vice president for institutional assessment at Texas A&M University and as director of assessment at North Carolina State University, Dr. Bresciani led university-wide initiatives to embed faculty-driven, outcomes-based assessment in the curriculum. She has led reforms in outcomes-based assessment program review, assessment of general education, quality enhancement, and assessment of the cocurricular. Dr. Bresciani has been invited to present and publish her findings on assessment and is a leading author of books on assessing student learning and outcomes-based assessment program review. Dr. Bresciani has a PhD in administration, curriculum, and instruction from the University of Nebraska and a master of arts in teaching from Hastings College.

Kathleen M. Callahan is a residential learning coordinator in the Division of Student Life and academic associate for University College at Winthrop University in Rock Hill, South Carolina. Raised in Greensboro, North Carolina, she earned a bachelor of arts with honors in sociology at North Carolina State University and a master of education in college student affairs at the University of South Florida. In June 2010, Ms. Callahan was named NASPA Region III New Professional of the Year. She is pursuing a PhD in higher education administration.

Dr. Evette Castillo Clark works as assistant dean of students at Tulane University and teaches a freshman course called "Leadership: Power, Politics, and Change." She is also an adjunct faculty member teaching graduate students in the College of Education and Human Development at the University of New Orleans. Dr. Clark has worked in higher education since 1991 at New York University; University of San Francisco; Laney Community College in Oakland, California; UC Berkeley; California State University, East Bay; San Diego State University; and Tulane University. She is also a past national co-chair of the Asian and Pacific Islander Knowledge Community of the National Association of Student Personnel Administrators (NASPA) and board member of the National Academic Advising Association (NACADA). Currently, Dr. Clark serves on the editorial board for the *College Student Affairs Journal* (2008–2011) and NASPA's board as the national director of knowledge communities (2011–2013). She earned a bachelor of arts in sociology from the University of California, Irvine; a master of arts in student personnel administration in higher education from New York University; and a doctorate in education in international and multicultural education at the University of San Francisco. Her areas of research, publication, and speaking concern college students of color, creating a pipeline of undergraduate students to careers in student affairs, strategic planning in student affairs, and leadership in higher education.

Dr. Kathy Cavins-Tull is vice chancellor for student affairs at Texas Christian University and previously served as vice president for student affairs and dean of students at Illinois Wesleyan University. She earned her bachelor of arts in sociology and psychology and master of science in college student personnel at Western Illinois University and her PhD in educational administration and foundations at Illinois State University. Her professional experience encompasses supervising campus life and student support services at public and private universities. She served as adjunct faculty in college student personnel programs at Western Illinois University and Illinois State University and as facilitator for Western Illinois University's *Higher Values for Higher Learning* strategic planning process. Her professional interests include creating seamless learning environments for students, designing effective support services for students, and helping students become engaged leaders in their communities. She is active in the National Association of Student Personnel Administrators (NASPA) Small Colleges and Universities Division and is a member of American College Personnel Association (ACPA).

Dr. Linda Clement is vice president for student affairs at the University of Maryland, a position she has held since 2001. She began her career at the University of Maryland in 1974 as a staff member in the departments of resident life and orientation. From the late 1970s until 2000, Dr. Clement served as director of undergraduate admissions and later as assistant vice president for academic affairs. Her career also included a brief stint as the president's chief of staff in 2000. Dr. Clement's portfolio in the Division of Student Affairs includes oversight of 15 departments, 1,500 employees, 48% of the campus land and space, and a $160 million budget. Additionally, she is an affiliate associate professor in the Department of Counseling and Personnel Services, where she teaches and advises master's and doctoral students. Outside the university, Dr. Clement has served as a trustee and chair for The College Board. In addition, she frequently engages in scholarly research and has authored numerous journal articles and book chapters, as well as her own book, *Effective Leaders in Student Services: Voices from the Field*. As a testament to her extraordinary university involvement, Dr. Clement has received several awards, including Outstanding Woman of the Year, Greek Advisor of the Year, Black Faculty and Staff Association Award for Student Diversity Initiatives, and the Thomas Magoon Distinguished Alumni Award from the Counseling and Personnel Services Department in College of Education. She earned a BA from the State University of New York at Oswego, an MA from Michigan State University, and a PhD from the University of Maryland.

Dr. Allison Hawkins Crume is assistant vice president for student affairs and adjunct faculty in the higher education program at Florida State University (FSU). She provides support in leadership and management in finance and planning, human resources, assessment and research, and marketing and communications. Dr. Crume has held positions in assessment and research, staff development, student programming, and policy development. Before entering the student affairs field, she was a high school social studies teacher. Dr. Crume earned a bachelor of science in history and a master of teaching in broad field social science from Georgia College and State University. She received a doctorate of philosophy in higher education administration from Florida State University, where she was a Hardee Scholar. She is an active member of the National Association of Student Personnel Administrators (NASPA), having served on the Region III Board for the past six years. Her research interests include campus governance, women in higher education, staff development, graduate preparation, and supervision. She and her husband live in Tallahassee with their three boys.

Dr. Leslie Dare is director of student affairs technology services at North Carolina State University. Her primary responsibility is providing leadership for the Division of Student Affairs in technology, communications, and distance education, including strategic planning for the division and its 35 units, and representing the division and its units in campus-wide technology planning, policies, and initiatives. She manages the technology staff that supports units and users within the division, with responsibility for academic and administrative computing, classroom technologies, Web development, and special applications. Dr. Dare has researched, written about, presented on, and taught on technology's role in student affairs, focusing on technology administration and planning, the use of technology in delivering student services and development programs, and the impact of technology on students' behavior. Dr. Dare has been at North Carolina State University since 1989, including eight years as the university's discrimination and harassment officer before returning to the Division of Student Affairs in her current position. She earned a bachelor's degree from Marshall University, and a master's degree and doctorate from North Carolina State University. She recently served as the national co-chair of the Technology Knowledge Community for the National Association of Student Personnel Administrators (NASPA).

Allyn Fleming is director of planning and administration for the Division of Student Affairs at the University of California, Santa Barbara. She has held this, or similar positions in student affairs, since 1993 and has worked in higher education since 1989. In her current role as chief of staff and confidential advisor to the vice chancellor for student affairs, she coordinates human resources, communications, and professional development functions for the division and is responsible for long-range and strategic planning. During her 18-year tenure, she has helped lead three division-wide planning efforts for 25 departments and co-authored a guide to departmental planning. She also oversees the grievance process for student discrimination complaints and privacy rights violations. In collaboration with Michael Young, UCSB's vice chancellor for student affairs, she has created keynote presentations on topics such as generations in the workplace, millennial students, student mental health, wellness programs, best practices, and the future of student services. She co-founded UCSB's Management Development Group, a professional development program for student affairs professionals that has served as a model for similar programs at other universities, and has presented nationally on professional development for staff in higher education. In 2005 she was named a campus "Unsung Heroine" by UCSB's Professional Women's Association.

Dr. Jerrid P. Freeman is currently serving as an enrollment management strategic planning consultant at Northeastern State University and previously served as director of student affairs auxiliary facilities and an adjunct assistant professor in the Higher Education Leadership program at The University of Arkansas. He has previously held positions in student affairs at Elon University, The University of North Carolina at Chapel Hill, Bowling Green State University, and the University of Nebraska at Kearney. Dr. Freeman received his bachelor of science in secondary mathematics, physics, and coaching from the University of Nebraska at Kearney and his master of arts in college student personnel from Bowling Green State University. He completed his doctorate in higher education administration from North

Carolina State University. Dr. Freeman is a certified emotional intelligence evaluator and has served on the board of the North Carolina Housing Officers Association. He has also chaired NASPA's national volunteer committee for three years and currently serves as research chair for Region IV-West. He has received the NASPA Region III New Professional Award and the Region IV-W Rising Star Award. Some of his research interests and areas of publication and presenting are integrated strategic planning (ISP), spirituality, student retention, leadership, and the changing economy's affect on higher education and underserved populations in the United States.

Chris Heltne serves as director of communications for student affairs at Duke University and is responsible for leading the conceptual development and branding processes for websites, major projects, and publications within the division, as well as serving on the University Crisis Communications Team. Since his arrival, Heltne has developed communications plans for a variety of issues, including career advising during the economic downturn, health outreach during the H1N1 outbreak, hiring Duke's first Muslim chaplain, and communications outreach to students during a campus emergency. He works with a broad range of students and other campus partners to adjust his communications approach. Before coming to Duke, Heltne was communications director for Washington, D.C.–based Conservation International (CI), where his emphasis on consistent messaging and strategic branding helped CI to increase its audience. Heltne has also been a reporter with the *Boulder Daily Camera* in Boulder, Colorado; a marketing specialist for an academic book publisher; a designer for a D.C.-based child safety nonprofit; a project manager for a marketing firm; and a professional beer brewer.

Kyle Johnson is associate provost for information and learning resources at SUNY Institute of Technology in Utica, New York. In that role he provides vision, strategic and operational planning, and day-to-day oversight to a newly created campus organization that combines a number of SUNYIT groups, including information technology services, library services, instructional resources, tutoring, instructional design, and distance education. Previously he was chief technology officer and director of enterprise applications for Guilford College, where he was responsible for providing active leadership, including vision and long-range planning, for information technology and services; integrating information technology (academic and administrative computing, media services, application/Web development, and telecommunications) into all aspects of the institution; and close cooperation with faculty, library, and other academic and administrative departments in meeting technology needs and developing and finding support for innovative uses of technology in fulfilling the mission of Guilford College. Before that, Kyle served for a decade as the director of IT for student affairs at Duke University. In his earlier position as director of IT for student affairs at Duke University, he provided strategic and long-range planning for technology use in student affairs, including residential and student activity spaces; developed and articulated strategy for support of the division's technology infrastructure, including growing the department as division needs increased; acted as project manager for significant technology projects within the division and as technical liaison for institutional projects; and provided representation on the university's Information Technology Advisory Council.

Dr. Sherry Mallory is associate dean of students at Western Washington University; previously, she served as Western's special assistant to the vice president for student affairs and academic support services. She is also an adjunct instructor in the Student Affairs Administration program, teaching the capstone seminar, "Current Issues in Student Affairs/Higher Education." Dr. Mallory earned a PhD in higher education from the University of Arizona and a BA in psychology from the University of California, Santa Cruz. Before arriving at Western, she served as assistant to the vice chancellor for student affairs at the University of Arkansas and as director of research and assessment for student life at the University of Arizona. She is an active member of the National Association of Student Personnel Administrators (NASPA), and is co-chair-elect of the Women in Student Affairs Knowledge Community. Previously, she served on the NASPA Board of Directors as chair of the Public Policy Division; on the planning committees for the 2002 and 2009 national conferences; and as a member of the Region IV-W, V, and VI advisory boards. She is currently a member of the editorial boards of the *Journal of College Student Affairs* and the *Journal of Student Affairs Research and Practice* and, in 2010, received the Region V Fred Turner Award for Outstanding Service to NASPA.

Nick M Rammell is currently pursuing a law degree at Brigham Young University. In May 2011 he completed a master's degree in higher education leadership at the University of Arkansas. He worked as a graduate assistant to Dr. Ashley Tull and coordinated professional development programming for the Division of Student Affairs. Mr. Rammell earned a bachelor of social work with honors from Brigham Young University–Idaho (BYU–Idaho), and before enrolling at BYU–Idaho, he served a two-year mission in Las Vegas, Nevada, for The Church of Jesus Christ of Latter-day Saints.

James Rychner serves is founding director of development and external relations for the Division of Student Affairs at the University of Maryland. He has more than 25 years of experience in student affairs administration, marketing, and fund-raising. In 2002, under the leadership of Vice President for Student Affairs Linda M. Clement, he originated the development and external relations unit in the Division of Student Affairs and has been responsible for garnering over $9 million in Maryland's Division of Student Affairs' ongoing campaign to support programs and initiatives.

Under his leadership, the student affairs development operation at Maryland has grown from a "one-person shop" to a nationally recognized office with three professional staff and numerous student interns dedicated to securing financial support via individual gifts, corporate partnerships, and public and private grants. He has held significant administrative positions at Maryland since 1988 and has presented nationally on student affairs fund-raising. He is also active in the National Association of Student Personnel Administrators (NASPA) and Council for Advancement and Support of Education (CASE) and is a member of the Association of Fundraising Professionals (AFP). In addition, he has consulted nationally in marketing and development.

Bernie Shulz is special assistant to the vice president of campus life at American University. His diversified background encompasses more than 18 years of experience in higher education administration with positions in residence life and housing, fraternity and sorority life, student activities, judicial affairs, community relations, and overall student affairs administration. He has overall responsibility for campus life's technology and Web management, assessment initiatives, divisional staff development programming, and Web communications, and he chairs the Student Achievement Award Selection Committee and represents Campus Life on University Project Teams and Committees. He earned a bachelor's degree in political science from Radford University, a master of education in student personnel services and higher education administration from the University of South Carolina, and a master of public administration from The Maxwell School of Citizenship and Public Affairs at Syracuse University. He is currently a doctoral student in the Higher Education Administration program at George Washington University and has been an active member of NASPA since 1994, with memberships in the fraternity/sorority, technology, and assessment knowledge communities. He currently serves as public policy liaison for knowledge communities, which includes membership on the Public Policy Division Leadership team.

Dr. Bette M. Simmons began her professional higher education experience in 1980 as assistant to the dean of students at County College of Morris, giving her the opportunity to truly appreciate the value of a community college education. Since being at the college, she has held positions as counselor, assistant to the president, assistant dean of student development, and dean of student development, and currently is vice president of student development and enrollment management. As the senior student affairs administrator on campus, Dr. Simmons supervises the staff and programs in academic advisement, admissions, athletics, campus life, career services and cooperative education, counseling services, dean of students, enrollment services, financial aid, health services, records and registration, and the Women's Center. She has also sat on the board—nationally and regionally—of the National

Association of Student Personnel Administrators (NASPA) and has held many volunteer positions within the association, of which she has been a member for 20 years. Additionally, she is a college evaluator for the Middle States Association of Colleges and Secondary Schools and has taught graduate-level courses in the Master's Program of Supervision, Leadership, and Administration at Seton Hall University, and has been a guest lecturer in the Board Leadership Institute at Seton Hall as well as in the Student Affairs in Higher Education Program at Montclair State University. She earned an EdD in higher education administration from Seton Hall University and a master of arts in counseling from Montclair State University.

academic advising, 182

academic skills and student support director, 44

access
  and accountability for general learning, 116
  community colleges and, 169, 185
  expectations for, 16, 171
  human resources departments and, 85
  need for, 3, 130, 131
  technology and, 5

accountability
  accreditation and, 35, 43, 44
  and the role of the SSAO, 78
  auxiliary services and, 105
  chief of staff and, 97
  expectations for, 16, 130, 206
  for general learning, 116, 118
  professional development and, 193

accreditation, 35, 43, 44, 116–117

adaptive change, 1–2, 7, 13–14, 131–134, 144, 208, 210

admissions, 8, 15, 172, 177–178

American College Personnel Association (ACPA), 86, 88, 90–91, 119, 166, 172–173, 200

American Council on Education (ACE), 135–136, 172

assessment. *See also* research and assessment
  as a transforming force, 129
  at smaller institutions, 161
  outcomes-based, 115, 138, 200
  political resistance to, 138
  technology and, 118, 120

Assessment Skills and Knowledge (ASK) Content Standards for Student Affairs Practitioners and Scholars (ACPA), 119

assistant to the vice president/chancellor or chief of staff

future needs, 82–83
sample job descriptions, 79–80
successes and challenges, 80–82
survey of current practices, 42–43
titles, reporting structures, areas of responsibility, 78–79

Auburn University, 108

auxiliary services
  challenges, 100
  commercial enterprises *vs.* higher education, 111–112
  current practices, 41–42
  emerging roles, 9–10, 106–107
  future needs, 109–111
  history, 104–106
  job descriptions, 107–108
  overview, 103–104

benchmarking, 146

blogs, 73

Bohlman and Deal's human resource frame for change, 137–139

branding, 68–71, 75

Bryson's ten steps to change, 143

budget issues. *See also* economic factors and scarce resources
  auxiliary services and, 91
  community colleges, 170, 174–175
  planning and, 143–145
  smaller institutions, 150, 151, 156
  vertical functioning and, 20

budget management, 9, 41–43, 78–79, 86

campus recreation center, 41. *See also* auxiliary services officers

campus-community liaison, 44

career advancement. *See* professional development

career services, 66, 151, 164, 176, 183
CAS Professional Standards for Higher
    Education, 86, 156, 196–197, 200
certification, 117. *See also* accreditation issues
change
    adaptive and transformational, 1, 131–134
        (*See also* adaptive change; transforma-
        tional change)
    and student affairs, 3–7
    assessing readiness for, 135–136
    evaluation and implementation of,
        145–146
    in roles and responsibilities, 81–82
    mission statements and, 196
    models for, 136–139
    planned, 2, 133–134
    processes for, 139–143
    professional development and, 189–203
    resistance to, 134–135
    restructuring resources for, 143–145
    within student affairs organizations, 7–11
chief of staff (or director of administration)
    at University of California, Santa Barbara
        (UCSB), 98–99
    at Virginia Tech, 97–98
    challenges and future trends, 100–102
    current practices, 42–43
    evolving functions, 96–97
    historical influences, 96
    overview, 94–95
    sample job descriptions, 99–100
civic-student outreach coordinator, 44
Clery Act, 97
cloud computing, 56
collaboration
    cross-unit, 16–18, 24
    human resources and professional devel-
        opment and, 87
    in community colleges, 174
    in smaller institutions, 150
    in staff development, 189
    need for, 6, 18
    organizational structure and, 26–28, 132
    professional development and, 189, 190,
        198, 199, 202–204
    strategies for, 29–30

College and University Professional Associ-
    ation for Human Resources (CUPA-
    HR), 85
Columbia University Teachers College, 190
communication
    immediacy of, 5
    lateral and vertical, 15, 17, 18, 24, 26, 29
    organizational structure and, 132, 133, 139,
        141, 145
    roles and responsibilities, 95, 96–97 (*See
        also* communications and outreach
        officers)
    survey of current practices, 78–79
communications and outreach officers
    future needs for, 73–74
    historical developments, 69–70
    overview, 68–69
    reporting structures, 70–71
    sample job descriptions, 71–73
    survey of current practices, 39–40
community colleges, specialist roles and
        structures in
    challenges for, 174–175
    overview, 169–171
    student affairs models and, 171–174
    student affairs responsibilities in, 175–185
community resources, 44
conference and event coordinator, 44
Congruence Model of Change (Nadler),
        136–137
consumerism, students, 4–5, 35, 170, 171
cost constraints. *See* economic factors and
        scarce resources
cost-centered budgeting, 144
Council for the Advancement of Standards
        in Higher Education (CAS), 86, 156,
        196–197, 200
counseling services, 173, 181–182, 183
crisis management, 70–71, 78, 90, 95, 97
cross-organizational specialists, 8–9, 38–44
cross-training, 142, 159–160, 176, 203
cross-unit collaboration, 16–18, 24, 27
customer-service orientation, 89, 107, 153,
        170, 185

dashboards, 146
dean of students, 184

demographic shifts, 3, 22, 35, 105, 129, 169–170
development officer (DO) position
  challenges and future trends, 63–66
  historical background, 59
  reporting structures, 60–61
  sample job descriptions, 61–63
  survey of current practices, 38
differentiation, 17, 18, 21. *See also* specialization
dining services, 41, 103, 106, 107
director of academic skills and student support, 44
director of administration, 42–43. *See also* chief of staff (or director of administration)
distance education, 50, 52, 102, 190, 197, 201–202
diversity
  and mission statements, 196
  as a core value, 158
  as a transforming force, 129
  auxiliary services and, 105
  increase in, 3–4, 15, 130, 171
  technology and, 96
double-loop learning, 30, 199
Draft and Noe's approach to organizational design, 19–20
Duke University, 71–72

economic factors and scarce resources
  auxiliary services and, 109
  chief of staff functions and, 96
  communications and, 70
  effect on change, 35
  effect on enrollment, 3
  effect on implementing change, 134
  in community colleges, 174–175
  meeting the challenge of, 6, 22
  restructuring resources for change, 143–145
  technology and, 55–56
education. *See* professional development
emergency planning, 97
empowerment, of student affairs professionals, 141
Engstrom, Cathy, 65

enrollment, 3, 175
evaluation, of progress toward change, 141–142, 145–146. *See also* research and assessment
event coordinator, 44
evidence-based decision making, 120. *See also* research and assessment

Facebook, 73
federal and state mandates, 44, 97, 130, 132, 179
flickr, 73
financial aid, 96, 138, 170, 176, 178, 179
Florida State University (FSU), 88–89
food services, 41, 103, 106, 107. *See also* auxiliary services officers
for-profit training and consulting firms, 192–193
Foursquare, 74
Fragmented Generation, 56
functional structure, 25–26
functionally specialized structures, 16, 23–25
fund-raising, 59. *See also* development officer (DO) position

Galbraith's approach to reorganizational design, 19–20
general learning, 116–117, 120
globalization, 4–5, 35, 130
graduate programs. *See* human resources and professional development

health services, 15, 160, 173, 183
housing, 15, 16, 41, 50, 55, 103, 107, 131, 179
human development facilitator model, 172
human resource frame for organizational change (Bolman and Diehl), 136–137
human resources and professional development
  examples of services, 87–89
  experiences in, 87
  historical development of, 84–87
  in smaller institutions, 160–161
  professional development coordinator job descriptions, 89–91

recommendations, 91
survey of current practices, 40–41
hybrid organizational structures
    definition, 25
    external environment and, 210
    organizational change and, 130–131, 211,
        214
    roles and responsibilities and, 60, 198,
        206, 208, 209

in loco parentis, 171
institution types. *See* community colleges;
    smaller institutions; Winthrop College
integration, 17
interdisciplinary teams, 17
international students, 179–180
Internet, 73
intramural operations, 41. *See also* auxiliary
    services officers

Jelsema, Martin, 69–70

Kotter's eight-stage model for change,
    139–143

leadership, 25, 35, 110, 133, 140
Leadership in Energy and Environmental
    Design (LEED) project, 117
League for Innovation in the Community
    College model of student affairs, 175
Lewin, Kurt, 136

maintenance, facility, 42, 104, 107
maintenance model of student affairs, 172
Managing Student Affairs Effectively (Upcraft
    and Barr), 167–168
marketing, 68, 69, 177–178, 191, 197
matrix structures
    context for, 14, 25–27
    organizational change and, 131–132,
        138–139, 141–142, 208
measurable outcomes, 55
media relations, 9, 37, 39, 40, 70, 160
mental health issues, 97
mission
    of community colleges, 170–172, 175

organizational restructuring and, 19,
    22–25, 30, 36, 131–132, 143, 145
specialist positions and, 36
student affairs professional preparation
    and, 195–197, 199
mission drift, 133, 146
mobile computing, 56
morale, 26, 141, 150, 167

Nadler, D. A., 136–137
National Association of Student Personnel
    Administrators(NASPA), 37, 51, 59–60,
    86, 90, 91, 119
National Labor Relations Act (Wagner Act),
    85
National Labor Relations Board, 85
New Leadership Alliance for Student
    Learning and Accountability, 117
New Professionals Institute (NPI), 88

O'Reilly, Tim, 56
online learning, 35, 50, 52, 102, 197, 201
organizational design, 19, 21–22, 102, 132
organizational restructuring. *See also* hybrid
    organizational structures; matrix
    structures
    culture changes and, 142
    elements of, 7–9
    impact of, 210–214
    models for, 136–139
    need for, 6–7, 16–19, 22–25
    new approaches to, 19–22
    roles and responsibilities in, 28–30
    work flow in, 27–28
Orton and Wieck's approach to organiza-
    tional design, 21–22, 102
outcomes-based assessment, 115, 138, 200

Patriot Act, 97
performance indicators, 141, 146, 209
personnel. *See* roles and responsibilities
planned change, 2
Planning, Programming, and Budgeting
    Systems (PPBS), 144
political frame for organizational change, 132,
    133, 135, 137, 138, 172

PPBS (Planning, Programming, and
     Budgeting Systems), 144
process
   change and, 132–136
   for organizational design (Galbraith),
     19–20
   for redesigning roles and responsibilities,
     29–30
   models for the change process, 136–145
process structure, 25–26
professional associations, 160, 189–193,
     200–203, 213
*Professional Competency Areas for Student
     Affairs Practitioners* (ACPA & NASPA),
     90, 119
professional development. *See also* human
     resources and professional development
   changing role for, 194–201
   complexity of, 189–194
   comprehensive approach to, 201–203
   coordinators, 89–91
   historical development of, 86–87
program budgeting, 144
project managers, 162–164, 166

Reauthorization of Higher Education Act,
     97
records, 178–179
recruiting
   staff, 40–41, 85, 91–92, 152
   students, 55, 116, 153, 161, 177–178
reframing model of change (Bolman and
     Deal), 137–139
regional accreditation, 117–118
registration, 172, 178–179
research and assessment
   competencies and skills for, 118–119
   current practices, 43
   current trends, 116–118
   future possibilities, 119–120
   history, 114–116
   job descriptions, 119, 123–125
residential life. *See* housing
responsibility-centered budgeting, 144
restructuring. *See* organizational
     restructuring

retention and graduation rates, 44, 55, 57, 85,
     97, 145, 153, 167, 170–171
rituals and change, 138–139, 156–157
roles and responsibilities. *See also* community
     colleges; smaller institutions
   auxiliary services, 106–107
   change in, 81–82
   communications, 95, 96–97
   cross-organizational specialists, 8, 38–44
   current and emerging challenges in,
     207–209
   current practices in, 37–38, 209–210
   evolution of, 34–37
   in organizational restructuring, 28–30

scorecards, 146
SCVNGR, 74
Second Life, 74
senior student affairs officers (SSAOs), 9,
     34–35, 78, 176
services, 4, 5, 23, 97
silo structure, 6, 34, 68, 74, 111, 130, 159, 176
smaller institutions, 150–155. *See also*
     Winthrop University
social media, 56
special students, 184–185
specialization, 16, 23–25
sports and recreational programs, 183
standards, 88, 119, 156, 174, 191–193, 195–203
state and federal mandates, 44, 97, 130, 132,
     180
strategic management, 145–146
structural frame for organizational change,
     137–138
student activities, 180–181
student affairs organizations, 15–22. *See also*
     organizational design; organizational
     restructuring; roles and responsibilities
student consumerism, 4–5, 35
student information coordinator, 44
Student Learning Imperative (ACPA), 166
Student Personnel Point of View Statement
     (American Council on Education), 172
student union, 41. *See also* auxiliary services
     officers
students as resources, 164–165

symbols as a frame for organizational change,
138–139

*Taking Charge of Change: A Primer for
Colleges and Universities* (Eckel, Green,
Hill, & Mallon), 135
teams, 29. *See also* collaboration
technology
assessment and, 118, 120
challenge of, 4–5, 35
communications and, 73–74
community colleges and, 174
current practices in, 39
evolving chief of staff functions and, 96
specialist positions in, 37
technology officers
challenges and future trends, 55–56
current practice, 39
historical development, 49–51
institutional examples, 51–53
position descriptions, 53–55
Texas A&M University, 87–88
traditional structures, 23
transfer and matriculation, 182
transformational change, 1, 146, 208, 210
transforming forces
accountability, 129, 130
assessment, 129 (*See also* research and
assessment)
changing demographics, 129

cost constraints, 129 (*See also* economic
factors and scarce resources)
diversity/multiculturalism, 129, 130 (*See
also* diversity)
international competition, 129
new teaching and learning approaches, 129
reliance on technology, 130 (*See also*
technology)
trust, 133–134
Tumblr, 74
Twitter, 73

University of Arkansas, 106–108
University of California, Santa Barbara
(UCSB), 98–99
University of Illinois at Urbana-Champaign,
61–62
University of Maryland, 60–61, 62–63, 91
University of South Florida, 101
urgency, 140

Virginia Tech, 72–73, 97–98, 98–99, 100
vision, 68, 131–132, 140, 141, 143

Winthrop University
human resources, 159–161
overview, 155–157
project manager program, 162–164
reporting structure, 165–166
student employees, 164–165
successes and challenges, 166–168

Also available from Stylus

Becoming Socialized in Student Affairs Administration
A Guide for New Professionals and Their Supervisors
Edited by Ashley Tull, Joan B. Hirt, and Sue Saunders

"Articulates a common framework that holds significant promise for both improving student affairs practice and enhancing the quality of new professionals' work life. When taken as a whole the text achieves its stated goal of illuminating 'student affairs administrators of all ranks on the importance of socialization and the role they can play in socializing their new employees'."—*Journal of College Student Development*

"The focus on professional socialization and, in particular, its influence on the retention of new professionals, differentiates this book from the many texts targeted at new professionals in student affairs and their supervisors. This book offers insights useful to several audiences, and is likely to contribute to the successful integration and retention of new student affairs professionals."—*The Review of Higher Education*

Contested Issues in Student Affairs
Diverse Perspectives and Respectful Dialogue
Edited by Peter M. Magolda and Marcia B. Baxter Magolda

What is your level of understanding of the many moral, ideological, and political issues that student affairs educators regularly encounter? What is your personal responsibility to addressing these issues? What are the rationales behind your decisions? What are the theoretical perspectives you might choose and why? How do your responses compare with those of colleagues?

Contested Issues in Student Affairs augments traditional introductory handbooks that focus on functional areas (e.g., residence life, career services) and organizational issues. It fills a void by addressing the social, educational and moral concepts and concerns of student affairs work that transcend content areas and administrative units, such as the tensions between theory and practice, academic affairs and student affairs, risk taking and failure; and such as issues of race, ethnicity, sexual orientation, and spirituality. It places learning and social justice at the epicenter of student affairs practice.

The book addresses these issues by asking 24 critical and contentious questions that go to the heart of contemporary educational practice. Intended equally for future student affairs educators in graduate preparation programs, and as reading for professional development workshops, it is designed to stimulate reflection and prompt readers to clarify their own thinking and practice as they confront the complexities of higher education.

Student affairs faculty, administrators, and graduate students here situate these 24 questions historically in the professional literature, present background information and context, define key terms, summarize the diverse ideological and theoretical responses to the questions, make explicit their own perspectives and responses, discuss their political implications, and set them in the context of the changing nature of student affairs work.

Each chapter is followed by a response that offers additional perspectives and complications, reminding readers of the ambiguity and complexity of many situations.

Each chapter concludes with a brief annotated bibliography of seminal works that offer additional information on the topic, as well as with a URL to a moderated blog site that encourages further conversation on each topic and allows readers to teach and learn from each other, and interact with colleagues beyond their immediate campus.

Sty/us

22883 Quicksilver Drive
Sterling, VA 20166-2102

Subscribe to our e-mail alerts: www.Styluspub.com